LOADED with
Daily
Blessings

LOADED with

Daily Blessings

By James E. Temidara

XULON PRESS

Xulon Press
2301 Lucien Way #415
Maitland, FL 32751
407.339.4217
www.xulonpress.com

Printed in the United States of America

Paperback ISBN-13: 978-1-66283-627-5
Hard Cover ISBN-13: 978-1-66283-628-2
Ebook ISBN-13: 978-1-66283-629-9

FOREWORD

by
Jentezen Franklin

I can think of no better way to start your day than spending three minutes each morning reading a devotional meditation from the LOADED with DAILY BLESSINGS produced through The Living Word for Today. Each day is filled with scripture and an encouraging word from the scriptures that will not only encourage you, but it will speak directly into your life and every situation you will encounter. Only the living word of God can do that. In addition to a powerful and timely scripture there is also a brief exhortation to serve as a reminder of just how powerful your God really is and how blessed you are in all circumstances.

In a day and age when our lives can become so filled with activity, it's reassuring to know just how powerful three or four minutes can be when you pause to see what God has in store for you every day you are willing to stop and listen. The title LOADED with DAILY BLESSINGS is filled with promises because God's holy scriptures are both: they are alive and always relevant and every word you read is activated and true the day you pause to read it.

If you are looking for an in-depth Bible Study this is not the book for you. But if you are looking for God's voice to be spoken into your life in a powerful way, this book provides a Rhema word that will well up like a spring and overflow into your life the rest of the day.

Pastor Jentezen Franklin
Founding Pastor, Free Chapel;
Author and Televangelist

ENDORSMENTS

I am pleased to endorse "Loaded With Daily Blessings." Written by Dr James E. Temidara. An experienced Healthcare/Hospice Spiritual Care Counselor and Minister,
who clearly demonstrates a keen capacity for connecting with saints and sinners. Not only with the terminally Ill and recovering patients, but is also adept in explaning God's Holy Word, in which he points up God's many profound Daily Blessings.
Dr. Curtis E. Smith
Author / Minister

I have been blessed and edified by different Christian devotionals through the years. "Loaded with Daily Blessings" stands out with unique scriptural insight that is destined to be a classic. Thank you Reverend James Temidara!
Pastor Daniel Santa Cruz

Loaded with Daily Blessings is an inspiration book grounded in the word of God. James Temidara brings forth understanding and application of the abundant provisional blessings God has readily loaded for our daily lives. As an intercessor, I find this revelation profitable to prayer. I am thankful for this teaching.
Janet and Jerry Garcia

It is such a poor life if there is no word for us who have no choice but to struggle and live in a life that repeats every day. The reason why we can enjoy peace and true rest is because there is God who bears all our burdens.
Pastor James tells us precious words like life every day, so it becomes a great driving force for my soul.
-Lena Barrington

Having had the privilege of being a first hand user of the Devotional, "Loaded with Daily Blessings", I regard it a daily spiritual capsule for the nourishment of my soul, and therefore recommend it to anyone with a desiring and thirsty quest.
Isaac Adeyemi,
Senior / Founding Pastor

LOADED with DAILY BLESSINGS is a compendium of very rich and at the same time very easy to read and understand Daily Devotional Meditations covering several aspects of Christian Doctrinal subjects to satisfy the spiritual appetite of all Christians irrespective of the denominations.
Rev. Engr. Silver Asuwata,
Senior Pastor

This book of meditation relates God's words to daily living and invokes peace, happiness and encouragement. Reverend Temidara has set forth a pathway to achieving a fearless life.
Dr. Lilly Barba, MD

Through this letter, I herey vouch for the strong moral fiber, spiritual, honesty, troustworthiness, professionalism, and integrity of Dr. Temidara. I have known Dr. Temidara for several years when working together to serve terminally ill patients and have maintained that professional friendship. The daily devotional messages have touched several lives positively and I strongly believe this book will be a tremendous asset to everyone seeking divine closeness. I'm appreciatve to Dr. Temidara for publishing this book and his selfless acts towards the people here in America and globally. Thank you.
Alhaja A. Akande
FNP, PMNP-BC, MSN, RN

James E Temidara's devotional became a part of our Channels of Hope daily messages and it was highly appreciated as a companion that helped many pass through the murky waters of COVID-19 infection & loss of loved ones. Read this book to hear the rhema word in season straight from the Lord...
Pontsho K Segwai,
Field Operations Officer, World Vision, South Africa;
Channels of Hope Mentor, World Vision International;
(This Daily Devotional is shared with World Vision globally)

DEDICATION

This book is dedicated primarily to the triune God, who gave me life eternal, called and keeps sustaining me in His service to mankind.

Secondarily, to:

- My parents who raised me in a Christian home where daily family devotion and church attendance were none negotiable, but mandatory.
- My spiritual mentors, from village catechists to renown international leaders and Bible scholars.
- My mentees and children, both biological and spiritual who are spread all over the world. You helped to shape my character and integrity.

To God be the glory!

James E. Temidara
LIVING WORD for TODAY
P. O. Box 2432,
Santa Fe Springs, California 90670 USA

TABLE OF CONTENTS

JANUARY 1:

LOADED with DAILY BLESSINGS—(Ps. 68:19)-#1

"Blessed be the LORD,
Who daily loads us with benefits,
The God of our salvation." (Ps. 68:19)

Welcome to the new year, which is the beginning of a new chapter of our lives. While we rejoiced in His presence throughout the previous years and blessed His holy name for so many insights and blessings we received from Him, we are, however, honored to be among the living who ushered in this new year. Praise the Lord!

In one of my recent morning devotions, the Lord impressed it upon my spirit that all the benefits received from Him so far are just in preparation for the amazing blessings He has reserved for His own in the coming years. The theme: Loaded with Daily Blessings was announced into my ears to be the theme for the year.

In Psalm 68, David starts the song with a battle cry: "Let God arise, Let His enemies be scattered." We see throughout this song of David, the battle and victory of the Lord over the hosts of enemies of His people. The result is taking the enemies captive and bringing spoils to God's children with loaded benefits daily.

Through the grace granted to me, I hereby declare that the Lord of hosts will rise up for you daily, scatter all your enemies like smoke, melt them like wax in His fire, and load you daily with all the goods and blessings you deserve to run your race and be a blessing to yourself and others!

He has taken back all that the enemy has stolen from you, and He's giving them back to you in multiple folds. This year is **loaded with daily blessings** for you and your loved ones in Jesus Christ's name!

Have a happy and prosperous New Year in His presence!

LIVING WORD for TODAY

January 2

LOADED with DAILY BLESSINGS (Ps. 68:19)-#2

You're loaded with daily blessings! Whether you feel it or not, this is the Word of God to you if you belong to Him. Live by faith daily with this in mind.

One of the powerful weapons the Lord has given to us to tap into the realms of His victory and blessings is music. Singing the right song can open the windows of heaven for divine interventions on behalf of the singer.

I encourage you to saturate your mind daily with scriptural songs of praise, worship, and testimony of who God is to you, and sing them out of your mouth. There are many inspirational worship contemporary songs in YouTube these days, which are capable of lifting up your spirit. As you worship and give testimony to God for what you're believing Him for this year, the songs will activate your faith every time you sing them along with the singers. The Book of Psalms also contains songs from David and others as they expressed their feelings and prayed to God in songs.

May the Lord fill your heart and mouth with new songs to praise and worship Him this year.

Have a year loaded with blessings in His presence!

JANUARY —LIFE

LIVING WORD for TODAY—January 3:

LOADED with DAILY BLESSINGS (Ps. 68:19)-#3

LIFE—3

"Therefore I say to you, do not worry about your life, what you will eat or what you will drink; nor about your body, what you will put on. Is not life more than food and the body more than clothing?" (Matt.6:25)

Everyday when you wake up, say to yourself: "I'm loaded with blessings today."

The first and most important benefit/blessing you have daily from God is your life. There's nothing to give in exchange for it. Every blessing depends on your life. Without it, you cannot enjoy any benefit.

Jesus Christ our Lord asked the worriers, "Is not life more than food..." And later, He warns the covetous, "Take heed and beware of covetousness, for one's life does not consist in the abundance of the things he possesses (Luke 12:15).

So as you start the day, always know that you're more than what you have or don't have. You're loaded with life from God, and thank Him for it.

Life is for the living!

Have a beautiful day in His Presence!

LIVING WORD for TODAY—January 4:

LOADED with DAILY BLESSINGS (Ps. 68:19)-#4

LIFE—4

"And the LORD God formed man of the dust of the ground, and breathed into his nostrils the breath of life; and man became a living being." (Gen. 2:7)

Human beings are not a product of evolution but carefully designed by God the Creator. What makes us alive is the breath of the Almighty God in us, and when that breath is withdrawn, life is gone and decay sets in.

The Bible says: "The Spirit of God has made me, And the breath of the Almighty gives me life" (Job 33:4).

So never take your life for granted; it is the life of the Almighty. Life is what makes the world to flourish. Plants, insects, animals, and humans depend on life to exist. Without life, there is no existence. So let us do whatever it takes to preserve life on earth and not destroy it, for life is a gift from God.

I pray that you and I will continue to enjoy the quality of life that comes from the Almighty God this year and beyond.

Have a blessed day in His presence!

LIVING WORD for TODAY—January 5:

LOADED with DAILY BLESSINGS (Ps. 68:19)-#5

LIFE—5

"Because Your lovingkindness is better than life, My lips shall praise You. Thus will I bless You while I live; I will lift up my hands in Your name." (Ps. 63:3–4)

Life is good! But there are times when death is better than life. Once life has lost its quality and potentials, it is better to die than to live without meaning and hope. Life without quality and dignity is just existence, and it's not worth living.

David in the Bible recognized this fact while wandering from cave to cave in the wilderness; hence, he cried out to God and said: "Your lovingkindness is better than life..." (Ps. 63:3). What David is saying is life is not worth living under God's rejection.

It is my prayer today that whatever we do to make it through in life would be within the confines of the Lord's approval.

Have a prosperous day in His presence!

LIVING WORD for TODAY—January 6:

LOADED with DAILY BLESSINGS (Ps. 68:19)-#6

LIFE—6

"...For what is your life? It is even a vapor that appears for a little time and then vanishes away. Instead you ought to say, 'If the Lord wills, we shall live and do this or that.'" (James 4:14–15)

Life is good; enjoy it to the fullest! But what does life mean to you? Life means different things to many people, depending on their age, status, exposures, experiences, faiths, environments, cultural upbringings, and families.

Here are some quotes about life:

"You only live once, but if you do it right, once is enough" (Mae West).

"In three words I can sum up everything I've learned about life: it goes on" (Robert Frost).

"Insanity is doing the same thing, over and over again, but expecting different results" (Albert Einstein).

The Bible has a lot to say about life. In our text today, life is compared to vapor that appears for a little time and vanishes away. This tells us that life on earth is very brief. Because of its brevity, let us allow the Giver to guide it to its meaningful purpose.

Enjoy your day with **loaded blessings!**

LOADED with DAILY BLESSINGS (Ps. 68:19)-#7

LIFE—7

"Before I formed you in the womb I knew you,
Before you were born I sanctified you;
I ordained you a prophet to the nations." (Jer. 1:5)

According to the individual's date of birth (DOB), life on earth starts at birth. However, according to God, each of our lives has been planned by Him in His foreknowledge before we were conceived by our parents. With this in mind, know that you're not on earth by accident. God the Creator planned your earthly journey in the eternity past in His mind, and at the right time, with the consent of your parents, He made it happen.

Your destiny has been planned by the Lord of the whole universe, but it is your responsibility to discover it. With His help, as you let Him be your Shepherd, you will discover it and live to fulfill your purpose on earth. So you have so much to live for. You're loaded with potentials!

Have a blessed day in His presence!

LIVING WORD for TODAY—January 8:

LOADED with DAILY BLESSINGS (Ps. 68:19)-#8

LIFE—8

"And this is eternal life, that they may know You, the only true God, and Jesus Christ whom You have sent." (John 17:3)

Great men and women who have contributed so much to the development of the world, and our molded thoughts have much to say about life. But none of them ever attributed life to themselves. Only our Lord Jesus Christ did.

Here are some quotes:

"To live is the rarest thing in the world. Most people exist, that is all." -Oscar Wilde

"Don't cry because it's over, smile because it happened." -Dr. Seuss

"You've gotta dance like there's nobody watching,

Love like you'll never be hurt,

Sing like there's nobody listening,

And live like it's heaven on earth." -William W. Purkey

While we can learn a lot by reflecting on these notable quotes, none gives us the full meaning and fulfillment to our lives as knowing Jesus Christ, the Author of eternal life.

According to Him, life is more than earthly existence. It is unending with quality. So you can enjoy life to the fullest on earth as you live for God through Jesus Christ, and when it is over here, you will enter into the realm of unending bliss.

What a blessed hope!

Have a great day **loaded** with **blessings** of **life**!

LIVING WORD for TODAY—January 9:

LOADED with DAILY BLESSINGS (Ps. 68:19)-#9

LIFE—9

"Jesus said to him, 'I am the way the truth and the life. No one comes to the Father except through Me.'" (John 14:6)

In one of the *I am* sayings of our Lord, He made it categorically clear that He is the life. No one can say that except Jesus Christ because He is the Giver of life. He is also the Author of eternal life. Life has no meaning and fulfillment except through Christ. One major blessing you can enjoy through Him today is eternal life. Eternal life is a quality of life, which Christ guarantees those who believe in Him. It is not just the life we're going to enjoy in heaven, but eternal life is enjoyable here now as you put your trust in Jesus Christ.

Enjoy your blessing of eternal life today and always as you, by faith, commit it to Him who alone can save it.

Have a great day **loaded** with **life**!

LIVING WORD for TODAY—January 10:

LOADED with DAILY BLESSINGS (Ps. 68:19)-#10

LIFE—10

"All things were made through Him, and without Him nothing was made. In Him was life, and the life was the light of men." (John 1:3–4)

"All things..." All we long for, all our desires, all we want to become, all our blessings—all were made by Jesus Christ our Lord.

In Him is life! Real life is in Jesus Christ. I resent those who make Christianity look dull, uninteresting, boring, and irrelevant. People who listened to Jesus Christ during His earthly ministry witnessed a huge difference between Him and the religious practice of the day. He spoke with life; He interacted with people with life. He preached, taught, healed, and even corrected people with life. He is the life and life-giver—not just our breath of life, but life in all areas of living!

Has life gone out of your daily life? Has everything you do become a chore and you're just struggling and managing to maintain and make things work? Maybe your life is on a survival mode.

Go to the Life-Giver now and learn from Him (Matt. 11:28–30). He will rekindle your fire and passion.

Life is to be enjoyed, not endured!

Enjoy your life today and beyond to the fullest in His presence!

LIVING WORD for TODAY—January 11:

LOADED with DAILY BLESSINGS (Ps. 68:19)-#11

LIFE—11

"For God so loved the world that He gave His only begotten Son, that whoever believes in Him should not perish but have everlasting life." (John 3:16)

Last night as I was worshiping the Lord, He told me to ask everyone who has been following this daily devotional and the theme for this year to ask for a specific blessing to be added to his or her cart of loaded blessings on this 11th day of the first month in the year, and He promised to do it. I've asked Him for mine, and I urge you to ask Him for a specific blessing this day.

Our God is a generous giver! He gives out of His nature of love. The Bible says, "He who did not spare His own Son, but delivered Him up for us all, how shall He not with Him also freely give us all things?" (Rom. 8:32). So the problem isn't God, but human pride.

Nothing is too difficult for our God to do. So humble yourself before Him and ask in faith. He will honor your faith and grant your heart's request this day in Jesus Christ's name!

Have a lovely day loaded with blessings!

LIVING WORD for TODAY—January 12:

LOADED with DAILY BLESSINGS (Ps. 68:19)-#12

LIFE—12

"For God so loved the world that He gave His only begotten Son, that whoever believes in Him should not perish but has everlasting life." (John 3:16)

Life is our first blessing that we received from God. Without life, there is no hope, but while there's life, there is hope.

But we must distinguish between two types of life. These are: earthly life and eternal life.

1. Earthly Life: This is a common life available to every living being. It is the life given to us by God the Creator to live, grow, and function on earth. This is a common gift from God to every creature. We must always thank God for being alive.
2. Eternal Life: This is a quality of life that God gives to those who humbly recognize their sinfulness, and by faith, receive Jesus Christ as their Lord and Savior. This is a simple gift that anyone can receive and enjoy. But human pride, religious beliefs, and ignorance make it so difficult to accept. It takes the supernatural work of the Holy Spirit for the gift of eternal life to be received, which grants us the benefit of a relationship with God.

Jesus Christ is the giver of earthly life and eternal life. So we praise and worship Him for these blessings daily. I pray that no one with the first life will miss the second life, which is our destiny.

Enjoy your daily blessings in His presence!

LIVING WORD for TODAY—January 13:

LOADED with DAILY BLESSINGS (Ps. 68:19)-#13

LIFE—13

Life is good, and let us enjoy it to the fullest!

Talking about our earthly life, I found a quote from Mother Theresa, which is thought-provoking, and let me share it with you for your meditation:

> Life is an opportunity, benefit from it.
>
> Life is beautiful, admire it.
>
> Life is a dream, realize it.
>
> Life is a challenge, meet it.
>
> Life is a duty, complete it.
>
> Life is a game, play it.
>
> Life is a promise, fulfill it.
>
> Life is sorrow, overcome it.
>
> Life is a song, sing it.
>
> Life is a struggle, accept it.
>
> Life is a tragedy, confront it.
>
> Life is an adventure, dare it.
>
> Life is luck, make it.
>
> Life is too precious, do not destroy it.
>
> Life is life, fight for it.
>
>   - Mother Theresa

I pray we all realize the blessings of life as we continue on our earthly journeys.

Have a blessed day in His presence!

LIVING WORD for TODAY—14:

LOADED with DAILY BLESSINGS (Ps. 68:19)-#14

LIFE—14

"Man who is born of woman is of few days and full of trouble. He comes forth like a flower and fades away; He flees like a shadow and does not continue." (Job 14:1–2)

Our earthly life can be divided into three parts, just like the day: morning, afternoon, and evening. Just like the day is brief, so are our lives on earth, no matter how long we live.

In the morning, from birth to sixteen or eighteen years of age, we're dependent on parents or guardians to make choices for us regarding where to be born, live, grow up, what school to attend, and so on. We are dependent and influenced by their decisions.

In the afternoon part, ages sixteen through the dying days, we are in control of our lives. We make choices of careers, friends, partners, marriages, associations, religions, investments, habits, and the list goes on. At this stage of life, not everyone has equal time and opportunities. Some of us are blessed with long life, while many are less fortunate.

The evening part is when we get old and retire from work. This age varies for many. Some retire early while some work till they could no longer work due to old age. Not everyone is privileged to reach this age.

The text in Job chapter 14 reminds us of the brevity of the earthly life and how to seriously live with a purpose. Everyday we live is a gift from the Lord; let us appreciate and make the best of it. I pray we all live and enjoy the full lifespan God has assigned to each of us in Jesus Christ's name! Our time is in His hand.

Have a productive day full of blessings!

LIVING WORD for TODAY—January 15:

LOADED with DAILY BLESSINGS (Ps. 68:19)-#15

LIFE—15

"Bless the LORD, O my soul;
And all that is within me, bless His holy name!
Bless the LORD, O my soul,
And forget not all His benefits." (Ps. 103:1–2)

Life is the greatest asset we all have. Everything hangs on it. Your fat bank accounts, properties, investments, work, careers, marriages, and family with all the benefits of this world—all depend on being alive. Hence, David, in Psalm 103, exclaims: "Bless the LORD, O my soul; And all that is within me, bless His holy name!"

Before thinking about all the benefits we receive from God, we must thank Him that our living souls can enjoy those benefits. So the first thing to do every morning when you wake up is to bless the Lord for keeping you alive to enjoy the blessings of the day. Being alive to see each new day is a blessing.

Celebrate the Lord and your life everyday.

Have a great day loaded with blessings!

LIVING WORD for TODAY—January 16:

LOADED with DAILY BLESSINGS (Ps. 68:19)-#16

LIFE—16

"Every moving thing that lives shall be food for you. I have given you all things, even as the green herbs." (Gen. 9:3)

Have you ever thought of this fact that human life on earth is dependent on other living things for survival? Without water, plants, herbs, trees and animals, survival of human life on this planet would be impossible. We shouldn't take all these for granted but cherish and preserve them because they're God's common blessings for our survival.

They are not to be worshiped but utilized for our wellbeing. Look around you, everything you see that adds quality to your life comes from other living things created by God. So let us always be thankful to God, who gives life and all that preserves it.

Live and enjoy God's daily blessings for your life!

LIVING WORD for TODAY—January 17:

LOADED with DAILY BLESSINGS (Ps. 68:19-#17

LIFE—17

"...Yes, all that a man has he will give for his life." (Job 2:4)

How much is a human life worth? Sometimes when we are in difficult situations in life, we exercise thoughts of worthlessness. Many suicides, which are preventable, are committed due to thoughts of worthlessness. But let it be said clearly, life belongs to God, and any act of intentionally taking human life is a crime against God and humanity.

Even Satan, our worst adversary, recognized the great value of human life in his dialogue with God when he declared: "Yes, all that a man has he will give for his life" (Job 2:4).

God puts His highest premium on human life, and that's why He sent His only begotten Son Jesus Christ to die and redeem us. Human life is eternal and transcends the present life. So let's do whatever it takes to preserve life and cherish our lives. Your life is priceless, so enjoy it to the fullest before God daily.

Have a great day loaded with blessings!

LIVING WORD for TODAY—January 18:

LOADED with DAILY BLESSINGS (Ps. 68:19)-#18

LIFE—18

"Hear, O Israel; The LORD our God, the LORD is one!
"You shall love the LORD your God with all your heart, with all your soul and
with all your strength." (Deut. 6:4–5)

One of the struggles we go through in life as we grow up is the struggle for identity. Questions springing up in our minds are:

1. Who am I;
2. Why am I here;
3. How do I fit in; and
4. What is my goal or purpose in life?

These questions may sound simple, but they're crucial to our enjoyment and fulfillment in life. Every creature that has breath apart from humans has no problem with this struggle. The fish in the ocean knows its identity and purpose. It doesn't try to fly like the bird nor want to live on a tree.

But humans struggle with who they are and why they're here. The statement of purpose God gave to the Israelites and reaffirmed by our Lord Jesus Christ in Mark 12:29–31 is meant for all mankind.

To know who you are is to know your origin. You and I came from one living God. He put us here to love and serve Him, and one day, He will take us back individually to Himself to account for our lives on earth.

This is the core of finding our purpose and fulfillment on earth. I pray we all come to the full meaning of this statement of purpose for our lives on earth and live to fulfill it.

Have a day **loaded** with **blessings!**

LIVING WORD for TODAY—January 19:

LOADED with DAILY BLESSINGS (Ps. 68:19)-#19

LIFE—19

*"Surely goodness and mercy shall follow me
All the days of my life..."(Ps. 24:6)*

Today's date is unique. I was going to follow up on our topic of yesterday's devotion when the Lord changed my mind to declare the special blessing of Psalm 23:6a upon you today.

I hereby declare upon you and your loved ones that certainly the goodness and mercy of the Lord will pursue and overtake you for each of the remaining days, months, and years of your life in Jesus's mighty name! Amen and amen.

Thank the Lord for the blessings He has in store for you this year and the gift of faith He is building up in your heart to receive them.

Enjoy your day with **loaded blessings!**

LIVING WORD for TODAY—January 20:

LOADED with DAILY BLESSINGS (Ps. 68:19)-#20

LIFE—20

"And you shall love the LORD your God with all your heart, with all your soul, with all your mind, and with all your strength. This is the first commandment. And the second, like it, is this: 'You shall love your neighbor as yourself.' There is no other commitment greater than these." (Mark 12:30–31)

Everyone who would like to have a successful life must live with purpose. And to live with purpose, there must be a vision statement.

Our purpose in life is two-fold:

- To love God with all our beings without any reservations; and
- Secondly, to love our neighbors as we love ourselves.

Any life established on these fundamental principles is a fulfilled life. All other desires we may have should flow from these principles. So to have a meaningful life here on earth and hereafter is to have a simple statement of purpose, which is focused on the Lord's prescription from today's text. Without it, life has no direction. God wants you to enjoy your life to the fullest with Him and others. So live with the vision of who you are and what you're here for.

Have a purposeful day **loaded** with **blessings**!

LIVING WORD for TODAY—January 21:

LOADED with DAILY BLESSINGS (Ps. 68:19)-#21

LIFE—21

"I call heaven and earth as witnesses today against you, that I have set before you life and death, blessing and cursing; therefore choose life, that both you and your descendants may live; that you may love the LORD your God, that you may obey His voice, and that you may cling to Him, for He is your life and length of days..."(Deut. 30:19–20)

God's plan for our lives on earth is loaded with good things, such as long life, good health, blessings, and good quality of life. But the choices we make sometimes interfere with God's plan for us.

Therefore, it is important to cling to God as He directs us. When we choose to love Him with all our hearts, He leads us daily in the paths of righteousness, which glorify Him and bring blessings to us.

The choices we make in life also determine the condition of our hearts and lifestyles we live. So commit to God through our Lord Jesus Christ, who, by the Holy Spirit, spreads the love of God abroad in our hearts to love Him and others.

Enjoy your freedom of choice to be **loaded** with **blessings** today!

LIVING WORD for TODAY—January 22:

LOADED with DAILY BLESSINGS (Ps. 68:19)-#22

LIFE—22

"Keep your heart with all diligence, For out of it spring the issues of life." *(Prov. 4:23)*

We're blessed with life by the Creator. That life is pure and reproductive. However, as we grow and get exposed to the world, the vanities of this present evil age find their ways into our hearts and pollute the purity of life given to us by God. Hence, it is necessary for guarding our hearts and watching out for what we allow to take roots in them.

Bad habits don't become lifestyles overnight. They take time to grow their deep roots in us before producing fruits, which affect the negative outcome of our lives. What is true of bad habits is also true of good habits that have positive impacts on our lives.

The Scripture is full of counsel to guide us on putting away bad habits from our hearts and allowing the good ones to develop our lives positively. I recommend reading one chapter of the Book of Proverbs in the Bible daily. The Holy Spirit doesn't work in a vacuum but through the Word of God planted in the soil of our hearts. So begin to plant the Word of God in the soil of your heart, and watch how it will take deep roots and transform your life for the better over time.

"Good friends, good books, and a sleepy conscience: this is the ideal life."– Mark Twain

Have a great day **loaded** with **blessings!**

LIVING WORD for TODAY—January 23:

LOADED with DAILY BLESSINGS (Ps. 68:19)-#23

LIFE—23

"For whoever finds me finds life. And obtains favor from the LORD." (Prov. 8:35)

Reading good books should begin with the Bible, which is the book of all books. The Bible is the Word and wisdom of God.

In Proverbs chapter 8, wisdom is personified and speaks to us in a personal pronoun. Wisdom is life and the source of obtaining favor from the Lord. It is amazing that Jesus Christ our Lord is called the wisdom of God.

"...but to those who are called, both Jews and Greeks, Christ the power of God and the wisdom of God." (1 Cor. 1:24)

So put on Christ daily and let Him rule and direct your life. You will never be the same again, but will be transformed from glory to glory.

Have a glorious day **loaded** with **blessings!**

IVING WORD for TODAY—January 24:

LOADED with DAILY BLESSINGS (Ps. 68:19)-#24

LIFE—24

My son, do not forget my law,
But let your heart keep my commands;
For length of days and long life : And peace they will add to you." (Prov. 3:1–2)
"Hear, my son, and receive my sayings, And the years of your life will be many."(Prov. 4:10)

There are some blessings God bestows upon us without any conditions. These are common benefits of life from the Creator to all the living. But there are many blessings that are conditional.

Many of us desire long life with the quality of good health and prosperity. These blessings, most of the time, come with the lifestyles we choose. Living daily by the Word of God may sound naive and unpopular, but the benefits are great. So decide daily that you're going to live by the living truths of God's Word, regardless of what your relationship circles may say, and you will enjoy good and long life. The Lord will support your decision and grant you His power to live by His Word.

Have a great day **loaded** with God's **benefits!**

LIVING WORD for TODAY—January 25:

LOADED with DAILY BLESSINGS (Ps. 68:19)-#25

LIFE —25

"The fear of the LORD leads to life, And he who has it will abide in satisfaction; He will not be visited with evil." (Prov. 19:23)

God promised to load us with daily blessings. That's His desire for all His children with no exception regardless of who we are or where we live. "The earth is the LORD's, and all its fullness" (Ps. 24:1).

But we have the responsibility to tap into the rainfalls of God's blessings. When we allow our hearts to be governed by the fear of the Lord, we are making a statement that we want His blessings to flow to us and our families. This is a universal principle that works anywhere and at all times.

The Bible says: "Keep your heart with all diligence, For out of it spring the issues of life..." (Prov. 4:23–27). Read all the verses in this passage of Proverbs and also Psalm 34:12–19. These are specific Scriptures with loaded promises of blessings to those who are ruled by the fear of God. May the Holy Spirit establish His fear in our hearts, and may we allow Him to lead us daily as God's children to where we can flourish with His blessings.

Have a blessed day with His **loaded blessings!**

LIVING WORD for TODAY—January 26:

LOADED with DAILY BLESSINGS (Ps. 68:19)-#26

LIFE —26

"Remember now your Creator in the days of your youth,
Before the difficult days come,
And the years draw near when you say, 'I have no pleasure in them.'" (Eccles. 12:1)

Life is the greatest asset that any of us living has and must be handled with care.

How should we handle life securely? The best life's security is to keep it in the hands of the One who created it—God. This is the wise counsel of King Solomon after experiencing all the best life could offer. In his counsel to us in Ecclesiastes 12, he reminded us:

1. Our mortality; no matter how good and great, life is very brief;
2. This world is not our eternal home. We will individually go to our eternal home one day (Eccles. 12:5);
3. The human's physical body is from the dust and will return there at death (12:7);
4. The human's spirit will return to God, who gave it at death (12:7). The spirit never dies but lives on;
5. All human's achievements and accumulations will become vanity upon vanities (12:8). None will go with us to our eternal home;
6. The fear of God and doing His will stay with us forever (12:13); and
7. God will bring every human's deeds on earth into judgment, including secret things, whether good or evil (12:14).

Therefore, the best we can do with our lives now is to commit them to the Savior, who has already been judged for our sins and live for Him daily by faith.

Have a beautiful day **loaded** with **God's blessings!**

LIVING WORD for TODAY—January 27:

LOADED with DAILY BLESSINGS (Ps. 68:19)-#27

LIFE—27

"So teach us to number our days, that we may gain a heart of wisdom." (Ps. 90:12)

From the day of birth into the world, life on earth starts declining for each of us. Everyday we're alive is a subtraction from the days allotted to us by the Creator. Hence, the Scripture instructs us to number our days with God's help.

Celebrating birthdays is one of the events to count our days. But what do we do on our birthdays? Let me recommend an important component to be added to your birthday event: self-evaluation. This should include: Life Review and Life Preview.

Life Review:

- Affirmation of the right and good choices you've made in life; you're not a failure; affirm some good things you've done in life;
- Correction and learning from mistakes you've made; some mistakes may be irreversible, but you can learn life's lessons from them; and
- Forgiveness and forgetting the past mistakes and regrets and move on; never allow your past mistakes to dominate and control your life. God's blessings and opportunities are fresh and new every day. So connect with God's blessings and possibilities for your life daily.

His faithfulness is great and new every morning. He loves you (to be continued).

Have a great day **loaded** with His **blessings!**

LIVING WORD for TODAY—January 28:

LOADED with DAILY BLESSINGS (Ps. 68:19)-#28

LIFE—28

"Brethren, I do not count myself to have apprehended; but one thing I do, forgetting those things which are behind and reaching forward to those things which are ahead, I press toward the goal for the prize of the upward call of God in Christ Jesus." (Phil. 3:13–14)

There are stages of achievement in life. In life review, we affirm our accomplishments, lay memorial stones to mark them, and give glory to God.

But we never have the mindset of arriving. Life on earth is full of challenges, and we must confront them. Therefore, we must always have goals before us.

Life preview allows us to look ahead. Like Paul, we put behind our past glories and move forward to things that are ahead of us; pressing toward our ultimate prize of upward call of God in Christ Jesus.

Here are some questions to be considered in Life Preview:

- What does the future hold for me;
- What legacies am I leaving behind for the next generation;
- What about End of Life (EOL) matters? How prepared are you? Do you have a Living Trust and durable power of attorney; and
- Are you sure of where you will spend your eternity?

Are there places or people you would like to see or books you want to write? The bucket list goes on.

At the end of the day, have a sense of fulfillment that you've lived well and done your best. Leave the rest for others. Life goes on!

Enjoy your day of **loaded blessings!**

LIVING WORD for TODAY—January 29:

LOADED with DAILY BLESSINGS (Ps. 68:19)-#29

LIFE—29

"For what will it profit a man if he gains the whole world, and loses his own soul? Or what will a man give in exchange for his soul?" (Mark 8:36–37)

As we wrap up this month's series on **life** in our daily devotional, let us consider some closing thoughts.

1. Life is the greatest gift from God the Creator to mankind;
2. Everything we have or want to be is dependent upon life;
3. Without life, there's no hope, but while there's life, there is hope;
4. Life on earth is temporary and brief, but human souls live on eternally, either in heaven or hell;
5. At death, we take nothing we've acquired on earth with us but the fear and love of God;
6. Jesus Christ came to the world to redeem mankind and give abundant life to whoever believes in Him; and
7. Life is good, so let us live it in such a way that we make it better for others.

Your thoughts?

I pray that you enjoy your life to the fullest with the quality of eternal life that Christ gives.

Have a blessed day with **loaded blessings** to others.

LIVING WORD for TODAY—January 30:

LOADED with DAILY BLESSINGS (Ps. 68:19)-#30

LIFE—30

"For we brought nothing into this world, and it is certain we can carry nothing out." (1 Tim. 6:7)

"And the world is passing away, and the lust of it; but he who does the will of God abides forever." (1 John 2:17)

In bringing this series to an end, let me challenge you with the words of eighteenth-century revivalist, John Wesley:

> Do all the good you can
>
> In all the ways you can
>
> To all the people you can
>
> At all the times you can
>
> As long as you can.
>
> - John Wesley

Thank God for His blessing of life to complete the first month of the year. May He preserve us with quality of life for the rest of the year and many more to come.

Have a pleasant day/night with God's **loaded blessings!**

LIVING WORD for TODAY—January 31:

LOADED with DAILY BLESSINGS (Ps. 68:19)-#31

LIFE—31

"Death and life are in the power of the tongue.

And those who love it will eat its fruit." (Prov. 18:21)

A closing thought on life: the power of the tongue; the Bible says there's power of life and death in our tongues. Because of that, use your tongue to speak life to yourself and your loved ones daily. Use your tongue to bless and not to curse because your words are powerful. Speak to yourself and others what God says about you and them. This is one of the Lord's conditions for living long and prospering.

"Who is the man who desires life, And loves many days, that he may see good?

Keep your tongue from evil, And your lips from speaking deceit.

Depart from evil and do good; Seek peace and pursue it." (Ps. 34:12–14)

May the Lord help us to put our tongues under the control of the Holy Spirit, moment by moment.

Have a pleasant day with the **daily blessings** of **life!**

FEBRUARY—LOVE

LIVING WORD for TODAY—February 1:

LOADED with DAILY BLESSINGS (Ps. 68:19)-#32

LOVE—1

"For God so loved the world that He gave His only begotten Son, that whoever believes in Him should not perish but have everlasting life." (John 3:16)

Next to the blessing of **life**, which we're loaded with, is the blessing of **love**. Notice how much love people express to newborn babies when they are born into this world. Almost everybody in their communities displays spontaneous joy and love to them and their parents. There's also rejoicing in heaven for every child born into the world.

No wonder God so loved the world! How would you like to be born into a loveless world and home full of hate?

Please note: Without love, life is unsustainable in this world.

It takes love for mothers to feed, nurse, and protect their vulnerable dependent children. Just as the mother's love for her baby is natural, so is God's love for the world derived from His nature. "...for God is love" (1 John 4:8).

In this month of February, we're going to explore more about what true love is, how to experience it, and express it to others.

I pray that you will be loaded with the blessing of God's love to transform you and the world around you.

Have a happy month **loaded** with the **blessing** of love!

LIVING WORD for TODAY—February 2:

LOADED with DAILY BLESSINGS (Ps. 68:19)-#33

LOVE—2

"In this the love of God was manifested toward us, that God has sent His only begotten Son into the world, that we might live through Him. In this is love, not that we loved God, but that He loved us and sent His Son to be the propitiation for our sins." (1 John 4:9–10)

God is love, and true love comes from God. But before we go too far into the applications of love, let us explore the meaning of love.

Our English word for love comes from four Greek words.

1. *Eros*–from where we have the word *erratic*. In Greek mythology, Eros is the Greek god of love and sex (Google).

   This word is never used for love in the original language of the New Testament Bible, which is Greek.

2. *Phileo*–represents tender affection (John 21:15–17). In this brief dialogue between Christ and Peter, the Lord uses the greatest word for love, "agapao," to ask for Peter's commitment, but Peter replies Christ with a lesser word, "phileo," in his response. Jesus asks Peter: "Do you agapao me more than these?" Peter replies: "Yes, Lord; You know that I phileo You" (John 21:15). Later in verse 17, the Lord comes down to Peter's level of affectionate love. Phileo is the root word for philanthropy-kindness and Philadelphia-brotherly love.

3. *Agape*-(noun), or *Agapao*-(verb). This word is used in the New Testament Bible "to describe the attitude of God toward His Son (John 17:26), the human race, generally (John 3:16; Rom. 5:8), and the believers in the Lord Jesus Christ (John 14:21) (W. E. Vive, An Expository Dictionary of Biblical Words, p.692).

"Love can be known only from the actions it prompts." (W.E. Vine)

So *love* in the New Testament is used in the last two Greek words, phileo or agape/agapao. Our devotional will focus on these two words.

Have a lovely day with God's **loaded blessings!**

LIVING WORD for TODAY—February 3:

LOADED with DAILY BLESSINGS (Ps. 68:19) -#34

LOVE—3

"Be kindly affectionate to one another with brotherly love, in honor giving preference to one another..." (Rom. 12:10)

In our devotional message yesterday on the subject of love, the fourth Greek word for love was omitted. Please take note: The fourth Greek word is *storge,* representing, "family love, the bond among mothers, fathers, sons, daughters, sisters, and brothers" (Jack Zavada).

The Enhanced Strong's Lexicon defines *storge* as "cherishing one's kindred, especially parents and children and wives and husbands; loving affection; prone to love."

The word *storge* is not used in the Greek New Testament except in Romans 12:10 quoted above, where it is combined with *phileo. Philostorge* is used by Paul for "brotherly love." Though this word is not used in the Bible, the idea is, however, spread out in the whole Bible. So we have, *eros, phileo, agape/agapao,* and *storge;* four different words with different meanings in Greek for our English word for love.

May the Lord open our minds of understanding to grasp the concept of love; most importantly, the agape love in our relationships with God and one another.

Enjoy your day/night with God's **loaded blessing** of **love**!

LIVING WORD for TODAY—February 4:

LOADED with DAILY BLESSINGS (Ps. 68:19)-#35

LOVE—4

"And we have known and believed the love that God has for us. God is love, and he who abides in love abides in God, and God in him." (1 John 4:16)

The Bible is a book of God's relationship with mankind. One of the attributes of God that is well pronounced throughout this relationship is love. Everything about God is love, even in His judgments. So the Bible is a love story about God and humanity.

We cannot experience and express true love without God in us. All human love is limited to *eros, storge,* and *phileo.* The highest love is agape, and no one can express it without the Holy Spirit because it is His fruit (Gal. 5:22).

Therefore, to be loaded with God's kind of love, we must receive by faith His regeneration of life and be filled with His Spirit.

Please make being filled with the Holy Spirit your earnest prayer daily to bear His fruit of love. You can only give what you have, and you're known by your fruit.

Have a lovely day with God's **loaded blessings!**

LIVING WORD for TODAY—February 5:

LOADED with DAILY BLESSINGS (Ps. 68:19)-#36

LOVE—5

"He brought me to the banqueting house,
And his banner over me was love." (Song of Sol. 2:4)

Without love, life is miserable and cannot be sustained for too long. We all need love and the feeling of being loved. Only those who have received the gift of love can produce its fruits to bless others since we cannot give what we don't have.

When people treat you with hate and cruelty, know that they're just releasing what they have in them to you. Your response is to release what is in you to them.

Have you received the love of God that is in Christ Jesus? Do you feel loved by God daily in this hostile world full of hate? Let me assure you that, just as the Shulamite lady assured the daughters of Jerusalem of King Solomon's love for her, God's love is His banner over you in the midst of conflicts and struggles of life.

You are loved by the King of the whole universe! So dispense God's love in you to others daily, regardless of what they may dump on you.

"His banner over you is love!"

Have a lovely day **loaded** with **His blessing** of **love!**

LIVING WORD for TODAY—February 6:

LOADED with DAILY BLESSINGS (Ps. 68:19)-#37

LOVE—6

*"Who redeems your life from destruction,
Who crowns you with lovingkindness and tender mercies." (Ps. 103:4)*

One of the commonly used words in the Old Testament Bible for love is *lovingkindness*. With God, love does not stand alone. It is tied to kindness.

In the Hebrew language, the original language in which the Old Testament Bible was written, the word for *lovingkindness* is "chesed." This same word is used for steadfast love, faithfulness, mercy, goodness, grace, and devotion (W. E. Vine). This word is loaded with meaning in the Bible .

Chesed is connected to God's redemption of His people. By His "chesed," we are redeemed from destruction. But notice in Psalm 103:4, God also crowns us with His "chesed"—His lovingkindness. Whenever God sees us, He sees His crown of lovingkindness, grace, tender-mercy, compassion, and goodness upon our heads. The enemy of our souls also sees God's crown of "chesed" upon our heads, so he's not able to touch us.

Therefore, live with confidence, and rejoice and bless the Lord for the crown you wear on your head daily. You're so loaded with all the components of God's lovingkindness.

Have a great day with His **loaded blessings!**

LIVING WORD for TODAY—February 7:

LOADED with DAILY BLESSINGS (Ps. 68:19)-#38

LOVE —7

"Because Your lovingkindness is better than life,
My lips shall praise You." (Ps. 63:3)

Life is nothing but empty and miserable without the lovingkindness (chesed) of God. Life may offer us many blessings that come with travails, but God's blessings associated with His favor are without travails.

Do you recognize God's lovingkindness (chesed) upon your life? Then respond to God daily as David did in this psalm (Ps. 63:3–6). He utilized seven components of his personality to praise and worship God as Thomas Le Blanc indicates.

1. His lips-vs. 3; My lips shall praise You;
2. His tongue-vs. 4; Thus will I bless You while I live; and
3. With his hands-vs. 4; I will lift up my hands in Your name.

    (4-7 to be continued).

Praising and worshiping God in the Bible were not quiet and reserved. They involved actions of total human beings. So don't be quiet about God's lovingkindness in your life. It is all about your life. Be proud about it and share it with others so they, too, can trust the Lord.

David says: "My soul shall make its boast in the LORD" (Ps. 34:2).

Have a pleasant day with HIS **loaded blessing** of **love**!

LIVING WORD for TODAY—February 8:

LOADED with DAILY BLESSINGS (Ps. 68:19)-#39

LOVE—8

"Because Your lovingkindness is better than life... My soul shall be satisfied as with marrow and fatness, And my mouth shall praise You with joyful lips. When I remember You on my bed, I meditate on You in the night watches." (Ps. 63:3–6)

Because God's lovingkindness (chesed) is better than our very beings, we must join David in the Bible to praise and worship Him with seven members of our bodies and faculties of our minds. These are lips, tongues, hands, and:

4.   Will-vs. 5; "my soul shall be satisfied as with marrow and fatness."
5.   Mouth-vs. 5; "And my mouth shall praise You with joyful lips."
6.   Memories-vs. 6; "When I remember You on my bed."
7.   Intellect-vs. 6; "I meditate on You in the night watches." (Thomas Le Blanc, The Treasury of David)

Take a few minutes daily to reflect on the goodness, lovingkindness, mercies, and favors of God in your life, family, and loved ones. Praise Him for His blessings, but above all, worship Him by total surrender of your life to Him to do His will all the days of your life. The Lord will feel honored about your decision.

Have a blessed day/night with God's **loaded blessings!**

LIVING WORD for TODAY—February 9:

LOADED with DAILY BLESSINGS (Ps. 68:19)-#40

LOVE—9

*"For the mountains shall depart
And the hills be removed,
But My kindness shall not depart from you, Nor small My covenant of peace be removed,
Says the LORD, who has mercy on you." (Isa. 54:10)*

Another rendering of chesed or hesed in our English Bible is steadfast love. That is the word used for kindness in NKJV of our text for today.

On this fortieth day of the year, the Great **Lord** of the universe asked me to remind you of His promise that His steadfast love will never depart from you nor His covenant of peace be removed from you and your loved ones! His mercy will follow you for the rest of the year and far beyond.

Continue to live under His covenant, and no weapon formed against you shall ever prosper. This is the word of the Lord for you today.

Enjoy your day with **loaded blessing** of His **love!**

LIVING WORD for TODAY—February 10:

LOADED with DAILY BLESSINGS (Ps. 68:19)-#41

LOVE—10

"Through the LORD'S mercies we are not consumed,
Because His compassions fail not.
They are new every morning;
Great is Your faithfulness.
The LORD is my portion, says my soul,
Therefore I hope in Him." (Lam. 3:22–24)

The steadfast love of God is related to His covenant. God's covenant love to His people can never be broken because it is not bilateral but unilateral.

It does not depend upon human imperfection but upon the absolute perfection of God. That is why His chesed or hesed cannot fail. His great love, mercies, and compassions are spontaneous to His children.

It was out of His unfailing love that made Him send His Son, Jesus Christ, to the world to atone for our sins. God knows we're messed up and will always be. So His steadfast love has made a provision through Christ's sacrificial death on the Cross. So receive His love daily by dumping all your mess in His cleansing blood to be clean. His hesed love is new every morning; great is His faithfulness! That's what sustains us.

Enjoy your day with His abundant love!

LIVING WORD for TODAY—February 11:

LOADED with DAILY BLESSINGS (Ps. 68:19)-#42

LOVE—11

"Who is a God like You,
Pardoning iniquity And passing over the transgression of the remnant of
His heritage?
He does not retain His anger forever, Because He delights in mercy.
He will again have compassion on us,
And will subdue our iniquities.
You will cast all our sins Into the depths of the sea." (Mic. 7:18–19)

There is no god that can measure up to our living God.

One of His attributes is that He forgives and forgets.

His greatest love to humanity is the forgiveness of sins. Human beings are essentially sinful, and God is absolutely holy. To relate to humans, God, in His steadfast love and mercy, provided a bridge. That bridge is His only Son Jesus Christ. God took our sins away into the depth of sea of forgetfulness. God doesn't see those who are in Christ as sinners but as His holy children. He did this out of His compassionate love and mercy (hesed).

Thank God for the gift of love from the King of the whole universe! Let us embrace His love, enjoy its delivering power, and share it with others in the circle of our relationships.

Have a lovely day **loaded** with the gift of **love**!

LIVING WORD for TODAY—February 12:

LOADED with DAILY BLESSINGS (Ps. 68:19)-#43

LOVE—12

"And the LORD passed before him and proclaimed, 'The LORD, the LORD God, merciful and gracious, long suffering, and abounding in goodness and truth...'" (Exod. 34:6)

When faced with uncertainties, an unknown future, surrounded by people who are fickle in faith, enemies within and without, mountain of problems, and you don't know what to do, your best bet is to go to the Lord and hang your hopes and directions upon Him.

His name and nature were revealed to Moses as he led the children of Israel through a hostile environment, which changed many of them negatively. But God saw His faithful ones through.

Instead of being **loaded** with what's going on around you, let the Lord transform and **load** you with His mercy, grace, longsuffering, goodness, and truth. He is our Source of everything we need to live. His nature is **love**!

Have a gracious day **loaded** with **His love**!

HAPPY VALENTINE'S DAY!

LIVING WORD for TODAY—February 13:

LOADED with DAILY BLESSINGS (Ps. 68:19)-#44

LOVE—13

"Oh give thanks to the LORD, for He is good!
For His mercy endures forever.
Let the redeemed of the LORD say so, Whom He has redeemed from the hand
of the enemy..." (Ps. 107:1–2)

God's steadfast love surrounds humanity like the oceans. There's nowhere we go that His love is not seen. But the greatest expression of His love was demonstrated in redemption. God, out of His great mercy (chesed), bought us back from the slave market of our enemy.

The same lovingkindness of God that bought us back to Himself also cleanses and preserves us daily from the corruption and enticements of this present evil age.

So if you're saved, you're among the redeemed, and the praises of the Lord should fill your mouth daily regardless of the pressures of the world you may be going through.

"Let the redeemed of the LORD say so;" "His lovingkindness endures forever!" We don't earn it, but it is freely bestowed upon us by our gracious loving Savior.

So affirm and enjoy God's benefit of love daily and be a loving person.

Have a blessed day with His **loaded love!**

LIVING WORD for TODAY—February 14:

LOADED with DAILY BLESSINGS (Ps. 68:19)-#45

LOVE—14

"But I say to you, love your enemies, bless those who curse you, do good to those who hate you, and pray for those who spitefully use you and persecute you, that you may be sons of your Father in heaven; for He makes His sun rise on the evil and on the good, and sends rain on the just and on the unjust." (Matt. 5:44–45)

Having learned about the loving nature of our God as revealed to us in the Bible, let us begin to learn how to demonstrate the love of God in our lives if we have God in us.

Firstly, true love, which is the agape-God-kind-of-love does not discriminate in expressing goodness and kindness to others. God's love is available to everyone anywhere.

Secondly, true love expresses goodness and kindness, even to our enemies who hate and persecute us. That's why we don't see God's thunder striking down the terrorists that kill the innocents. God loves them but hates their barbaric sinful acts.

Thirdly, God's love is the true and sincere love by which we measure our own love. Christ is our model of love.

God is love, and Jesus Christ came to demonstrate it to us, even in a world full of hatred and hostility. So if He lives in us, we have no option but to love like Him. Whenever we fall short of His standard of love, we must go to Him for help.

Have a lovely day with **loaded love** to give to those you're in contact with.

LIVING WORD for TODAY—February 15:

LOADED with DAILY BLESSINGS (Ps. 68:19)-#46

LOVE—15

"This is my commandment, that you love one another as I have loved you.

Greater love has no one than this, than to lay down one's life for his friends." *(John 15:12–13)*

The Ten Commandments are summarized in two statements in the Bible: Love God with your whole life, and love your neighbors as yourself. (Mark 12:29–31)

Jesus Christ reaffirmed these statements in His teachings and laid more emphasis on the second. In fact, He made loving one another His new commandment to His disciples before He left the world. Why? Because our love for God can only be measured in the way it is demonstrated to people, especially His children.

Since God is invisible, our love for Him is in the spirit. But what is in our hearts must be put into action in concrete terms for the people we see and deal with. John, the apostle, makes it even more imperative for us to the point of laying down our lives for the brethren. "By this we know love, because He laid down His life for us. And we also ought to lay down our lives for the brethren" (1 John 3:16).

This is the greatest of all God's commandments to us.

May the Lord help us to constantly abide in Christ so He can produce His fruit of love in us daily.

Have a loving day with His **loaded blessing** of **love**!

LIVING WORD for TODAY—February 16:

LOADED with DAILY BLESSINGS (Ps. 68:19)-#47

LOVE—16

"Beloved, if God so loved us, we also ought to love one another.
No one has seen God at any time. If we love one another, God abides in us, and
His love has been perfected in us." (1 John 4:11–12)

The triune Godhead is Spirit, and no human being can see Him and live. Jesus Christ is the perfect manifestation of God in human flesh for humans to know how God is. Christ is the embodiment of God's love. People who lived with Him when He was here on earth saw and testified that all they've read, heard, and thought of God were seen in the man Jesus Christ. They all came to one conclusion that Jesus Christ, whom they lived with, was God in human body. You can read about their testimonies in the Gospels, the books they wrote about Him, the Bible.

So we can see the demonstrations of God's love by how Christ lived, His acts of compassion, healings, feeding the hungry, teaching and showing the way to God, giving life to the dead, forgiving sins, restoring hopes, and finally, laying down His life to save the world.

It is impossible for anyone to love according to God's standard without knowing Jesus Christ. Hence, our knowledge of Him and His Spirit in us releases God's love through us to benefit others.

Pray that you will not just be fascinated by the deeds of Christ but be transformed by His Spirit into His image daily.

Have a blessed day with **God's loaded blessings!**

LIVING WORD for TODAY—February 17:

LOADED with DAILY BLESSINGS (Ps. 68:19)-#48

LOVE—17

"But whoever has this world's goods, and sees his brother in need, and shuts up his heart from him, how does the love of God abide in him?
My little children, let us not love in words or in tongue, but in deed and in truth."
(1 John 3:17–18)

The message of love in the Bible becomes specific and personal to us. Just as our faith in God, our love for God and the brethren must also lead to action.

The same word, love, is used as a noun and verb in English. But in Greek, it is, agape (noun) and *agapao* (verb). Just as God's love for the world led Him to give His only begotten Son as a substitutionary sacrifice to take away our sins, so must our love for God and others lead us to actions.

Love without action is dead!

So let your love, my love, lead us to help others in need around us. Although we cannot save the world, only God can; but we can change the world around us for good through our acts of agape love.

Pray that the Lord will lead you to someone you can help today without expecting anything in return.

Have a great day with **His loaded blessings!**

LIVING WORD for TODAY—February 18:

LOADED with DAILY BLESSINGS (Ps. 68:19)-#49

LOVE—18

"For you, brethren, have been called to liberty, only do not use liberty as an opportunity for the flesh, but through love serve one another.

For all the law is fulfilled in one word, even in this: 'You shall love your neighbor as yourself.'" (Gal. 5:13–14)

Loving one another is not an option for Christians but a duty, which we owe one another. While it is important to celebrate our freedom from the devil and all his devices, the Bible, however, draws a balance for our freedom. Our freedom is from the kingdom of Satan into the kingdom of Christ.

The law that governs the kingdom of Christ is the law of the Spirit, and the law of the Spirit is agape love. The fruit of pure love is the evidence of true Christianity.

God will always bring people to us to demonstrate how much we love Him. Please be sensitive to the opportunity coming your way to put God's love in your heart into action daily. None of us can escape this.

Have a blessed day with **His loaded blessings** of **love**!

LIVING WORD for TODAY—February 19:

LOADED with DAILY BLESSINGS (Ps. 68:19)-#50

LOVE—19

"But earnestly desire the best gifts. And yet I show you a more excellent way. Though I speak with the tongues of men and of angels, but have not love, I have become sounding brass or a clanging cymbal." (1 Cor. 12:31; 13:1)

Now we come to the greatest chapter on love in the Scriptures ever written under the inspiration of the Holy Spirit. The title of the chapter is taken from the preceding verse, which ends Paul's explanation of the gifts of the Holy Spirit in 1 Corinthians 12.

Agape love is more excellent than any gift that God the Holy Spirit may bestow on us.

The first on the list of gifts compared to love in 1 Corinthians 13 is the gift of speech. People who are eloquent in speech are easily recognizable in the crowd and can easily become leaders. But let us beware of people who are gifted in making excellent speeches in the church because they can be the weakest in character.

We should always be patient in our approval of people because of the way they are persuasive in their speeches.

Demonstration of love is the supreme measure of a man or woman of God. Let agape love be the motivation of all that you do in life and ministry, and you will be approved by God.

Have a great day with **loaded blessings** of **His love**!

LIVING WORD for TODAY—February 20:

LOADED with DAILY BLESSINGS (Ps. 68:19)-#51

LOVE—20

"And though I have the gift of prophecy, and understand all mysteries and all knowledge, and though I have all faith, so I could remove mountains, but have not love, I am nothing." (1 Cor. 13:2)

The prophetic gift, word of knowledge, and supernatural faith are parts of the powerful gifts that produce miracles. Anyone operating these gifts is highly honored and elevated by the congregation anywhere. These apostolic gifts are needed in the church today and always, especially in the age that questions the reality of Christ's resurrection.

The Christians' answer should be more than persuasive arguments, but in demonstrations of the power of the gospel of Christ in changed lives, and signs and wonders.

In fact, Paul, the apostle, operated in all these gifts and still considered himself nothing without love, which is the fruit of the Spirit and more excellent than these gifts.

So in all your getting, be sure to get love because, without it, all our gifts are useless

May the fruit of agape love operate more in our lives daily than any gift we may possess.

Have a blessed day **loaded** with the **blessings** of **love!**

LIVING WORD for TODAY—February 21:

LOADED with DAILY BLESSINGS (Ps. 68:19)-#52

LOVE—21

"And though I bestow all my goods to feed the poor, and though I give my body to be burned, but have not love, it profits me nothing." (1 Cor. 13:3)

It is possible to be an altruistic person without agape love. The gift of altruism is an act of benevolent giving out of selfless love for the welfare of others or mankind. Individuals with this gift may also exhibit the behavior of martyrdom. Many early Christians, including Paul, the author of this epistle, were martyrs for Christ. And many Christians today are still being martyred for their faith. However, it is possible to do all these acts out of pride of becoming a hero and have nothing to do with agape love.

So let us always examine our motives for what we do and ask ourselves the purpose of doing them.

I pray the Holy Spirit to examine and correct any wrong and selfish motives in us as we express our generosities to others.

Have a pleasant day/evening with God's **loaded blessings** of **love!**

LIVING WORD for TODAY—February 22:

LOADED with DAILY BLESSINGS (Ps. 68:19)-#53

LOVE—22

"Love suffers long and is kind, Love does not envy, love does not parade itself, is not puffed up." (1 Cor. 13:4)

Love is excellent and supreme. This is clearly stated in verses one through three. No gifts we display can replace the agape love in our lives.

Love is easy and simple.

From verses four through seven, we see the easiness and simplicity of love. Agape love is not difficult and complicated. The most difficult people you could ever deal with are those who pretend to be what they are not. Their ways of life are complicated and not straightforward. Try to avoid them. Religious groups are full of them. Jesus Christ calls them hypocrites.

But the opposite is the agape love. People whose lives are controlled by agape love are easy to deal with because they have nothing to hide. Even when people are unkind to them, they are still kind because the fruit in them is love. They have no time to brag about what they have other than boasting in the Lord and of His glory in them. Agape love has no room for pride and arrogant behaviors. Love is not puffed up but humble.

I pray the Holy Spirit of God to fill our hearts with His fruit of love daily in all our dealings, even with difficult and complicated people. May His love manifest in us so we can be easy to relate to in our circles of relationships.

Have a great day with **His loaded blessings** of **love!**

LIVING WORD for TODAY—February 23:

LOADED with DAILY BLESSINGS (Ps. 68:19)-#54

LOVE—23

"...does not behave rudely, does not seek its own, is not provoked, thinks no evil..." *(1 Cor. 13:5)*

This love chapter in the Bible, 1 Corinthians 13, should be a mirror through which we look into our hearts daily. Actually, it has been suggested that love should be replaced with God in the chapter because everything that love does or doesn't can only be found in God. That's why this kind of love is not human but the fruit, which the Holy Spirit produces in a Christian who lives a surrendered life to Him.

You can teach a dog to fly, but it's not going to happen because dogs don't fly; that's not their nature. Agape love is not in the human nature but the product of God the Holy Spirit in a committed Christian life. So live by the Spirit, and what is impossible with human nature will be made possible in you by Christ.

Have a peaceful day/evening with **God's loaded blessings!**

LIVING WORD for TODAY—February 24:

LOADED with DAILY BLESSINGS (Ps. 68:19)-#55

LOVE—24

"...does not rejoice in iniquity, but rejoices in the truth..." (1 Cor. 13:6)

There is a clear line of demarcation between godliness and ungodliness, just as a difference between light and darkness.

Those who are filled with the Holy Spirit are not only known by the gifts of the Spirit they exhibit, but by the fruit they produce. Agape love is the unquestionable fruit. Since love does not rejoice in iniquity, those who bear it will not approve those who practice iniquity nor associate with them. Our love for sinners is to show them the Savior by our actions and character. The Bible condemns those who don't practice the abominable sins of sinners but approve and are happy with their deeds (Rom. 1:32).

May the Holy Spirit spread His love abroad in our hearts daily so we can become light and salt in our communities.

Have a beautiful day/evening with God's **loaded blessings!**

LIVING WORD for TODAY—February 25:

LOADED with DAILY BLESSINGS (Ps. 68:19)-#56

LOVE—25

"...bears all things, believes all things, hopes all things, endures all things." (1 Cor. 13:7)

True love is discerning, and because it has pure eyes of the Spirit, it discerns the truth from error. Hence, it bears all things, believes all things, hopes all things, and endures all things.

I believe "all things" in this verse are things according to the will of God. "And we know that all things work together for good to those who love God, to those who are the called according to His purpose" (Rom. 8:28).

There are situations God may allow in the lives of His children, which may not be what they expect, but because the fruit of the Spirit, which is love, operates in them, they will endure to the end. Agape love gives us the enduring grace with the positive attitude of hope.

May Christ Jesus in His love release His abundant grace to your life today and always, to live through all things God may allow to come your way for His glory and your blessings!

Have a great day with His **loaded blessings!**

LIVING WORD for TODAY—February 26:

LOADED with DAILY BLESSINGS (Ps. 68:19)-#57

LOVE—26

"Love never fails. But whether there are prophecies, they will fail; whether there are tongues, they will cease; whether there is knowledge, it will vanish away." (1 Cor. 13:8)

     3. Agape Love is eternal and supernatural (8-13).

In the preceding verses of this love chapter of the Bible, Paul, the apostle, shows us how:

1.   Agape love is excellent and supreme above all gifts.
2.   Agape love is easy and simple in character.

In the last section of the chapter, we will discover how:

3. Agape love is eternal and supernatural. "Love never fails." While all our gifts and the manifestations of spiritual gifts in our lives come to an end, agape love will continue with us to our eternal destinations. Why? Because agape love is God, and God is eternal. Since love will live with us forever, let us cultivate it more in our lives and avoid any temporal personal benefits that may suppress it in our lives.

I pray the Lord to reveal to us daily the eternal and supernatural nature of agape love, and empower us to let it reign supreme in our dealings with people around us.

Have a lovely day with God's **loaded blessings!**

LIVING WORD for TODAY—February 27:

LOADED with DAILY BLESSINGS (Ps. 68:19)-#58

LOVE—27

"For we know in part and we prophesy in part.
But when that which is perfect has come, then that which is in part will be done
away." (1 Cor. 13:9–10)

As long we are in the human body, we can never live a life of absolute perfection. We will always have some shortcomings. This does not make us complacent but challenges us to keep improving and believing for the best.

This is what Paul seems to have in mind in verse ten. Everything we do or have now, even in the exercise of spiritual gifts, is imperfect. But once we leave the mortal body to the spirit body, our imperfections give way to perfection. Until then, we continue to live in progressive perfection.

Our love for the Lord and others will continue to grow, just like a child grows into adulthood. So let us continue to grow and improve in our love relationships for the things of God and toward the people the Lord brings our way day by day.

Have a great day with His **loaded blessings!**

LOADED with DAILY BLESSINGS (Ps. 68:19)-#59

LOVE—28

"When I was a child, I spoke as a child, I understood as a child, I thought as a child, but when I became a man, I put away childish things." (1 Cor. 13:11)

In wrapping up this beautiful chapter of love, Paul, the apostle, describes the condition and development of a church contending with each other about spiritual gifts. Whenever the exercise of spiritual gifts is causing division among God's people, it is an indication of childishness and lack of growth in love.

In a follow-up to this chapter, Paul, in chapter 14, uses the analogy of unity in the Godhead and human body to describe how growing in love harmonizes the body of Christ instead of tearing it apart.

The message to us is we all need to stop childish behaviors in pursuing and being carried away by manifestations of the spiritual gifts. Rather, we should grow up in Godlike love. It is also noteworthy to understand that agape love is childlike love and not childish. The two concepts are not the same. While we should get rid of childish behaviors in our love relationships, we should never stop childlike love, which is simple, uncomplicated, and unconditional.

May we continue to grow up to be like our Heavenly Father in love (Matt. 5:43–48).

Have a lovely day with God's **loaded blessings!**

LIVING WORD for TODAY—February 29:

LOADED with DAILY BLESSINGS (Ps. 68:19)-#60

LOVE—29

"For now we see in a mirror, dimly, but then face to face. Now I know in part, but then I shall know just as I also am known.
And now abide faith, hope, love, these three, but the greatest of these is love." (1 Cor. 13:12–13)

Love is the greatest and eternal. Everything else will fail, but love never fails.

As I remarked at the beginning of this chapter of love, I will repeat again. 1 Corinthians 13 should be a mirror through which we examine ourselves daily to see if we're still in faith. We live by faith and always hope for a better future here now. But the time is coming when we shall see our Lord, whom we believe and hope for, face to face. By then, we would not need faith and hope anymore. But love stays with us forever. May the Lord reveal our deficiencies to us and create a contrite spirit in us so we can continue to grow in love daily.

Have a happy night/day with God's **loaded blessings** of **love!**

MARCH—HEALTH

LIVING WORD for TODAY—March 1:

LOADED with DAILY BLESSINGS (Ps. 68:19)—#61

HEALTH—1

"BLESS the LORD, O my soul;
And all that is within me, bless His holy name!
Bless the LORD, O my soul,
And forget not all His benefits:
Who forgives all your iniquities,
Who heals all your diseases." (Ps. 103:1–3)

Thank God for another month of **loaded blessings**! In January, we were loaded with the blessing of **live**, and in February, with the blessing of **love**. Now in March, we're being blessed with **health**. Oh praise His holy name!

We hear a lot in the news these days of a new virus from China that has just invaded our world called coronavirus or COVID-19. The virus itself is mild and not as deadly as speculated. However, the fear of it is deadlier than the virus itself.

In the midst of this pandemic, what should be the Christian's attitude? During our daily devotional this month, we will consider the benefit of good health that God has made available to us and see how, by faith, we can appropriate it into our lives daily.

But let us begin by joining David to appreciate what our Lord is doing in our health daily. He "heals us from all our diseases." Note that it is from "all" and not some or part, but "all." This is enough to give us the assurance that we're covered and protected from all viruses, including COVID-19. Your health is totally guaranteed, including your family, during this month and beyond, in Jesus Christ name!

Have a healthy month **loaded** with God's **blessing** of good health!

LIVING WORD for TODAY—March 2:

LOADED with DAILY BLESSINGS (Ps. 68:19)—#62

HEALTH—2

"BLESS the LORD, O my soul;
And all that is within me, bless His holy name!
Bless the LORD, O my soul,
And forget not all His benefits:
Who forgives all your iniquities,
Who heals all your diseases," (Ps. 103:1–3)

Health is wealth. A healthy body is needed to be happy, make wealth, and enjoy life.

Hence, the Lord promised to consistently be the Healer of His children.

The entrance of sin into the world opened the gateways of sicknesses and diseases to mankind. It is important to know that forgiveness of sins precedes healing of diseases.

While it is difficult to live in the sin-sick world without being sick, it is, however, refreshing to know that the children of God have more than the medical doctors to take care of them when they are sick. They have the **Lord** of all flesh, who forgives all their iniquities and heals all their diseases.

So be sure to claim His forgiveness for all your sins daily through the cleansing blood of Jesus Christ. And when sick, prayer of faith to the Lord is the first cause and ongoing, even while seeking medical treatments.

I pray the Lord to keep us healthy, all the days of our lives, and speedily intervene in our healings whenever we're sick.

Have a healthy day/evening with His **loaded blessings!**

LIVING WORD for TODAY—March 3:

LOADED with DAILY BLESSINGS (Ps. 68:19)-#63

HEALTH—3

"So Abraham prayed to God; and God healed Abimelech, his wife, and his female servants. Then they bore children; for the LORD had closed up all the wombs of the house of Abimelech because of Sarah, Abraham's wife." (Gen. 20:17–18)

While not everyone who is sick or afflicted with one disease or the other can be said to be suffering because of his or her sins, it is, however, noteworthy to see the correlation between sin and sickness in the Scriptures.

The entrance of sin into the world brought sickness and disease, which affect all creatures. Therefore, whether we're holy or sinful, we can lose our health as a result of ignorance, lack of proper diet, disobedience and sins of others, communicable diseases, heredity, environmental pollution, and lack of proper hand hygiene.

In the first recorded case of prayer of healing in the Bible, the sickness of Abimelech, the king of Gerar and his household in Genesis 20, was a result of sin. God had to intervene and instructed the king in his dream to do restitution to Abraham before healing could occur through Abraham's prayer.

So let us be careful how we live and know that our actions can have unhealthy effects on others. Thank God for His benefits of forgiveness of iniquities and healing of all diseases, regardless of their causes. These benefits belong to the children of God. So always claim them for your health when you're sick.

Have a blessed day with His **loaded blessings!**

LIVING WORD for TODAY—March 4:

LOADED with DAILY BLESSINGS (Ps. 68:19)-#64

HEALTH—4

"...and said, 'If you diligently heed the voice of the LORD your God and do what is right in His sight, give ear to His commandments and keep all His statutes. I will put none of the diseases on you which I have brought on the Egyptians. For I am the LORD who heals you.'" (Exod. 15:26)

One of the revelation names of God is Jehovah Raphah: the LORD who heals. This name was revealed to Moses in the desert as he led Israelites to the Promised Land.

It was a time of crisis of no water to drink, and when they found a river they could drink from, it was toxic. The Israelites complained to Moses, and he took their complaints to God in prayer. God's solution was through a tree for healing the water and forgiving the crowd for sinning. The tree pointed to the cross of Jesus Christ, which is the remedy for human sins and sickness.

In this passage, God tied sickness to sin and healing to obedience. So to stay healthy, we must accept God's solution for sin and sickness. The solution is twofold; the death of Christ on the cross and our obedience to accept it. God is always interested to heal. All we need to do is always go to Him first, with a contrite spirit, and claim Him as our Healer.

Have a healthy day with His **loaded blessings!**

LIVING WORD for TODAY—March 5:

LOADED with DAILY BLESSINGS (Psa.68:19)—#65

HEALTH—5

"So you shall serve the LORD your God, and He will bless your bread and your water. And I will take sickness away from the midst of you.
No one shall suffer miscarriage or be barren in your land; I will fulfill the number of your days." (Exod. 23:25–26)

Divine health is God's provision for His children. The Bible is loaded with promises of God to keep us healthy and make us live to fulfill the number of our days here on earth.

These promises are direct and applicable to any of His children who believes them. When a doctor prescribes medicine to cure a disease, it is up to the patient to take the prescription drug to be healed. The doctor is not going to force it on the patient.

So divine health is provided and always available to the obedient children of God. The Lord will not force them on us if we refuse to take them. Believe His words for health in the Bible and apply them to your life and household daily. You will live in divine health and fulfill the number of your days on earth.

Have a great day/ evening with God's **loaded blessings!**

LIVING WORD for TODAY—March 6:

LOADED with DAILY BLESSINGS (Ps. 68:19)-#66

HEALTH—6

"My son give attention to my words,
Incline your ear to my sayings.
Do not let them depart from your eyes; Keep them in the midst of your heart;
For they are life to those who find them.
And health to all their flesh." (Prov. 4:20–22)

There are many sicknesses and diseases in the world today due to disobedience.

A visit to the medical institutions around will convince any honest person of this fact. While all sicknesses may not be a direct result of personal disobedience of the sick person, it is, however, clear that our hospitals, mental health centers, drugs and alcohol rehabilitation centers, and so on, are full of patients who have violated and abused simple principles of healthy living.

There are many blessings of living a normal, moral, and obedient life. One of them is good health. God promised good life and health to His children. But it is our responsibility to obey and follow His instructions in the Bible to benefit from them.

The lifestyle you live now is a seed being planted that will grow to your future harvest of physical and mental health. So live well and follow the blueprints of God and healthcare to enjoy a healthy old age.

"For they are life to those who find them. And health to all their flesh" (Prov. 4:21).

Have a blessed day with His **loaded blessings**!

LIVING WORD for TODAY—March 7:

LOADED with DAILY BLESSINGS (Ps. 68:19)-#67

HEALTH—7

"And the LORD will take away from you all sickness, and will afflict you with none of the terrible diseases of Egypt which you have known, but will lay them on all those who hate you." (Deut. 7:15)

We hear so much today in the news media of a new disease afflicting people all over the world called COVID-19. Schools are closed in some cities and counties, billions of dollars are being voted to fight it, and masks are sold out in stores to protect the spread of this virus disease. This could be one of the signs of end time predicted in the Bible.

But in the midst of these fears and commotions, God's covenant of protection to His own should be heard louder: "I will afflict you with none of these terrible diseases." But you must be marked with the seal of God on your forehead. The seal of God is the Holy Spirit in those covered by the blood of Jesus Christ.

God is still in control of whatever may be happening in the world, and He knows His own. So if you're a child of God, relax and don't be afraid. Follow the health rules, but also know that you're under the protective covenant of God—you and your household. You shall not be afflicted with the COVID-19 virus nor any other in Jesus Christ's name!

Have a peaceful day with **God's loaded blessing** of **health!**

LIVING WORD for TODAY—March 8:

LOADED with DAILY BLESSINGS (Ps. 68:19)-#68

HEALTH—8

"Because you have made the LORD, who is my refuge,
Even the Most High, your dwelling place,
No evil shall befall you,
Nor shall any plague come near your dwelling;
For He shall give His angels charge over you,
To keep you in all your ways." (Ps. 91:9–11)

This prayer of Moses for the children of Israel in Goshen is relevant for all the children of God in the world today and beyond. Just as different plagues were widespread in Egypt, and the Lord put His protective covering around His people, He wants to do the same for us in these days of the COVID-19 virus and many that may still show up. I pray:

"No evil shall befall you, nor shall any plague come near your dwelling."

But you have to make the **Lord** your refuge and dwelling place. This means:

- Being contrite in the spirit;
- By faith, receiving the cleansing of the blood of Jesus Christ daily; and
- Affirming your relationship with the risen Christ by claiming your rights as a child of the Most High God. Please note: This does not exclude you from following the universal health precautions, most importantly, hand hygiene.

Let us add knowledge to our faith in the Lord.

Have a healthy day/ evening with God's **loaded blessings!**

LIVING WORD for TODAY—March 9:

LOADED with DAILY BLESSINGS (Ps. 68:19)—#69

HEALTH—9

"Fools, because of their transgressions,
And because of their iniquities, were afflicted." (Ps.107:17)

Health is wealth. It is when we're healthy that we can make wealth. A sick person in the hospital bed or at home is concerned about one thing: regaining back health.

The Lord our God is the source of good health. His means of keeping us healthy may be divine or human; hence, God's healing for our bodies does not preclude medicines, good nutrition, proper rest, sleep, and regular, moderate exercises.

But sometimes God's children wander away from God and walk in their own stupid ways. God's way of getting their attention and calling them back to their senses could be through the affliction of sickness and disease.

Whenever this happens, we must do like the children of Israel did in their afflictions. They cried to the Lord in repentance, and He delivered them. "Then they cried out to the LORD in their trouble, And He saved them out of their distresses."

Never discount the power of prayer of faith in times of affliction. Our merciful God hears and answers the cries of faith of His children, and He will deliver.

Enjoy a peaceful day with His **loaded blessing** of **health**!

LIVING WORD for TODAY—March 10:

LOADED with DAILY BLESSINGS (Ps. 68:19)—#70

HEALTH—10

"He sent His word and healed them,
And delivered them from their destructions." (Ps. 107:20)

Psalm 107 is a good read for anyone going through distress and affliction. It is divided into five sections, with each starting with a refrain of thanksgiving for God's deliverance in times of trouble and affliction.

It is noteworthy to see in verse 20 the means by which God heals. God heals by His spoken Word! Jesus Christ our Lord, when He came in flesh, demonstrated the power of the spoken Word of God in healing and deliverance from the power of demons. At no time did He pray to heal and deliver the sick. He simply spoke the Word.

A Roman centurion captured this concept when he came to Jesus to seek deliverance for his servant, who was paralyzed and dreadfully tormented at home. While Jesus wanted to go and heal the servant in the centurion's home, this military officer recognized the power of a spoken word by a person of authority. He said to Jesus: "But only speak a word, and my servant will be healed" (Matt. 8:8). And that's what Jesus did, and the servant was healed.

Are you in distress or affliction? Speak the Word of God to your situation. If you've prayed and there seems to be no change, try to speak the Word and claim God's promises relating to your situation. Remember:

"Many are the afflictions of the righteous, But the LORD delivers him out of them all" (Ps. 34:19).

The Lord will deliver you and grant you good health in Jesus Christ's name!

Have a great day **loaded** with His **blessings**!

LIVING WORD for TODAY—March 11:

LOADED with DAILY BLESSINGS (Ps. 68:19)-#71

HEALTH—11

Here is the word of the **Lord** to His covenant children in these days of the novel coronavirus pandemic threatening nations of the world:

"Fear not, for I am with you;
Be not dismayed, for I am your God.
I will strengthen you,
Yes, I will help you,
I will uphold you with My righteous right hand." (Isa. 41:10)

And Jesus Christ prayed to God the Father for us:

"I do not pray that You should take them out of the world, but that You should keep them from the evil one. They are not of the world, just as I am not of the world" (John 17:15–16).

You can take these words of assurance of God's presence and protection with you as you go about your normal life and business. No virus nor disease will ever come near you and your loved ones in Jesus Christ's name!

Have a healthy day **loaded** with **His blessings!**

LIVING WORD for TODAY—March 12:

LOADED with DAILY BLESSINGS (Ps. 68:19)-#72

HEALTH—12

"He who dwells in the secret place of the Most High
Shall abide under the shadow of the Almighty.
I will say of the LORD, He is my refuge and my fortress;
My God, in Him I will trust." (Ps. 91:1–2)

We're in the world but not of the world. The Lord intentionally spreads us all over the world to represent Him. Therefore, we're Christ's ambassadors.

However, many things happen in the world that affect us. The impact of the current novel COVID-19 pandemic is already having serious impact in the world economy. Schools are closed, stores/shopping malls are deserted, the stock market is trading very low, and people are losing their investments. The traveling industries are not left out. Flights are being canceled, and many are changing their plans to travel. Think of how many missions trips will be affected. In fact, I had to cancel my mission trip to Europe and Africa in April, which I had bought flight tickets for since January when President Trump announced the travel ban from Europe to America on Wednesday. Even churches are closing their doors and going online. So the impact affects all of us, especially in the underdeveloped countries. And we don't know how long it is going to take us to return to normalcy.

In the midst of all the chaos and confusion, let not your heart be troubled. Reaffirm your faith daily in the Lord and declare: "He is my refuge and my fortress; My God, in Him I will trust" (Ps. 91:2). God is real, and He takes care of His own.

Have a safe day/ evening with His **loaded blessings**!

LIVING WORD for TODAY—March 13:

LOADED with DAILY BLESSINGS (Ps. 68:19)-#73

HEALTH—13

"Surely He shall deliver you from the snare of the fowler
And from the perilous pestilence.
He shall cover you with His feathers,
And under His wings you shall take refuge,
His truth shall be your shield and buckler." (Ps. 91:3–4)

We live in perilous times predicted millenniums ago by our Lord and His holy prophets and apostles. The current crisis of COVID-19 is just one of them. Throughout human history, mankind has survived many devastating diseases and crises. So let us be assured that we will surely survive the current pandemic of coronavirus.

Let us, however, beware of many religious leaders/preachers taking advantage of human miseries and fears to advance their personal gains. They promise false hopes and easy ways out of any problem. Every new crisis that has confronted mankind has always led to scientific research for a durable solution. Of course, God is the source of all durable solutions; hence, no one should discountenance medical science interventions and over-spiritualize the current crisis.

The fact that underdeveloped countries are not reporting the numbers of victims testing positive to coronavirus doesn't mean that the disease is nonexistent there. It may be because of poor or lack of modern diagnostic equipment.

While we support the efforts of civil authorities and medical science worldwide to find a vaccine for the treatment of the coronavirus disease, we, the people of biblical faith should, however, study more of God's Word, build our hopes in the promises of God to keep us healthy, and live daily by faith in His words. Don't be caught up in "the snare of the fowlers" who prey and profit on human fears and ignorance. Know the truth and let the truth of God's word make you free. Read Psalm 91 and other relevant passages.

Enjoy a fear-free life with **His loaded blessings!**

LIVING WORD for TODAY—March 14:

LOADED with DAILY BLESSINGS (Ps. 68:19)-#74

HEALTH—14

"You shall not be afraid of the terror by night,
Nor of the arrow that flies by day,
Nor of the pestilence that walks in the darkness,
Nor the destruction that lays waste at noonday." (Ps. 91:5–6)

Our divine health plan covers us twenty-four seven and all aspects of our lives. So we don't have to be afraid. There's so much fear in the news these days—even about the unknown concerning the new virus. Stores are emptied of supplies as people troop in grooves to buy their daily necessities in case they are self-quarantined for days. It is good to plan ahead, but when our plans are dictated by fears, then where is our faith?

"His truth shall be your shield and buckler."

Our major problem is that we listen to the daily news more than what God promises us in His Word. In less than a month, many Christians know more about the novel coronavirus than they know the Bible. It is the truth of God's Word that will deliver us in times of trouble.

His promise is to protect us from:

- Terror by night;
- Arrows that fly by day;
- Pestilence in darkness; and
- Destruction that occurs in the noonday.

So we're totally covered by the Most High God.

Even our comprehensive health insurance, which costs us so much in monthly premiums, doesn't cover us that much.

So let us live by faith in God's promise for our health instead of fear of what may not happen to us. Remember this, "Fear has torment" (1 John 4:18). Fear is a painful sickness. Keep loving the Lord and reading His love messages to you in the Bible, and you're covered.

Have a lovely day **loaded** with **His blessing** of **health**!

LIVING WORD for TODAY—March 15:

LOADED with DAILY BLESSINGS (Ps. 68:19)-#75

HEALTH—15

"A thousand may fall at your side,
And ten thousand at your right hand;
But it shall not come near you.
Only with your eyes shall you look,
And see the reward of the wicked." (Ps. 91:7–8)

While we continue to pray for God's intervention to remove the new virus, COVID-19, which is disrupting the normal life and business of our world today, and grant wisdom to those in authority for right directives to save lives, we must, however, not be distracted from our primary Source of good health.

In Psalm 91 and throughout the Bible, we see clearly:

1. God's plan for our health.
   He wants His people to be healthy; and

2. God's presence in our health.

He is actively involved in our health.

In Psalm 91, the **Lord** and His personal pronoun are used about eighteen times to indicate His involvement.

Later in the Scriptures, we shall also see: God's price, prescriptions, and purpose for our health.

As we continue to obey the directives of our respective civil authorities in controlling the spread of the coronavirus and other viruses, let us put our faith in the Lord and trust Him daily because He has a durable health plan, which He already paid for by His blood. So you and your household are covered.

Enjoy your health plan with all the **daily benefits!**

LIVING WORD for TODAY—March 16:

LOADED with DAILY BLESSINGS (Ps. 68:19)-#76

HEALTH—16

It is time for Christians, the people of faith in the Lord Jesus Christ, to start saying what God says about their health. The medical institutions, civil authorities, and the news media are well equipped with the necessary information about what's going on with diseases and how to slow down or stop the spread around us. Let us give them credit for what they are doing.

But as Christians, are we equipped with what our Lord is saying about our health? If so, let us speak about it to ourselves and spread the message to others to balance whatever they may be hearing from the other side. Here is what the Almighty God says about your health:

> Because you have made the LORD, who is my refuge, Even the Most High, your dwelling place, No evil shall befall you,
>
> Nor shall any plague come near your dwelling;
>
> For He shall give His angels charge over you, To keep you in all your ways, In their hands they shall bear you up,
>
> Lest you dash your foot against a stone.
>
> You shall tread upon the lion and the cobra,(these are symbols of demons and destructive viruses and diseases)
>
> The young lion and the serpent you shall trample underfoot (Ps. 91:9–13).

And our Lord Jesus Christ affirmed this passage to His disciples when He was with them, and He is affirming it to you today.

"Behold, I give you the authority to trample on serpents and scorpions, and over all the power of the enemy, and nothing shall by any means hurt you."

These are the words of the Lord. "Nothing shall by any means hurt you."

Let us start living out what we believe and be healthy all the days of our lives!

Have a great day with **His loaded blessings!**

LIVING WORD for TODAY—March 17:

LOADED with DAILY BLESSINGS (Ps. 68:19)-#77

HEALTH—17

"Because he has set his love upon Me, therefore I will deliver him;
I will set him on high, because he has known my name.
He shall call upon Me, and I will answer him;
I will be with him in trouble;
I will deliver him and honor him." (Ps. 91:14–15)

God never promised us a trouble-free life in this world, but He promised His presence with us through every situation we may face. Since the fall of mankind into sin, forces of good and evil have dominated our present world. Because mankind loves evil more than good, evil reigns.

But in the midst of chaos and troubles, God's presence brings peace, health, and wholeness to those who know and trust Him. In the concluding part of Psalm 91, we read the six "I will" of the Most High God promising His presence, deliverance, promotion, answers to prayers, and honor to those who love and trust Him.

So it doesn't matter what may be happening around you; what matters most is who is in you and who runs your life.

Emmanuel, God with us, reveals in you and me!

Have a peaceful day/ evening with **His loaded blessings!**

LIVING WORD for TODAY—March 18:

LOADED with DAILY BLESSINGS (Ps. 68:19)-#78

HEALTH—18

"With long life I will satisfy him,
And show him My salvation." (Ps. 91:16)

In this sixth "I will" of God in the concluding verse of this song, we have the Lord's promise of longevity to those who make Him their shelter and hiding place. Please note that not just long life is promised here, but long life with satisfaction.

It is not pleasant to live long in poor health and be a burden to the loved ones and community. Good quality of life is what satisfies us, and that's what the Lord promises us. But to enjoy this, we must dwell in the secret place of the Most High God and be covered with His salvation.

So there is no reason for God's children to panic about what is going on in the world today. God takes care of His own, and if it is not your time to go, you're not going to die. Just live a worry-free life and enjoy it to the fullest.

I pray the Lord will cover you with His presence wherever you are and fulfill His promise of good health in your life.

Let us keep those who are directly affected by the novel COVID-19 in our prayers so the Lord will comfort and bring complete healing to them and also protect their caregivers.

Have a healthy life with **God's loaded blessings!**

LIVING WORD for TODAY—March 19:

LOADED with DAILY BLESSINGS (Ps. 68:19)-#79

HEALTH—19

"GOD is our refuge and strength,
A very present help in trouble.
Therefore we will not fear,
Even though the earth be moved, And though the mountains be carried into the
midst of the sea." (Ps. 46:1–2)

One of my friends sent a post to me this morning about how Christians should be translating COVID-19. The acronym should be translated to:

Christ **O**ver **V**iruses and **I**nfectious **D**iseases

I think that's a smart way to turn the devil's battle against him.

Instead of being afraid of what has become the household name all over the world, we can rename it for our victory and health.

Because Jesus Christ is our refuge and strength, our very present help in trouble, we should not be afraid of any plague that may trouble the world. Christ has overcome all. Listen to what He says:

"These things I have spoken to you, that in Me you may have peace. In the world you will have tribulation; but be of good cheer, I have overcome the world" (John 16:33). So relax and enjoy His peace. Christ has overcome coronavirus!

Have a blessed day/evening with **His loaded health!**

LIVING WORD for TODAY—March 20:

LOADED with DAILY BLESSINGS (Ps. 68:19)-#80

HEALTH—20

"There is a river whose streams shall make glad the city of God, The holy place of the tabernacle of the Most High.
God is in the midst of her, she shall not be moved;
God shall help her, just at the break of dawn...
The LORD of hosts is with us;
The God of Jacob is our refuge. Selah" (Ps. 46:4–7)

In the midst of chaos, confusion, and uncertainties, don't allow fear to hold you hostage. Though the present situation around us is to stay home, yet we will make best use of the lock-in period to glorify the Lord, turn our homes into His tabernacle, and take care of ourselves. Let your faith be active and adaptable to any situation of life.

The **Lord** of hosts is with us, and He will crush coronavirus under our feet. "... and nothing shall by any means hurt you" (Luke 10:19).

Have a happy day/evening with **God's loaded blessings!**

LIVING WORD for TODAY—March 21:

LOADED with DAILY BLESSINGS (Ps. 68:19)-#81

HEALTH—21

"Be still, and know that I am God;
I will be exalted among the nations.
I will be exalted in the earth!
The LORD of hosts is with us,
The God of Jacob is our refuge. Selah" (Ps. 46:10–11)

The Lord will be exalted and glorified in our current situation of the COVID-19 pandemic. As we pray for divine interventions, let us be still and wait patiently for what He would do. Whatever He does will be to the benefit of His children. This is going to be another case of serendipity for those who believe and trust the Lord.

"And we know that all things work together for good to those who love God, to those who are the called according to His purpose" (Rom. 8:28).

"All things," including the coronavirus, will work for the good of Christ's kingdom and His children all over the world.

What Satan meant for evil, God will turn it around for our good in Jesus Christ's name!

Relax and have a restful day/night with **His loaded blessings!**

LIVING WORD for TODAY—March 22:

LOADED with DAILY BLESSINGS (Ps. 68:19)-#82

HEALTH—22

"He is despised and rejected by men,
A man of sorrows and acquainted with grief.
And we hid, as it were, our faces from Him;
He was despised, and we did not esteem Him." (Isa. 53:3)

God did not only plan, promise, and involve His presence for our health, but He paid the price for our wellness!

All our afflictions, sicknesses, diseases, and viruses have been placed upon our Burden-bearer, the Lord Jesus Christ. Our health is very costly, and we couldn't pay for it. None of us was good enough for the price. Only the perfect Lamb of God could do it (John 1:29).

Isaiah, the prophet in Israel, predicted His sufferings for us over five centuries before He was born. And when He came, the civil authorities of the day did not recognize Him. But the simple believers did. So be humble and put your trust in Him who has the power and authority to keep you healthy in the midst of any virus and disease. Jesus Christ paid for all of them to keep you healthy. You have the right to be whole through our Lord Jesus Christ!

Have a healthy life with HIS LOADED BLESSINGS!

LIVING WORD for TODAY—March 23:

LOADED with DAILY BLESSINGS (Ps. 68:19)-#83

HEALTH—23

"Surely He has borne our griefs
And carried our sorrows;
Yet we esteemed Him stricken,
Smitten by God, and afflicted." (Isa. 53:4)

Before the world was created, God in His infinite foreknowledge, knew the miseries, sorrows, and afflictions we would bring upon ourselves in the beautiful world He was going to give us. Therefore, He made a plan to pay the price for our wholeness, which was impossible for us to pay.

He put all our troubles upon Himself and carried them on the cross where they were crucified with Him (Col. 2:14).

So stop bearing the grief, afflictions, and sorrows the Lord has borne for you. Lay them on His cross. He paid for all our pains and sufferings on the Cross. There is no penance you and I can pay to remove the consequences of our sin. The cross of Jesus Christ, where He shed His blood and died, is the perfect price.

Remember the fact of Christ's cross in the midst of bombarding news of deadly diseases and viruses. **Jesus Christ** is **our health**.

Have a happy day with **His loaded benefits** of **health!**

LIVING WORD for TODAY—March 24:

LOADED with DAILY BLESSINGS (Ps. 68:19)-#84

HEALTH—24

"But He was wounded for our transgressions,
He was bruised for our iniquities;
The chastisement for our peace was upon Him,
And by His stripes we are healed." (Isa. 53:5)

Our thoughts and prayers are with many who are grieving the loss of their loved ones due to pandemic virus of COVID-19 and other silent killers, which no one is talking about. May the Lord of all comfort come alongside with them with His compassion and love.

It is noteworthy that Isaiah 53 used past tense, at the time of this prophecy, to foretell over five centuries ahead all that Jesus Christ our Lord would suffer for us to pay the price of our health. This should give us the assurance to know there's nothing happening to us today in the world that surprises God. He saw all in ages past, and has already made a provision for the cure.

Our health was a done deal before we were born. So whenever you're threatened by any sickness or virus, you have the right, if you're a child of God, to claim your healing, based on the finished work of Christ on the Cross. Every other prescription is secondary.

"The chastisement for our peace was upon Him,

And by His stripes we are healed" (Isa. 53:5).

Enjoy a healthy and virus-free life with **His loaded benefits!**

LIVING WORD for TODAY—March 25:

LOADED with DAILY BLESSINGS (Ps. 68:19)-#85

HEALTH—25

"All we like sheep have gone astray;
We have turned, every one, to his own way:
And the LORD has laid on Him the iniquity of us all." (Isa. 53:6)

The sheep always has the propensity to go astray. Hence, the rod and staff of the shepherd to protect and correct the sheep (Ps. 23:4).

This is the picture of humans. We're always prone to go astray and do things in our own ways, whether approved or unacceptable by our Good Shepherd. Sometimes sickness could be one of the corrective means the Shepherd uses to get our attention and return us to His fold. It is difficult, scripturally, to separate sickness from sin.

Regardless of our opinions, the good news is the mercy of God that paid the price for our freedom from sin and sickness.

"The LORD has laid on Him the iniquity of us all."

Thank God for the price our Lord Jesus Christ paid to take away our iniquities and diseases on the cross of Calvary. "It is finished." It is not based on your belief or mine. It is based on God's imperatives! So let us be comforted by what God's Word says and what Christ has done for us. "By His stripes we were healed." "The LORD has laid on Him the iniquity of us all." "It is finished."

Rest your faith on these divine statements daily and be free from fears and stubbornness to sin.

Enjoy your daily freedom in Him with **His loaded blessings!**

LIVING WORD for TODAY—March 26:

LOADED with DAILY BLESSINGS (Ps. 68:19)-#86

HEALTH—26

"And Jesus went about all Galilee, teaching in their synagogues, preaching the gospel of the kingdom, and healing all kinds of sickness and all kinds of disease among the people." (Matt. 8:23)

The ministry of Jesus Christ, when He came in the human flesh to identify with us, was holistic.

He taught the Scriptures, precept upon precept. He preached, proclaiming the good news of God's kingdom on earth. This is the limit of many modern preachers. But in Christ's ministry, preaching the gospel of the kingdom would be incomplete without the demonstration of the power of the kingdom of God to save and heal all kinds of sickness and disease among His audience.

Where did we get it wrong?

Preaching today has become, more or less, the social gospel. We seem to have surrendered the demonstration of the power of the gospel to the medical doctors. Please note that there were many physicians in the world during the time of Jesus. But He ministered deliverance and healing through the power of God. While He did not condemn the physicians, He proved that God's plan and purpose for His people were to be whole and healthy beyond what medicines could do.

The church needs to go back to her foundation to rediscover and practice the power of the gospel of Christ to deliver from sins, Satan, sicknesses, and diseases. This is the full gospel in the Bible.

Yes, Jesus Christ still has power to deliver from viruses, such as coronavirus and much more, but He is waiting for believers in Him to connect with Him for releasing it into their needs.

I pray that you would experience His power in your day-to-day life encounters. It is real!

Have a blessed day/evening with **His loaded benefits** of **healing**!

LIVING WORD for TODAY—March 27:

LOADED with DAILY BLESSINGS (Ps. 68:19)-#87

HEALTH—27

"Then His fame went throughout all Syria; and they brought to Him all sick people who were afflicted with various diseases and torments, and those who were demon-possessed, epileptics, and paralytics, and He healed them." (Matt. 4:24)

Jesus's ministry or our ministry? Whenever I read about Christ's ministry in the New Testament, I'm humbled and cry within me; where is the power of Christ in today's church?

Notice the three dimensions of Jesus's ministry in Matthew 4:23–24. He taught, preached the gospel of the kingdom, and healed all kinds of sickness and disease.

Another observation in this passage is the connection of demons with human's afflictions. Any sickness or disease that defies clinical or medical remedies can be considered demonic and requires divine intervention in Jesus Christ's name. Remember the Great Commission He gave to His disciples in Mark 16:15–18.

Let us measure our ministries with the standard of His ministry and be constantly challenged in our prayers for the manifestation of His power in our lives and ministries daily.

Have a healthy day with **His loaded blessings!**

LIVING WORD for TODAY—March 28:

LOADED with DAILY BLESSINGS (Ps. 68:19)-#88

HEALTH—28

"When evening had come, they brought to Him many who were demon-possessed. And He cast out the spirits with a word, and healed all who were sick, that it might be fulfilled which was spoken by Isaiah the prophet, saying:

'He Himself took our infirmities And bore our sicknesses.'" (Matt. 8:16-17)

Christ's mission on earth was and still is to deliver all who were and are being oppressed by the devil. We see this truth being played out in all His meetings with those who were sick in the New Testament. Note that all the sick who came to Jesus Christ in His meetings were all healed with no exceptions. There's no single reference in the New Testament of a sick person who came to Christ or who He encountered that was not healed.

When Matthew, one of His disciples, saw Jesus's healing ministry, he remembered the prophecy of Isaiah, written over five centuries before being fulfilled that:

"He Himself took our infirmities And bore our sicknesses" (Matt. 8:17; Isa. 53:4).

Whether you're healed or not, when prayed for in Jesus's name, does not change this truth. Let it be made clear that God wants His children to be healthy and whole! Let your faith be anchored on this fact of God's Word, which is forever settled in heaven.

Have a happy day/night with **His loaded blessings** of **health**!

LIVING WORD for TODAY—March 29:

LOADED with DAILY BLESSINGS (Ps. 68:19)-#89

HEALTH—29

"And behold, a leper came and worshiped Him, saying, 'Lord, if You are willing, You can make me clean.'
Then Jesus put out His hand and touched him, saying, 'I am willing; be cleansed.'
Immediately his leprosy was cleansed." (Matt. 8:2–3)

The question of whether it is the will of God to heal people can be answered in the above passage of Scripture. A leper came to Jesus and worshiped Him, not knowing if it was the will of Jesus to cleanse him from his disease. Mark 1:41 tells us that Jesus was moved with compassion and said, "I am willing; be cleansed." Immediately, the leper was cleansed.

Let us be more focused on the revealed will of God and leave the secret things to Him (Deut. 29:29). Why some people are healed by God and some are not is only known to Him. We can suggest some answers, but we must also accept the fact that now we know in part. So let us live by the truth He revealed to us.

If Christ could cleanse a leper by His words, then there's no virus or disease He cannot heal. I chose to live by faith in His living Word.

I pray that you would do the same when faced with health challenges. It is always the will of God for us to be healthy.

Have a healthy day with **God's loaded blessings!**

LIVING WORD for TODAY—March 30:

LOADED with DAILY BLESSINGS (Ps. 68:19)-#90

HEALTH—30

"Beloved, I pray that you may prosper in all things and be in health, just as your soul prospers." (3 John 2)

As we end this month, which has so far been the most challenging month in healthcare for many developed nations, I invoke the apostolic prayer quoted above upon you and your loved ones.

- It is the will of God for you to prosper in all things;
- It is the will of God for you to be in good health; and
- It is the will of God for your soul to prosper.

Make these affirmations daily, and let them mix with your faith, then expect and experience God's prosperity in all areas of your life.

This is why Christ came. This is why He died on the Cross.

This is why He rose from the dead. And this is why He sits at the right hand of the Father, interceding for us; prosperity in all things, including **health!**

Have a happy day/evening with **His loaded benefits** of **health!**

LIVING WORD for TODAY—March 31:

LOADED with DAILY BLESSINGS (Ps. 68:19)-#91

HEALTH—31

"And these signs will follow those who believe: In My name they will cast out demons; they will speak with new tongues; they will take up serpents; and if they drink anything deadly, it will by no means hurt them; they will lay hands on the sick, and they will recover." (Mark 16:17–18)

In this last day of the month of March, we need to be reminded of the purpose of our health. If the Lord has kept you healthy, it is a blessing you can share with others who are being afflicted with some health challenges.

In these days of COVID-19, which we don't even know what it is, other than what the world politicians and their medical cohorts are telling us, we need to rely more on the power our Lord bequeathed upon us to live victoriously over all the works of the enemy of our health.

We also need to use this same power to liberate those who are in the enemy's prison and being tormented by his demons and diseases. Our Lord left us in the world to represent Him.

He says: "As the Father has sent Me, I also send you" (John 20:21).

So believe Him and receive His mantle of deliverance to rescue the afflicted. Pray for wisdom and His direction as to how and where to represent Him. I pronounce His power on you to prosper in **health** all the days of your life! Nothing shall by any means hurt you and your loved ones in Christ's name!

Enjoy your life with **His daily blessings** of good **health**!

APRIL: REDEMPTION

LIVING WORD for TODAY—April 1:

LOADED with DAILY BLESSINGS (Ps. 68:19)-#92

REDEMPTION—1

"Bless the LORD, O my soul,
And forget not all His benefits:
Who forgives all your iniquities,
Who heals all your diseases,
Who redeems your life from destruction" (Ps.103:2–4)

Glory to God in the highest for seeing us through ninety-one days of the year. He who saw us through the first quarter will surely watch over us for the rest of the year and beyond.

Our broad theme for the year is: **loaded** with **daily blessings** (Ps. 68:19).

In January, we were refreshed with the blessing of **life**.

In February, it was the blessing of **love**, and in March, the blessing of **health**. Each of these blessings inspires and challenges us to live in the realms and realities of what God makes available to us daily.

During this month of April, our focus would be on the **Lord's redemption.** Please notice in Psalm 103:4, David uses the word "redeems" to describe God's benefits for us daily. While there was a major historical event of the redemption of mankind on the Cross by our Lord Jesus Christ, the effect of that finished redemptive work is, however, active in the present continuous tense in believers daily. So we're going to explore this topic during the month, and experience the benefits of our redemption.

May the Lord's redemption protect us from every satanic destruction going on in our world today.

Have a refreshing month with **His loaded blessings** of **redemption**!

LIVING WORD for TODAY—April 2:

LOADED with DAILY BLESSINGS (Ps. 68:19)-#93

REDEMPTION—2

"In Him we have redemption through His blood, the forgiveness of sins, according to the riches of His grace..." (Eph. 1:7)

Let us take a moment to appreciate our redemption—buying back from:

- Tyranny of Satan;
- Slavery to sins;
- Addiction to bad habits;
- Condemnation of hell fire;
- Labor and heavy ladling;
- Sicknesses and diseases;
- Laws and traditions of men;
- Religious traditions; and
- Fears and death.

Think of what you have been redeemed from and then celebrate your freedom to be:

- Who you're created to be;
- Holy and acceptable to God;
- Free from fears;
- Free from guilt and shame;
- Adopted into God's family;
- In commonwealth of Israel; and
- In God's Kingdom forever.

And how much did you pay for all these? Nothing because you can't afford the price. But somebody stepped up and paid the price for your ransom. All you can do is appreciate who paid the price, turn back, and worship Him. Give your life back to Him to own you forever.

Redemption, oh, what a wonderful story. Jesus Christ paid the price with His own blood. Let us live to glorify Him.

Have a great day with **God's loaded blessings** of **redemption**!

LIVING WORD for TODAY—April 3:

LOADED with DAILY BLESSINGS (Ps. 68:19)-#94

REDEMPTION—3

"...God, before whom my fathers Abraham and Isaac walked,
The God who has fed me all my life long to this day,
The Angel who has redeemed me from all evil..." (Gen. 48:15–16)

The word *redemption* is an important theological word in the Bible. Although the idea was introduced by God in the Garden of Eden after the fall of mankind, the first usage of the word was by Jacob as he blessed his grandsons, the sons of Joseph.

The word means: "Deliverance of persons, property that had been sold for debt" (Lev. 25:25).

A poor man may sell himself to a fellow Israelite or an alien living in Israel until the year of Jubilee (W. E. Vine, An Exposition Dictionary of Biblical Words, pp. 317-318). Leviticus chapter 25 gives stipulations relating to the law of redemption.

The first act of God when we believe in Him and yield our lives to Him is to buy us back from the evil one and all his evil devises. Mankind has sold himself and all his rights to the evil one, and it takes the supernatural power of God to deliver him. This truth was recognized by Jacob and must be accepted by us.

Only God has the right and means to pay the price of our redemption.

May the God of Jacob redeem you from all evil of these days and feed you throughout your days here on earth.

Have a blessed day/evening with His **loaded blessings!**

LIVING WORD for TODAY—April 4:

LOADED with DAILY BLESSINGS (Ps. 68:19)-#95

REDEMPTION—4

"Therefore say to the children of Israel: 'I am the LORD; I will bring you out from under the burdens of the Egyptians, I will redeem you with an outstretched arm and with great judgments.
'I will take you as My people, and I will be your God. Then you shall know that I am the LORD your God who brings you out from under the burdens of the Egyptians.'" (Exod. 6:6–7)

The concept of redemption:

The topic of redemption is a broad subject in the Bible. In the Old Testament, it involved a poor person who found himself in a situation beyond his power and in bondage. It also involved the redeemer.

The person who redeemed the one in financial difficulties or in bondage was known as a kinsman redeemer.

Ruth 4:5 summed up the responsibility of the kinsman-redeemer. He was responsible for preserving the integrity, life, property, and family name of his close relative or for executing justice upon his murderer. The greater usage is God, who promised, "I am the LORD; I will bring you out from under the burdens of the Egyptians, I will rescue you from their bondage, and I will redeem you with an outstretched arm and with great judgments" (Exod. 6:6) (Vine, p.318).

With this background, we can grasp the concept of redemption in the Old Testament Bible.

Just as God, with His outstretched arm, rescued and delivered Israelites from their bondage and slave masters in Egypt, Jesus Christ, our Kinsman Redeemer, has come to deliver us from bondage of the world, the devil, sins, sicknesses, and poverty. He says: "Therefore if the Son makes you free, you shall be free indeed" (John 8:36).

No matter what bondage you may experience now, if you will confess it to Christ and tell Him to set you free, He will step in and rescue you. He is our Redeemer!

Have a great day with **His loaded blessings!**

LIVING WORD for TODAY—April 5:

LOADED with DAILY BLESSINGS (Ps. 68:19)-#96

REDEMPTION—5

"You in Your mercy have led forth The people whom You have redeemed;
You guided them in Your strength
To Your holy habitation."(Exod. 15:13)

The concept of redemption in the Old Testament Scripture primarily refers to God's deliverance of His people, the Israelites, from the bondage in Egypt. This theme was echoed throughout their generations. "You have with Your arm redeemed Your people, The sons of Jacob and Joseph" (Ps. 77:13).

Their deliverance from bondage was an act of redemption by the **Lord** their God through His mercy. By the same power and mercy which He redeemed them, He also led and guided them through their wilderness journey until He settled them into the Promised Land, which He gave them. So there is a broader purpose for their deliverance.

What was true of them is also true of us in this church age. Jesus Christ redeemed us by His grace and leads us, day by day, by the power of the Holy Spirit as we travel to His destiny for us.

It is my prayer that we will continue to follow His guide to find rest for our souls daily, even in the midst of chaos and confusion of the world around us.

"God is our refuge and strength, a very present help in trouble" (Ps. 46:1).

Have a blessed week of our **redemption!**

LIVING WORD for TODAY—April 6:

LOADED with DAILY BLESSINGS (Ps. 68:19)-#97

REDEMPTION—6

"But now, thus says the LORD, who created you, O Jacob,
And He who formed you, O Israel:
'Fear not, for I have redeemed you;
I have called you by your name; You are Mine." (Isa. 43:1)

God's claim to ownership of humanity is expressed in this Scripture.

First, He created us. We're not just here by chance.

Second, He formed us individually with the shape and distinctiveness we portray.

Third, when we were lost, missed our bearings, then captured and enslaved by the forces beyond our control, He found us and bought us back (redeemed) to Himself.

The ancient nation of Israel was a typical example of God's ownership of all the nations of the world.

Those who recognize and understand this concept have no reason to be afraid regardless of the forces operating in the world around them. You belong to God by creation and redemption. No power here on earth, or in hell, can take you from Him except the one you give yourself to. Relax and let your Redeemer direct your life, and you will not fall into the trappings of the enemy who is trying to hold you captive to his desires.

Enjoy your life with **God's loaded blessings!**

LIVING WORD for TODAY—April 7:

LOADED with DAILY BLESSINGS (Ps. 68:19)-#98

REDEMPTION—7

"When you pass through the waters, I will be with you,
And through the rivers, they shall not overflow you.
When you walk through the fire, you shall not be burned.
Nor shall the flame scorch you." (Isa. 43:2)

This promise of God's protection is for the redeemed of the Lord only and not universal. While God, through His Son Jesus Christ, has redeemed the whole world to Himself, He, however, gives free will of choice to each person to accept His redemption and be in a covenant relationship with Him. To those who accept the invitation to be His, He promised to be with them in any situation.

There are many of His children at this time who are healthcare workers in the frontline, providing care to the victims of the coronavirus pandemic. All the physicians, nurses, clinical social workers, spiritual care counselors, medical technicians, administrators and first responders who are in covenant relationship with the Lord should feel free to claim this promise and be assured that they are not alone. The Creator of the universe, their Redeemer, is with them and will protect them from being infected by any virus, including COVID-19. Let us keep them in our prayers, and also for God's mercy upon other healthcare workers who don't know Him.

You, as a Christian, can also claim this promise whenever you're in any circumstance beyond your control. The Lord will see you through it all, according to His promise.

Have a great day with **His loaded blessings!**

LIVING WORD for TODAY—April 8:

LOADED with DAILY BLESSINGS (Ps. 68:19)-#99

REDEMPTION—8

"Therefore the redeemed of the LORD shall return, and come with singing unto Zion; and everlasting joy shall be upon their heads. They shall obtain gladness and joy; and sorrow and mourning shall flee away." (Isa. 51:11)

The deliverance of God's people, Israel, from bondage was an act of God, which demanded responsibility to be set apart and love their Redeemer. But Israel failed and fell in love with the pagan idols around them.

Their act of disobedience led to their captivity in Babylon—from bondage in Egypt to freedom and plenty in the Promised Land and then to captivity in Babylon.

But the mercy and compassion of God never abandoned them in their miseries. He raised prophets, like Isaiah, who prayed and prophesied for their release. Their future was depicted in Isaiah 51:11 and other passages in the Bible.

God's people all over the world may be going through a difficult time today as a result of disobedience and rebellion. But there is a remnant of intercessors praying and pleading for God's mercy upon our land. Their prayers will never go unanswered. The Lord will intervene on behalf of His people. He will fill us with gladness and joy. Sorrow and sighing shall flee away so that we can gather together again to worship Him without fear.

Let all the redeemed of the Lord be hopeful for a better tomorrow. COVID-19 is not the end. It is a passing season that will soon be history.

May the Holy Spirit fill your heart with songs of victory and make you see a better future coming your way.

Have a blessed day with His **loaded blessings!**

LIVING WORD for TODAY—April 9:

LOADED with DAILY BLESSINGS (Ps. 68:19)-#100

REDEMPTION—9

"For I received from the Lord that which I also delivered to you: that the Lord Jesus on the same night in which He was betrayed took bread; and when He had given thanks, He broke it and said, 'Take, eat; this is My body which is broken for you; do this in remembrance of Me.'
In the same manner He also took the cup after supper, saying, 'This cup is the new covenant in My blood. This do, as often as you drink it, in remembrance of Me.'" (1 Cor. 11:23–25)

The cost of redemption:

Congratulations for completing one hundred days of the year. The Lord who watched over us and saw us through these one hundred days will definitely keep us healthy and see us through the whole year and many more to come.

It is also important to note that in the text above, the Lord gave the institution of Holy Communion. The Lord shed His blood and died on the Cross to pay for our redemption. But before He went to the Cross, He did something significant. He celebrated His last Passover meal with His disciples. On that night, He inaugurated the new covenant, sealed by His blood. This brought an end to the old covenant, which was sealed by the killings of a sacrificial lamb.

The prophetic implications of what He did that night are crucial for us. The broken bread represents His body that would soon be broken through beatings to pay the price for our sickness and physical sufferings as predicted in Psalm 22 and Isaiah 53.

The cup of wine He drank and shared with His disciples represents His blood, which would soon be shed on the cross at Calvary to take away the sin of the world.

This was the price He paid to redeem us, and we must never forget it.

If it is possible for you, take a loaf of bread or a piece of cracker, break it, and eat it; pour some juice in a cup and drink it. As you do this, join the heavenly

hosts in Revelation 5:9–13 and worship the Lamb, our Lord Jesus Christ, who sits on the throne of heaven forever.

Have a reflective day/ night with **His loaded blessings** of **redemption**!

LIVING WORD for TODAY—April 10:

LOADED with DAILY BLESSINGS (Ps. 68:19)-#101

REDEMPTION—10

"But when the fullness of the time had come, God sent forth His Son, born of a woman, born under the law, to redeem those who were under the law, that we might receive the adoption as sons." (Gal. 4:4–5)

Both Jews and Christians have many things in common. They all trace their faith to the God of Abraham, Isaac, and Jacob. They also affirm their beliefs in the Old Testament Bible. But there is a huge difference. While Christians believe in the prophetic fulfillments of the old covenant in Jesus Christ, the Jews reject Him as the Messiah and are still looking forward to the coming of their messiah.

The same truth holds regarding the Passover. While the Jews look back to Goshen in Egypt in celebrating the Passover feast (Exod. 12), the Christians look back to Calvary on the cross for their Passover Lamb, Jesus Christ (1 Cor. 5:7; John 19:14–18).

Everyone must believe and confess this truth in Jesus Christ to be a Christian. God paid the price of our redemption through His Son so we can be adopted into His family and live by His Spirit. This is true Christianity. Let us celebrate our living faith daily. The death of Jesus Christ on the Cross is the perfect sacrifice for our redemption from Satan, sin, sickness, suffering, disease, and poverty.

Have a blessed day with **God's loaded blessings!**

LIVING WORD for TODAY—April 11:

LOADED with DAILY BLESSINGS (Ps. 68:19)-#102

REDEMPTION—11

"Christ has redeemed us from the curse of the law, having become a curse for us (for it is written, 'Cursed is everyone who hangs on a tree'), that the blessing of Abraham might come upon the Gentiles in Christ Jesus, that we might receive the promise Spirit through faith." (Gal. 3:13–14)

Our redemption is very costly!

It cost God His only begotten Son, and it cost the Son His life.

In Deuteronomy 28, we love to read verses one to fourteen, where blessings are pronounced upon those who obey the law of God. But starting from verse fifteen through verse sixty-eight, there is a long list of curses pronounced upon those who disobey the law. Every Jew and Christian should read this chapter to appreciate what Christ has done for us. The curse of the law was heavy, and it haunted the nation of Israel for generations. The curse still hangs on anyone who rejects the redemption of Christ and thinks he or she can live by the law.

But when Jesus Christ was hanged on the Cross (Deut. 21:23; John 19:31), He took upon Himself all the curses pronounced in the law for our disobedience and breaking the laws of God.

So we're no longer under the curses of the law but under the blessings of Abraham (Gen. 12:2–3; Rom. 4:7–11; Rom. 3:29–30) made available to believers in Christ Jesus through the Holy Spirit.

Thank God for the blessings now available through the death of Christ on the Cross to those of us who believe in Him. Stop working for God to be blessed and enter into the realm of His shower of blessings by believing in the finished work of Jesus Christ on the Cross for you. He also rose from the dead to make His resurrection life available to us.

May the power of the Spirit that raised Jesus Christ our Redeemer from the dead, banish fear of sickness and death in your life and home and bring new life to every dead potential in you.

Rejoice and celebrate His resurrection!

Have a happy day with His **loaded blessings** of **redemption!**

LIVING WORD for TODAY—April 12:

LOADED with DAILY BLESSINGS (Ps. 68:19)-#103

REDEMPTION—12

"So when Jesus had received the sour wine, He said, 'It is finished!' And bowing His head, He gave up His spirit." (John 29:30)

"But he said to them, 'Do not be alarmed. You seek Jesus of Nazareth, who was crucified. He is risen! He is not here. See the place where they laid Him.'" (Mark 16:6)

There are two short statements that sealed redemption history:

(1) It is finished! (John19:30); and

(2) He is risen! (Mark16:6).

In these six words, our **redemption** was completed.

When Jesus said, "It is finished!" what did He mean?

He meant, sin, sickness, suffering, misery, pains, and death are all paid for and no longer have control over His people.

Satan thought he had seen the end of Jesus when He said, "It is finished" and died on the Cross. But when the angel said, "He is risen," there were shockwaves in the Satanic kingdom. What the enemy meant for evil God has turned around for good.

It is my prayer for you that all the enemy meant for your evil, the resurrected Lord will turn them around for your good!

Enjoy your purchased redemption with all the **loaded blessings**!

LIVING WORD for TODAY—April 13:

LOADED with DAILY BLESSINGS (Ps. 68:19)-#104

REDEMPTION—13

"He who did not spare His own Son, but delivered Him up for us all, how shall He not with Him also freely give us all things?" (Rom. 8:32)

In our devotional this month, we've meditated on the concept of redemption, the cost of redemption, and with Christ's resurrection, let us see the consequences of our redemption.

Jesus Christ's resurrection from the dead bestows on believers in Him many benefits:

- He is risen to destroy the destroyer. (Heb. 2:14–15);
- He is risen to give us a living hope;
- He is risen to give us a living faith;
- He is risen to restore to believers in Him all things the enemy had stolen from them (Rom. 8:32); and
- He is risen to give us abundant life (John 10:10).

Christ's death and resurrection are the cornerstones of the Christian faith.

You and I have something to live for. We have a living faith in the living Lord of all things. So don't be afraid, but live boldly and confront all the challenges of the enemy trying to hold you bound in the grave of failures, pains, and regrets. Our Lord tore the bars of the grave away and rose from it triumphantly.

I pray that His resurrection power will quicken your faith to live daily in the fullness of His authority and blessings.

Have a great day/night with His **loaded resurrection benefits!**

LIVING WORD for TODAY—April 14:

LOADED with DAILY BLESSINGS (Ps. 68:19)-#105

REDEMPTION—14

"In Him we have redemption through His blood, the forgiveness of sins, according to the riches of His grace..." (Eph. 1:7)

The consequences of Christ's redemption are many. When Jesus Christ said, "It is finished" on the cross of Calvary and shed His blood, heaven recognized what was done, and God's presence, which was taken away from mankind in the Garden of Eden, was reopened.

God is absolutely holy, and mankind is absolutely sinful. The only price acceptable to God for forgiveness of human sins is the sinless blood. None of us is qualified to pay for our own sins, not to talk about the sins of the whole world. Only the perfect, sinless, Son of God, who took upon Himself the human body, could pay for the sins of the world.

Now any sinful person can gain access to the presence of Holy God and fellowship with Him through the blood of Jesus Christ.

"In Him we have redemption through His blood, the forgiveness of sins..." (Eph. 1:7)

Do not live without the assurance of knowing that your sins are forgiven by God. Living with your past, present, and future sins hanging over your head is an eternal disaster! But the blood of Jesus Christ, His Son, can cleanse you from all sins (1 John 1:7) if you come to Him daily with a contrite spirit.

Have a great day with **God's loaded benefits** of **forgiveness**!

LIVING WORD for TODAY—April 15:

LOADED with DAILY BLESSINGS (Ps. 68:19)-#106

REDEMPTION—15

"BLESSED is he whose transgression is forgiven,
Whose sin is covered.
Blessed is the man to whom the LORD does not impute iniquity, And in whose
spirit there is no deceit (Ps. 32:1–2)

Forgiveness of sins is the greatest blessing the death of Jesus Christ on the Cross brought to humanity. Every other blessing is a bi-product.

Forgiveness of sins releases us from God's judgment and any claim Satan may have over us. With forgiveness of sins, we're free from:

- God's condemnation;
- Satan's claims/accusations;
- Our own convictions of sin; and
- A guilty conscience.

Above all, we're free from slavery to sonship in God's economy.

The most important work of God through Christ in the world is reconciling the world to Himself, not imputing their trespasses to them, and has committed to the Christians the ministry of reconciliation (2 Cor. 5:18–19).

So be happy if you're saved from sins by the blood of Jesus Christ. You have the greatest blessing of God that you can also share with your family and friends. All other blessings from heaven are lined up for you.

Have a joyful day with **His loaded blessings!**

LIVING WORD for TODAY—April 16:

LOADED with DAILY BLESSINGS (Ps. 68:19)-#107

REDEMPTION—16

"Moreover, brethren, I declare to you the gospel which I preached to you, which also you received and in which you stand, by which also you are saved, if you hold fast that word which I preached to you—unless you believed in vain." (1 Cor. 15:1–2)

The consequences of redemption: the gospel:

The redemption of mankind Jesus Christ paid for with His own blood has been the basis of preaching the gospel since the first century, till now. There would have been no good news, which Christians have proclaimed through the centuries without the redemptive work of Christ.

So the gospel message we preach, which people receive, stand on, and by which they're saved, is the result of redemption.

Let us, therefore, be fully persuaded about what we believe and stand for to share it with others in our circles of influence and relationship. The core of the Christian message is redemption in Christ Jesus. So share it as the cure of human sufferings.

Have a victorious day with **God's loaded blessings!**

LIVING WORD for TODAY—April 17:

LOADED with DAILY BLESSINGS (Ps. 68:19)-#108

REDEMPTION—17

"For I delivered to you first of all that which I also received: that Christ died for our sins according to the Scriptures,
and that He was buried, and that He rose again the third day according to the Scriptures, and that He was seen by Cephas, then by the twelve."(1 Cor. 15:3–5)

The gospel:

The proclamation of the gospel is a major consequence of our redemption. But what is the gospel? Simply put, the gospel means the good news.

Think of what makes the headline news today; the bad news. The bad news travels faster than the good news.

Imagine how fast the bad news of coronavirus spread and became a pandemic disease all over the world within three months. There's no nation in the world today that doesn't know about COVID-19. Compare that to the good news of redemption for mankind; there are peoples, nations, and ethnic groups in the world today who still don't know about their redemption, which has spread for the past 2,000 years. Why?

Because the bad news spreads faster than the good news. The good news of salvation is what God gave us, His children, to spread.

Paul, the apostle, says: "For I delivered to you first of all that which I also received" (1 Cor. 15:3).

Has the good news of redemption reached you? Then spread it. It is the remedy for human's disease of sin. Stop spreading the bad news and spread the good news!

I speak the good news of Christ's deliverance from sins, diseases, sicknesses, death, mishaps, poverty, and miseries to your life and home today. No bad news will be heard about you, your family, and loved ones. Spread the same good news of Christ's deliverance to others as you have received.

Have a lovely day with His **loaded blessings!**

LOADED with DAILY BLESSINGS (Ps. 68:19)-#109

REDEMPTION—18

"For I am not ashamed of the gospel of Christ, for it is the power of God to salvation for everyone who believes, for the Jew first and also for the Greek." (Rom. 1:16)

The gospel is the power of God. What then makes the good news so powerful to change and transform life?

In our devotional Scripture yesterday (1 Cor. 15:3–5), we saw four components that make up the gospel of Jesus Christ. The gospel is incomplete without any of them.

Christ died for our sins according to the Scriptures.

The death of Jesus Christ was not a fairytale. It was predicted and documented centuries before it happened (Ps. 22:1, 6–8, 16–18; Isa. 53:1–12);

Christ was buried according to the Jewish culture of the time (Matt. 27:57–66). His burial was proof that He actually died;

Christ rose from the dead on the third day according to the Scriptures. His resurrection from the dead was prophesied and came to pass (Ps. 16:9–10; Matt. 28:1–10); and

Christ was seen after His resurrection from the dead by His disciples and many (Matt. 28:17–20; Luke 24:13–31; Acts 1:1–10).

These are the four cardinal pillars upon which the gospel of our redemption stands.

So we have more than a religion but the power of the Almighty God in our faith.

I pray that the power of the gospel will continue to transform your life and situations from glory to glory.

Have a great day/evening with God's **loaded blessings!**

LIVING WORD for TODAY—April 19:

LOADED with DAILY BLESSINGS (Ps. 68:19)-#110

REDEMPTION—19

"For in it the righteousness of God is revealed from faith to faith; as it is written, 'The just shall live by faith.'" (Rom. 1:17)

The major product of the power of the gospel is the righteousness of God. Nothing else is capable to produce this in humans' lives.

Good moral upbringing, education, disciplined lifestyle, and following sets of religious rules and rituals cannot produce the righteousness of God. The best they can produce are human righteousness, which, to God, are like filthy rags (Isa. 64:6). Only the gospel of Jesus Christ is able to make us righteous before God. This is the greatest power of the gospel.

The spiritual powers of darkness can produce many miracles and wonders to deceive, but they can never yield to God's righteousness.

So let us present the good news of our redemption with all clarity and see its power transforming lives in our societies with the righteousness of God.

Have a pleasant day/ evening **loaded** with His **blessings!**

LIVING WORD for TODAY—April 20:

LOADED with DAILY BLESSINGS (Ps. 68:19)-#111

REDEMPTION—20

"He has delivered us from the power of darkness and conveyed us into the kingdom of the Son of His love, in whom we have redemption through His blood, the forgiveness of sins." (Col. 1:13–14)

As we continue our meditation on the consequences of our redemption, let us express another important benefit made available to believers in Christ Jesus as a result of the price He paid for our redemption.

- The deliverance from the power of darkness and conveying us into His kingdom; Christians are people of the kingdom of God. The subject of the kingdom of God is a broad subject in the Bible. In my daily devotional, titled, "In His Presence," a section was devoted to it. But let us remember that when Christ died on the Cross, He opened the gate of the kingdom of God to every believer in Him to enter, even when they are still on earth.

    Peter, the apostle of Christ, describes Christians as:

- A chosen generation, a royal priesthood, a holy nation, His own special people (1 Pet. 2:9), so there's a nation or kingdom operating in the present nations and kingdoms of this world. That is the kingdom of Jesus Christ, which has been advancing by force since the Day of Pentecost, and the greatness of the kingdom would soon consume the kingdoms of this world to establish the eternal kingdom of Christ on earth. But for now, we advance the kingdom spiritually by the power of the Holy Spirit in us.

Please don't see yourself as an ordinary person if you're a born-again Christian. You are a person of the kingdom of God, and you can't really fit into the mold of the kingdoms of this world, which is under the power of darkness. Live daily as a kingdom person.

Have a great day with God's **loaded blessings!**

LIVING WORD for TODAY —April 21:

LOADED with DAILY BLESSINGS (Ps. 68:19)-#112

REDEMPTION—21

"Inasmuch then as the children have partaken of flesh and blood, He Himself likewise shared in the same, that through death He might destroy him who had the power of death, that is, the devil, and release those who through fear of death were all their lifetime subject to bondage." (Heb. 2:14–15)

The consequences of our redemption would be incomplete without mentioning our deliverance from death.

Our redemption, purchased by the blood of Jesus Christ, guarantees our victory over the devil and death. Since the fall of mankind into sin by the first man, Adam, death reigns with all its fears. "For as in Adam all die, even so in Christ all shall be made alive" (1 Cor. 15:22).

The devil should no longer threaten the children of God with the fear of death because anyone who is in Christ has passed from death to life (John 11:25–26).

So live your life without fear of death because you're a life carrier. Life lives in you and not death. The destroyer has been destroyed! Jesus Christ is our life!

Have a glorious day with His **loaded benefits** of **life!**

LIVING WORD for TODAY—April 22:

LOADED with DAILY BLESSINGS (Ps. 68:19)-#113

REDEMPTION—22

"...who delivered us from so great a death, and does deliver us; in whom we trust that He will still deliver us..." (2 Cor. 1:10)

Daily Deliverance

As long as we're in this world, which is described as "this present evil age," we're susceptible to various dangers and trappings of the evil one. Hence, our redemption insures us daily from the enemy's deadly attacks.

The fact that we're still alive for God proves that He had delivered us from many dangers in the past and preserved us till now. The same God, through Jesus Christ our Lord, who redeemed us from all evils of the past, is still covering us in whatever situation we are in now, and will protect us from any future attacks, no matter how brutal and deadly.

So keep trusting Christ, who is your Redeemer, for your daily security throughout your lifetime. Relax and fear not; you're a redeemed of the Lord. He watches over His own.

Have a peaceful day with His **loaded blessings** of **redemption**!

LIVING WORD for TODAY—April 23:

LOADED with DAILY BLESSINGS (Ps. 68:19)-#114

REDEMPTION—23

"Now when these things begin to happen, look up and lift up your heads, because your redemption draws near." (Luke 21:28)

The Consummation of Our Redemption

In our daily meditational devotion during this month, we're considering the subject of redemption under the broad theme for this year: **loaded** with **daily blessings**. Redemption is one of the blessings the Lord freely bestows on whoever will receive it from Him and be free.

We've studied:

- The concept of redemption;
- The cost of redemption;
- The consequences of redemption; and now
- The consummation of our redemption.

We're already redeemed by the blood of the Lamb of God (Jesus Christ) who took away the sins of the world. That perfect sacrifice was once and for all. But why are we still going through pains, struggles, tensions, fears, sins, sicknesses, diseases, demonic attacks, and death?

And why did the Lord say we should look up because our redemption draws near when we start to see the distress of nations?

The answers to these questions are simple and will be considered in our devotional for the remaining days of this month.

Please know that when our Lord Jesus Christ died on the Cross and rose from the dead on the third day, He paid the full price for the sins of humanity. He also set in motion the process of liberating the whole world from the tyranny of Satan, the prince of this earth.

What we're going through in the world now is part of the delivery process well known to women who have been through the labor pains of delivering a

baby. These pains are in stages before the final push to get the baby out. May God bless our mothers!

So the troubles we're witnessing in the world today are the labor pains of the final delivery of the world into the hands of its Redeemer for a new world order.

Let not your heart be troubled, but look up to the Lord and be ready for the complete benefit of your redemption.

Have a great day with His **loaded blessings**!

LIVING WORD for TODAY—April 24:

LOADED with DAILY BLESSINGS (Ps. 68:19)-#115

REDEMPTION—24

"And He said: 'Take heed that you not be deceived. For many will come in My name, saying, 'I am He,' and, 'The time has drawn near.' Therefore do not go after them." (Luke 21:8)

Signs of the consummation of our redemption are many. In fact, there are about fourteen signs given by our Lord Himself as recorded in Luke 21:8–27. Of course, there are more signs spread out in the Bible.

Let us look at a few of these signs as they relate to the last phase of our redemption.

The Lord warns us to take heed of many deceivers in His name. False prophets, false ministers, and ministries with false teachings have been part of the church from its inception. The early church and through the centuries had to wrestle with them. The goal of Satan is to contaminate and destroy the church from within; hence, the need for the five-fold ministry of true apostles, prophets, evangelists, pastors, and teachers in the church.

As the coming of the Lord draws near for the consummation of our redemption, we will witness more intense activities of false apostles, bishops, prophets, evangelists, pastors, and teachers who peddle and merchandise the Word of God for their personal gains and not for the glorification of Christ and edification of believers.

So watch out and stay with the basic principles of the Bible. Be careful how you go after miracles and miracle workers. Remember this: Unbelievers go after signs and wonders, but signs and wonders follow believers in Jesus Christ (Mark 16:17–18). Know God and His Word, and you will not be deceived.

Have a blessed day with God's **loaded benefits!**

LIVING WORD for TODAY-April 25:

LOADED with DAILY BLESSINGS (Ps. 68:19)-#116

REDEMPTION—25

"'But when you hear of wars and commotions, do not be terrified; for these things must come to pass first, but the end will not come immediately.'
Then He said to them, 'Nation will rise against nation, and kingdom against kingdom.'" (Luke 21:9–10)

The second coming of Christ is the grand finale of our redemption. But He did not leave His own in the dark to be led by false and sensational teachings about His coming.

He gave us warnings and signs to watch for: wars and commotions; nations rising against nations.

These are all part of the formation of our world. They did not start now; they've always existed and would continue in their intensities until the Prince of Peace comes to put an end to human kingdoms under the control of Satan.

The world has witnessed world wars, and it seems we're living through another one now. Modern warfare is changing from physical, military, and artillery combats to an invisible air attack. COVID-19 is an invisible world war that every nation is fighting right now.

But it's not going to be the end of the world. It will be over, and the present world will go on to confront other global disasters.

The Lord's counsel to us when these things begin to happen are:

- Don't be terrified. These things must come to pass and God would see His children through them; and
- Look up and lift up your heads, don't be depressed and distracted by threats and theories that don't edify. But be focused on the Lord and prepared for His coming in any form.

I pray the Lord to see us through the COVID-19 war and any depression that may result from it.

Rejoice in the Lord with His **loaded blessings!**

LIVING WORD for TODAY—April 26:

LOADED with DAILY BLESSINGS (Ps. 68:19)-#117

REDEMPTION—26

"And there will be great earthquakes in various places, and famines and pestilences; and there will be fearful sights and great signs from heaven." (Luke 21:11)

Earthquakes, famines, pestilences, and fearful sights from heaven—these will be common events in the world as the consummation of our redemption draws near.

There have been record earthquakes in various places in recent times, and experts are already warning world governments of the next pandemic, which will be global famines. With the swarms of locust invading many farmlands in East Africa and other regions of the world and farm workers staying at home due to the coronavirus, the stage is set for global famines.

But note the word "great" our Lord used to emphasize these events. These signs are already taking place in various parts of the globe; they will become more intense and then great. Find time to read the Book of Revelation and refresh your memory of the opening of the seven seals in heaven to wrap up the end of the world.

Again, the Lord's marching order to us as we witness the preambles of the catastrophic events to come:

- Don't be terrified. Fear is a sin; and
- Look up and be focused on the Lord who controls these events. He will take care of His own.

Have a peaceful day with God's **loaded blessings!**

LIVING WORD for TODAY—April 27:

LOADED with DAILY BLESSINGS (Ps. 68:19)-#118

REDEMPTION—27

"But before all these things, they will lay their hands on you and persecute you, ... "You will be betrayed even by parents and brothers, relatives and friends, and they will put some of you to death.
"And you will be hated by all for My name's sake.
"But not a hair of your head shall be lost. By your patience possess your souls."(Luke 21:12–19)

We live in the church age that was inaugurated by the outpouring of the Holy Spirit on the Day of Pentecost. The gospel of the kingdom of God being advanced by the Christian church has reached all nations on earth.

But it is also the age of conflicts; conflicts between light and darkness, truth and lies, Christians and unbelievers, and Christ and Satan. These battles will continue relentlessly until they usher in Christ, the Prince of Peace, who will put an end to all conflicts and reign with His redeemed on earth.

Until then, expect persecutions, betrayals, hatred, and even martyrdom, if you are a disciple of Jesus Christ, from the agents of Satan, who is the prince of this evil age.

Our consolation is the promise of our Savior to keep us safe in this troubled world. "But not a hair of your head shall be lost" (Luke 21:18). So be patient, our Redeemer is on His way with His rewards.

Have a beautiful day with His **loaded blessings!**

LIVING WORD for TODAY—April 28:

LOADED with DAILY BLESSINGS (Ps. 68:19)-#119

REDEMPTION—28

"And there will be signs in the sun, in the moon, and in the stars; and on the earth distress of nations, with perplexity, the sea and the waves roaring; men's hearts failing them from fear and the expectation of those things which are coming on the earth, for the powers of the heavens will be shaken." (Luke 21:25–26)

Biblical prophecies have multiple fulfillments. Some of the signs our Lord predicted in this chapter and elsewhere were directly related to the fall of Jerusalem in AD 70. However, this Olivet Discourse of Jesus with His disciples answers their triple questions about the destruction of the Jerusalem temple, the signs of His coming, and the end of the age (Matt. 24:3).

The part relating to Jerusalem and the dispersion of the Jews to the nations of the world has been completely fulfilled. Jerusalem is still being trampled by Gentiles. But we're now living in the times of "distress of nations, with perplexity," when people's hearts are failing them from fear and expectations of things to come. Since this is not an in-depth study on eschatology but a short devotional to inspire and empower us in our daily walk with the Lord, I pray that you will study the Bible and be familiar with Christ's predictions about the signs of His second coming.

May your heart be filled with God's courage to live a fear-free life in this end-time.

Have a blessed day/evening with God's **loaded blessings!**

LIVING WORD for TODAY—April 29:

LOADED with DAILY BLESSINGS (Ps. 68:19)-#120

REDEMPTION—29

"For we know that the whole creation groans and labors with birth pangs together until now. Not only that, but we also who have the firstfruits of the Spirit, even we ourselves groan within ourselves, eagerly waiting for the adoption, the redemption of our body." (Rom. 8:22–23)

The Cosmic Redemption

In these last two sessions of our series on redemption, let us consider the final stage of our redemption. Because of the sins of mankind, the whole creation of God has been distorted from what it was in the beginning.

When God created the world in Genesis 1, His verdict for each creation was, "it was good." But man's rebellion turned what was good into what is harmful. The whole creation has been groaning through birth pangs, eager to be reborn into its original beauty. The redemption Jesus Christ paid for with His blood included the whole cosmos.

When Christ comes back to earth, He will restore all things, including our bodies into their original conditions. This is our hope, the finality of our redemption. So let us live daily with this hope as we go through the imperfections of this present world. A new world order is coming, free from all viruses, death, and decay. The healthcare system will be folded up, and all healthcare workers will have to change their professions. Cheer up; it is going to happen!

Have a happy day with God's **loaded blessings!**

LIVING WORD for TODAY—April 30:

LOADED with DAILY BLESSINGS (Ps. 68:19)-#121

REDEMPTION—30

"Repent therefore and be converted, that your sins may be blotted out, so that times of refreshing may come from the presence of the Lord, "and that He may send Jesus Christ, who was preached to you before, whom heaven must receive until the times of restoration of all things, which God has spoken by the mouth of all His holy prophets since the world began." (Acts 3:19–21)

Christ, Our Redeemer and Restorer

Let us conclude this important subject of redemption with Saint Peter's appeal to the religious leaders and people in Jerusalem during the formation of the early church.

• It is possible to be very religious and even hold a position in the church without having a personal relationship with Jesus Christ.

- It takes true repentance from sins to be converted to Christ;
- Seasons of refreshing from God are designed for those who belong to the Lord;
- You can experience God's seasons of refreshing now, even in the midst of pandemic crisis;
- Jesus Christ will come again for the redeemed to restore all things in the world to their perfect conditions; and
- You can be converted or reconciled with Jesus Christ where you are now by confessing your sins to Him and affirming your commitment to His Lordship over your life.

Have a great day with His **loaded blessings** of **redemption!**

LIVING WORD for TODAY—MAY 1:

LOADED with DAILY BLESSINGS (Ps. 68:19)-#122

Good bye to April, and welcome, May!

As April, has gone away forever, may your pains, sorrows, disappointments, griefs, failures, lacks, and shortcomings disappear from you forever!

It is a new day, a new month with great expectations of God's faithfulness, forgiveness, favor, faith, friendship, finances, fulfillment, and future. I declare all of these to your life in Jesus Christ's name!

Music is a powerful tool to ignite and attract the presence of God and His ministering angels into your situations. So listen to some of the best praise and worship songs on YouTube. These collections of the yearly best praise and worship songs minister to me every time I listen to them, and I'm sure they will minister to you as well. You may also use them for your prayer walk and exercise even in your rooms.

May the great God of our salvation meet you at the point of your need and put His songs of praises in your mouth always.

Happy new month of May with God's **loaded blessings**!

MAY—FORGIVENESS

LIVING WORD for TODAY—May 2:

LOADED with DAILY BLESSINGS (Ps. 68:19)-#123

FORGIVENESS—1

"Bless the LORD, O my soul,
And forget not all His benefits:
Who forgives all your iniquities, Who heals all your diseases..." (Ps. 68:19)

Forgiveness of sins is one of the daily benefits we receive from God. While redemption is once and for all, a done deal price paid by Christ on the Cross with His blood, forgiveness of sins is a daily ongoing benefit available to believers in Christ Jesus.

Although the very moment penitent sinners accept Jesus Christ as their personal Savior, legally, they stand forgiven and justified before God, the Judge of the whole universe. However, because they still live in a sinful world with their sinful nature, they're prone to sin and fall short of God's holy standards. Hence, the divine provision for cleansing and forgiveness through the shed blood of Jesus Christ on a regular basis is needed.

This provision is a blessing that cannot be bought with money or birthright but given freely by grace from the Lord to those who are contrite in spirit. So it's worth our praise and worship to the Lord. During our devotional time this month, we're going to explore and experience God's provision, power, and practice of forgiveness in our daily living.

Have a great day/evening with His **loaded blessings!**

LIVING WORD for TODAY—May 3:

LOADED with DAILY BLESSINGS (Ps. 68:19)-#124

FORGIVENESS—2

"Bless the LORD, O my soul,
And forget not all His benefits:
Who forgives all your iniquities, Who heals all your diseases..." (Ps. 103:2–3)

Forgiveness of sins is related to the healing of diseases. In my years of directing spiritual care counseling in a busy medical center and coordinating the same service in various hospice care organizations, I have witnessed, firsthand, how unforgiveness stood in the way and prevented many patients from being healed and recovered until they let go and released those who had offended them. Likewise, many struggled to pass on in peace but could not until they were led into confessions and forgiveness of their own sins and then the release of those who had offended them before they could die in peace.

It has been discovered through many studies and observations that some sick patients who go to hospitals for treatments need more than medicine to be healed. They need spiritual and emotional care to recover. Forgiveness of sins is part of a holistic approach to physical, spiritual, and mental health.

David, the king and a man after God's heart in the Bible, knew this truth and experienced it in his own life (Ps. 51:8; 103:3). So never let a day pass by without opening your hearts to the Lord in prayer; first for your own cleansing of all known and unknown sins, and second, for forgiving and releasing those who have offended you. Living with a clear conscience is foundational to a happy life.

Have a restful day/night with God's **loaded blessings!**

LIVING WORD for TODAY—May 4:

LOADED with DAILY BLESSINGS (Ps. 68:19)-#125

FORGIVENESS—3

"I, even I, am He who blots out your transgressions for My own sake;
Put Me in remembrance;
Let us contend together;
State your case, that you may be acquitted." (Isa. 43:25–26)

Power to Forgive

Forgiveness of sins is a blessing given to us freely by grace. But who has the power to forgive?

The religious leaders of Jesus's day confronted Him with this question when He forgave a sick man his sins before healing him (Mark 2:7).

There's no controversy about the sovereign power of God to forgive human sins. This truth is well established in the Scriptures. It is not only in His nature, but also in His power to forgive our sins. He says:

"Come now, and let us reason together, Says the LORD,

Though your sins are like scarlet, They shall be as white as snow; Though they are red like crimson, They shall be as wool. If you are willing and obedient, You shall eat the good of the land" (Isa. 1:18–19).

So it is up to us to come openly before Him for our daily cleansing and forgiveness. He is the One who blots your sins away.

Have a good day with God's **loaded blessings** of **forgiveness!**

LIVING WORD for TODAY—May 5:

LOADED with DAILY BLESSINGS (Ps. 68:19)-#126

FORGIVENESS—4

"The LORD is merciful and gracious, Slow to anger and abounding in mercy. He will not always strife with us, Nor will He keep His anger forever. He has not dealt with us according to our sins, Nor punished us according to our iniquities." (Ps. 103:8–10) Forgiveness of sins affects all of us because

God deals with all His creatures with His tender mercies. Some people see God as a police officer who is out there watching for violators of His rules so He can cite and punish them. That is not the picture of God in the Bible but what religions painted Him to be. Of course, He will eventually judge the rebellious who flagrantly reject His mercies and choose to go in their sinful ways. But as far as His dealings with us from day to day, He is gracious, merciful, and lovingly caring for all His creations. There are common blessings of God, severally spread all over the universe for the benefit of His creatures because of His general principles of mercy (Matt. 5:44–45).

While God in His mercy is patient, He has, however, commanded everyone everywhere to repent and receive His forgiveness through Christ Jesus for free (Acts 17:30–31). Please receive the free gift of His forgiveness now and be transformed into who He created you to be.

Have a happy day/evening with His **loaded blessings!**

LIVING WORD for TODAY—May 6:

LOADED with DAILY BLESSINGS (Ps. 68:19)-#127

FORGIVENESS—5

"For as the heavens are high above the earth,
So great is His mercy toward those who fear Him;
As far as the east is from the west, So far has He removed our transgressions from
us."(Ps. 103:11–12)

The Scripture in this passage now moves from general to specific—from God's general bestowal of mercies to His creatures to His special mercy for those who fear Him.

With a display of poetical language, David describes to us how far God's mercy can go in forgiving the sins of those who are His own. God's mercy is limitless, just as high as the heavens are above the earth. In His limitless mercy, He also removes our sins far, as the east is to the west. When God forgives His own people, He forgets all about their past offenses. In fact, their sins are blotted out of His books.

Thank God for His forgiveness! But this special display of mercy is reserved for those who fear Him. The Holy Spirit spreads the love of God abroad in our hearts and makes true Christians hate sins by the fear of God.

If you're struggling with guilty feelings of something bad you've done in the past, which you're even ashamed of, it is time to be delivered and move on with divine approval if you love the Lord and serve Him. This message is sent to you.

"There is therefore now no condemnation to those who are in Christ Jesus, who do not walk according to the flesh, but according to the Spirit" (Rom. 8:1). Be healed!

Live by the Spirit and enjoy the limitless mercy of God for forgiving and forgetting your transgressions.

Have a peaceful day with God's **loaded blessings** of **forgiveness**!

LIVING WORD for TODAY—May 7:

LOADED with DAILY BLESSINGS (Ps. 68:19)-#128

FORGIVENESS—6

"As a father pities his children,
So the LORD pities those who fear Him.
For He knows our frame;
He remembers that we are dust." (Ps. 103:13–14)

The power to forgive sins on earth belongs absolutely to God our Creator and Father because of His infinite, immeasurable, and indescribable love and mercy.

When God instituted a covenant relationship with the children of Israel, He wanted to be their Father. But they didn't respond to Him as their Father; rather, they related to Him in a slave and master relationship.

However, the Lord never distanced Himself from them because of His covenant with their fathers, Abraham, Isaac, and Jacob. In progression of His love, He sent Jesus Christ, His son, to make that Father/children relationship possible. Anyone who receives Christ can now enjoy the Fatherhood of God in His mercy, lovingkindness, and compassion in a special family relationship not available to those who are outside the covenant.

Forgiveness of sins is part of the deal guaranteed to those who come to God through Christ and grieve for their sins. He promised to pity, deliver, and welcome them into His family (Ps. 103:13; Mal. 3:17; John 1:12).

This is the only way to change our frame of dust into the family of God.

May the Holy Spirit grant you the grace to enter and enjoy God's family blessings daily.

He loves you!

Have a great day with His **loaded benefits!**

LIVING WORD for TODAY—May 8:

LOADED with DAILY BLESSINGS (Ps. 68:19)-#129

FORGIVENESS—7

"'But that you may know that the Son of Man has power on earth to forgive sins'
—He said to the paralytic, 'I say to you, take up your bed, and go to your house.'
Immediately he arose, took up the bed, and went out in the presence of them all,
so that all were amazed and glorified God, saying, 'We never saw anything like
this!'" (Mark 2:10–12)

The power to forgive sins on earth belongs to God. But who else has power to grant forgiveness? In the next few days, we're going to examine in the Scriptures others who can forgive and release the flow of God's grace to remove the pains of sins.

Let us start with our Lord Jesus Christ. During His earthly ministry, He healed and delivered many from their sicknesses and diseases. Some, He let us know the sources of their problems, some, He didn't.

In the case of healing the paralytic man in our passage above, the Lord specifically said the source of the man's paralysis was a sinful lifestyle.

If his sins were not forgiven him, no amount of prayers, doctor's visits, medications, and therapies could have restored him. Jesus, knowing this, went straight to the root of the man's sickness and declared the power of forgiveness for his sins. This led to the religious leaders accusing Jesus of blasphemy, which was a sin punishable by death in Israel at that time because only God has power to forgive sins.

But Jesus made it clear to them that He was God in human flesh, and He has the same power to forgive any sins and heal sinners. So He healed the man with His word.

It is always important to examine ourselves when sick and also be cautious when praying for the sick to apply this principle. The prayer of faith and forgiveness of sins go hand in hand with healing the sick (James 5:15–16).

Have a great day with God's **loaded blessings!**

To be continued.

LIVING WORD for TODAY—May 9:

LOADED with DAILY BLESSINGS (Ps. 69:19)-#130

FORGIVENESS—8

"...'Son, be of good cheer; your sins are forgiven you...

'But that you may know that the Son of Man has power on earth to forgive sins'—then He said to the paralytic, 'Arise, take up your bed, and go to your house.'" (Matt. 9:2–6)

Sins paralyze our abilities to live a life of wholeness, which God designed for us on earth.

Hence, Jesus Christ came as God in the human flesh to forgive our sins and release God's grace to enable us to be whole and be who He wants us to be on earth.

While it can be said that not all sicknesses are directly the result of sins, it can also be argued that without the entrance of sins into the world, there would have been no acts of human disobedience and rebellion causing sicknesses and diseases.

Let us be humble enough to accept our weaknesses and flaws to invite the divine grace of forgiveness and wholeness into our situations daily. Maybe you're suffering now and feel forsaken by God because of your sins; hear the compassionate voice of Jesus Christ speaking to you right now: "Son or daughter, be of good cheer; your sins are forgiven you. Arise and walk."

Have better days ahead of you with God's **loaded blessings!**

LIVING WORD for TODAY—May 10:

LOADED with DAILY BLESSINGS (Ps. 68:19)-#131

FORGIVENESS—9

"Then He said to them, 'Thus it is written, and thus it was necessary for the Christ to suffer and to rise from the dead the third day, and that repentance and remission of sins should be preached in His name to all nations, beginning at Jerusalem.'" (Luke 24:46–47)

Wishing all our mothers and women in general, happy Mothers' Day!

Though Jesus Christ, as God in human flesh, had equal power with God to forgive sins while He was here on earth, He, however, acquired a transferrable authority of forgiveness through His death and resurrection for human sins.

After His resurrection, it took the revelation of the Holy Spirit for His disciples' eyes to be opened to know Him and understand the Scriptures about His forgiving power. Once the eyes of the early disciples of Jesus were opened to know this scriptural truth, they went everywhere, proclaiming forgiveness of sins in Jesus's name to people around them (Acts 2:38; 3:18–21).

Since Christ has acquired this authority through what He suffered, God has made Him the only mediator between God and mankind to forgive sins. So God is no longer forgiving sins directly, but through Jesus Christ. It is, therefore, a waste of time and effort to pray to God for forgiveness of sins without praying through Jesus Christ.

Let's teach and proclaim this truth clearly without fear or favor to all mankind everywhere.

Have a great day/evening with God's **loaded blessings!**

LIVING WORD for TODAY—May 11:

LOADED with DAILY BLESSINGS (Ps. 68:19)-#132

FORGIVENESS—10

"Again I say to you that if two of you agree on earth concerning anything that they ask, it will be done for them by My Father in heaven. For where two or three are gathered together in My name, I am there in the midst of them." (Matt. 18:19–20)

Who has the power to forgive sins on earth?

We've seen from the Bible that God the Father has absolute power to forgive sins. We've also seen how that authority and power were demonstrated by Jesus Christ, God the Son, during His earthly ministry. His name also becomes the transferring authority for remission of sins after His resurrection from the dead.

Now we come to the critical issue of others who have delegated power to forgive sins on earth.

The passage above is often quoted to support the authority of believers to bind and loose. But the context by which this authority was given to the church directly related to the forgiveness of sins.

A local gathering of two or three believers in Christ Jesus is called the church. Whenever they unite in agreement in any matter according to the will of God, Christ is present with them to bring to pass what they decree. A Christian who offends another Christian and refuses to admit it even after being confronted on the matter by other Christians can be reported to the elders of the church. After a careful examination of the offense and the elders find him or her guilty, the offending believer can repent and be declared forgiven by the elders of the church. But if not repented, the church elders can withdraw the fellowship of the church from him or her. This must be done with integrity and love to receive the backing of the Lord.

Try to be in unity with the local assembly of Christians you join for the flow of Christ's support and His gifts of grace into your life.

Have a great day with His **loaded blessings!**

LIVING WORD for TODAY—May 12:

LOADED with DAILY BLESSINGS (Ps. 68:19)-#133

FORGIVENESS—11

"This punishment which was inflicted by the majority is sufficient for such a man, so that, on the contrary, you ought rather to forgive and comfort him, lest perhaps such a one be swallowed up with too much sorrow.
Therefore I urge you to reaffirm your love to him." (2 Cor. 2:6–8)

The church is delegated with Christ's authority to forgive sins on earth. Whenever the church exercises this authority with the Spirit of Christ and in unity, God upholds her decision.

The biblical text above confirms this practice. The case in view refers to the act of sexual immorality in the Corinthian church (1 Cor. 5:1–7) reported to Paul. Since the man involved was not called to repentance by the church, Paul summoned the church in the name of the Lord Jesus Christ and His presence to commit the sinful member to Satan for his physical torture. The church did that, and the man later repented of his sinful lifestyle. Seeing how remorseful the man was, Paul called on the church to exercise the same authority of Christ used to commit him to Satan for his forgiveness, restoration, and comfort.

Let this case remind us that the grace of God is not a license to sin but the power of Christ to denying ungodliness and worldly lusts, living soberly, righteously, and godly in this present evil age with Christ's return in focus (Tit. 2:11–12).

Have a happy day with His **loaded blessings!**

LIVING WORD for TODAY—May 13:

LOADED with DAILY BLESSINGS (Ps. 68:19)-#134

FORGIVENESS—12

"So Jesus said to them again, 'Peace to you! As the Father has sent Me, I also send you.'
And when He had said this, He breathed on them, and said to them, 'Receive the Holy Spirit. If you forgive the sins of any, they are forgiven them; if you retain the sins of any, they are retained'" (John 20:21–23)

A Spirit-filled believer in the Lord Jesus Christ is not only forgiven but has the power to minister forgiveness of sins to sinners. This is a delegated authority, which the Resurrected Christ confers on them as they carry out His mission of spreading the good news of His kingdom on earth.

It is not difficult to understand this part of the Great Commission. But what about the other side of it—the power to retain people's sins? This is a crucial authority that any Spirit-filled Christian can release under the discernment of the Holy Spirit when confronted with oppositions to fulfill the missions of Christ. Read more about this in Acts 13:6–12 and the encounters of Moses with Pharaoh and his magicians in Egypt (Exod.7:8–12:33).

The same power of the Holy Spirit in us with which we release God's grace of salvation into sinners can also be used to release God's judgment upon hardening sinners who refuse to repent but continue to obstruct and pervert the truth of God's Word to others.

So be sensitive to the leading of the Holy Spirit as to when to swing the two edge sword of God's forgiveness. May the Lord guide us daily as we carry out His missions here on earth.

Have a refreshing day with His LOADED BLESSINGS!

LIVING WORD for TODAY—May 14:

LOADED with DAILY BLESSINGS (Ps. 68:19)-#135

FORGIVENESS—13

"And forgive us our sins,
For we also forgive everyone who is indebted to us..." (Luke 11:4)

Forgiveness of sins is a gift we daily receive freely from God and which we, in turn, give freely to others. Our Lord forgives us our sins even before we ask Him. Including forgiveness in our daily prayer is just to let us acknowledge before the Lord our imperfection and sinful nature. Just as we don't wait for our children to beg us for their forgiveness when they offend us before we do, so is our perfect Heavenly Father already forgiven us before we come to Him in prayer (Ps. 103:13–14). We come to Him in prayer to take what He already offered.

The same way we're forgiven, our Lord has endowed us with the power to forgive others who sin against us. Our Lord has a lot to say about our responsibility to forgive others if we're going to be effective in His kingdom. We shall explore this further in the days ahead.

So pray that the Lord will bring to your remembrance someone you need to forgive and release today so that your prayers will not be hindered.

Have a great day with His **loaded blessings** of **forgiveness!**

LOADED with DAILY BLESSINGS (Ps. 68:19)-#136

FORGIVENESS—14

"For if you forgive men their trespasses, your heavenly Father will also forgive you. But if you do not forgive men their trespasses, neither will your Father forgive your trespasses." (Matt. 6:14–15)

Forgiveness of sins is not only a gift we receive freely from God, but also what gives us the right to stand before the righteous God.

So we do have the power to forgive those who offend us.

We also need the power of forgiveness to operate in our lives and constantly release the flow of Christ's blessings to us and through us to others. This is the way our Master and Redeemer sets up His kingdom, and this is the way He wants us to function in it. The only right we have to ask Him to forgive our sins is our disposition of mind to forgive those who sin against us. This is very powerful!

Has anyone offended you lately? Please forgive and release that person. Remember this, as long as God's favor is upon your life, the enemy will always bring offenders across your way to obstruct the flow. Oftentimes, he uses people who are close to us. So watch out and always be ready to activate the power of forgiveness.

Have a lovely day with His **loaded blessings!**

LIVING WORD for TODAY—May 16:

LOADED with DAILY BLESSINGS (Ps. 68:19)-#137

FORGIVENESS—15

"Then Peter came to Him and said, 'Lord, how often shall my brother sin against me, and I forgive him? Up to seven times?' Jesus said to him, 'I do not say to you, up to seven times, but up to seventy times seven.'" (Matt. 18:21–22)

Forgiveness of sins affects all of us mortals, no matter how great or small, for **all** have sinned and fallen short of God's righteous standards.

The church, as the bride of Christ here on earth, consists of forgiven sinners, not perfect, but forgiven and pursuing perfection, which will not happen until Christ, the Bridegroom, comes to take His bride, the church, and make her perfect. Until then, we have to put up with individuals' imperfections and shortcomings in the church.

Peter's question to the Lord was the religious standard of forgiveness for the day. But Jesus's answer to Peter introduced a new standard requirement of the kingdom of God. Forgiving each other without limit is the norm of operating in Christ's kingdom. This may be difficult for humans, but with God, all things are possible.

Let us trust Christ to empower us daily with His Spirit so we can live to forgive and forget the mistakes, and even the intentional offenses our brothers and sisters may commit against us from day to day.

Have a happy day/evening with God's **loaded blessings!**

LIVING WORD for TODAY—May 17:

LOADED with DAILY BLESSINGS (Ps. 68:19)-#138

FORGIVENESS—16

"'So My Heavenly Father also will do to you if each of you, from his heart, does not forgive his brother his trespasses'" (Matt. 18:35)

Peter's religious question about forgiveness was answered by the Lord with the standard requirement of unlimited forgiveness in His kingdom. The Lord then followed up His answer with the parable of a king who wanted to settle accounts with his servants (Matt. 18:23–34). While the king forgave the servant who owed him the most debt after begging for mercy, this same servant could not forgive his fellow servant who owed him a far less amount and locked him in prison till he could pay back his debt.

The ungrateful servant in this parable represents us, Christians, and the fellow servant represents our fellow believers who may offend us. The Lord concludes this parable with a strong warning to us as we relate to our fellow Christians.

- Forgiveness must come from our hearts;
- Forgiveness should be unconditional; and
- Forgiveness is limitless.

May the Lord, by His Spirit, flood our hearts with His compassion daily so we can love and forgive those who offend us just as we are being forgiven by Him.

Have a great day with His **loaded blessings!**

LIVING WORD for TODAY—May 18:

LOADED with DAILY BLESSINGS (Ps. 68:19)-#139

FORGIVENESS —17

"...bearing with one another, and forgiving one another, if anyone has a complaint against another, even as Christ forgave you, so you also must do." (Col. 3:13)

Christian living in a community of other believers is challenging. Why? Because people we live with or relate to are from different backgrounds and diversities. What unites us together is the love of God in Christ our Lord.

Due to our peculiar backgrounds, we're bound to step on each other's toes. Sometimes we even rub our imperfections on others; hence, the admonition of "bearing with one another, and forgiving one another."

Complaining against one another is bound to happen from time to time, but we avoid a lifestyle of complaining about every mistakes made by others, and live with the spirit of forgiveness.

One of the problems of the world today, which is also in the church, is that no one likes to be corrected, even when done in love and by the appropriate authority. Everyone is right in whatever they do. The spirit of forgiveness does not eliminate correction in love but forbears with people who are going through the process of becoming who they ought to be in Christ Jesus. Our Lord is intolerant with those who refuse to change. Jesus is a life-changer, and so also His church.

So let us bear with one another as we are all, at one time or the other, going through some changes in our lives.

Pray always for patience, which is the fruit of love, to relate to others in Christ Jesus.

Have a happy day with His **loaded blessings!**

LIVING WORD for TODAY—May 19:

LOADED with DAILY BLESSINGS (Ps. 68:19)-#140

FORGIVENESS—18

"John came baptizing in the wilderness and preaching a baptism of repentance for the remission of sins.
Then all the land of Judea, and those from Jerusalem, went out to him in the Jordan River, confessing their sins." (Mark 1:4–5)

The power of forgiveness to restore is a major message of the Bible. But the Bible also emphasizes the importance of true repentance as a condition to forgiveness of sins. One of the weaknesses of the modern preaching is over-emphasis on the mercies and grace of God. Yes, God's mercies and grace are the pillars of our salvation.

But the Bible asks: "Shall we continue in sin that grace may abound?" The Bible's answer is: "Certainly not!" The Scripture abounds with teachings of God's goodness and mercies leading sinners to true repentance before the gift of forgiveness for restoration into God's standard of living.

So if you're struggling with sins, even as a Christian, know that it is God's mercy and grace creating restlessness and displeasure in you to repent, be forgiven, and be fully restored by the Lord to where you should be.

In the remaining days of this month, we're going to meditate more on this.

Pray that the Lord will continue His work in you by creating hatred for sins and true repentance to enjoy the full benefits of His forgiveness and mercies.

Have a blessed day with His **loaded benefits!**

LIVING WORD for TODAY—May 20:

LOADED with DAILY BLESSINGS (Ps. 68:19)-#141

FORGIVENESS—19

"Seek the LORD while He may be found,

Call upon Him while He is near. Let the wicked forsake his way, And the unrighteous man his thoughts; Let him return to the LORD, And He will have mercy on him;

And to our God, For He will abundantly pardon." (Isa. 55:6–7)

Forgiveness of sins is a free gift from God, but it must be received by humanity. Genuine repentance is how one receives this powerful gift.

Repentance means turning around to forsake wrongdoings and doing the right things. True repentance comes with godly sorrows and convictions of sins. Actually, this is the work of the Holy Spirit in believers (John 16:8; 2 Cor. 7:10).

So let us heed the call of the Lord and come to Him daily with genuine repentance so He can help us be cleansed from the filthiness of the flesh and spirit by His blood (2 Cor. 7:1).

Our God is merciful and always willing to abundantly pardon our sins if we come to Him with a contrite spirit.

If the Holy Spirit is convicting you of any sin in your life, don't brush it aside. Now is the time to confess it before the Lord and ask for His power to overcome temptations.

Have a great day **loaded** with His **blessings!**

LIVING WORD for TODAY—May 21:

LOADED with DAILY BLESSINGS (Ps. 68:19)-#142

FORGIVENESS—20

"From that time, Jesus began to preach and to say, 'Repent, for the kingdom of heaven is at hand.'" (Matt. 4:17)
"Then Jesus said, 'Father, forgive them, for they do not know what they do.'" (Luke 23:34)

Repentance and forgiveness of sins played a prominent role in the earthly ministry of our Lord Jesus Christ. The Lord's first statement as He started His public ministry was "Repent, for the kingdom of heaven is at hand" (Matt. 4:17). And His first of the seven last statements He uttered on the Cross before He died for our sins was a prayer of forgiveness. "Father, forgive them, for they do not know what they do" (Luke 23:34).

The implication of this tells us the main purpose of His coming to the world to die.

"For the Son of Man has come to seek and to save that which was lost" (Luke 19:10).

Repentance and forgiveness were side by side in His ministry, and so they must be in our ministries today.

May His Spirit perform a genuine work of repentance in our hearts daily so we can enjoy His blessing of forgiveness

Have a merry day with His **loaded blessings!**

LIVING WORD for TODAY—May 22:

LOADED with DAILY BLESSINGS (Ps. 68:19)-#143

FORGIVENESS—21

"'I say to you that likewise there will be more joy in heaven over one sinner who repents than over ninety-nine just persons who need no repentance.'" (Luke 15:7)

The power of forgiveness as demonstrated in the ministry of the Lord:

Our Lord spoke three parables in Luke chapter 15, each with the same conclusion. There is always a celebration in heaven whenever a sinner repents and returns to the Lord to receive forgiveness.

Ironically, these parables were spoken to silence the complaints of the religious leaders about Jesus's reception of sinners in His ministry. While Jesus accepted repentant sinners with open arms, the religious leaders kept them at arm's length. Christ's attitude to repentant sinners demonstrates the heart of God and His willingness to forgive sinners and welcome them into His kingdom without any reservations.

Feel free to come to Christ with all your load of sins, as long as you're willing to drop it at the feet of His cross, and see how He will cleanse and forgive you. He will even throw a party for the angels in heaven because of you. So instead of allowing your sins to pull you away from God, let them draw you closer to Him for deliverance. It is the sick that needs healing and not the healthy.

Have a refreshing day with His **loaded blessings!**

LIVING WORD for TODAY—May 23:

LOADED with DAILY BLESSINGS (Ps. 68:19)-#144

FORGIVENESS—22

"And he arose and came to his father. But when he was still a great way off, his father saw him and had compassion, and ran and fell on his neck and kissed him." (Luke 15:20)

There are many lessons we can learn from the story of the Prodigal Son in the Bible as told by our Lord Jesus Christ.

(1) Many of God's children always take God's grace and blessings for granted to live a wasteful and carefree life;

(2) God allows storms of adversity to come to His children to get their attention when they walk away from Him;

(3) God's storms of adversity will always lead to godly sorrow, which produces humility and repentance in His children;

(4) True repentance will always lead God's children back to Him and not far away from Him;

(5) God's heart of love is always yearning and waiting for His runaway children to come back home;

(6) Nothing pleases God the Father more than seeing His stray away children come back to Him; and

(7) God will always receive back, with great celebration, His sinful children who repent and come back to Him regardless of the sins committed.

So be encouraged to come back to your Heavenly Father with repentance. His forgiveness and royal garments of blessings are waiting for you.

Have a great day **loaded** with His **forgiveness**!

LIVING WORD for TODAY—May 24:

LOADED with DAILY BLESSINGS (Ps. 68:19)-#145

FORGIVENESS—23

"'...Woman, where are those accusers of yours? Has no one condemned you?'
She said, 'No one, Lord.' And Jesus said to her, 'Neither do I condemn you; go
and sin no more.'" (John 8:10–11)

The power of forgiveness as demonstrated by the Lord to the woman caught in the act of adultery could only be understood with the mind of God's infinite love and mercy as against societal norms.

Jesus was busy teaching people in the Temple, and suddenly there was an interruption by the religious leaders. A woman was brought before Him to be executed for breaking the moral law established by God through Moses. The hypocrisy of the religious leaders could be seen by them excluding the woman's partner in the act. It takes two to commit adulterous sin.

But instead of Jesus focusing on the woman, He turned the allegation against the accusers and condemned them by their conscience. The lady was forgiven by the Lord with a command: "go and sin no more." Please note that Jesus did not approve the sinful act of the woman but delivered her from guilt and condemnation by His power of forgiveness.

The power of the Lord's forgiveness goes far beyond addressing the act of sins, but also grants the power to be set free from sinful lifestyles. If you're being forgiven and still struggling with the same sin, it is time to seriously pray for the power to be delivered by the Lord. And He will answer your prayer if you mean it from your heart.

Have a victorious day **loaded** with His **forgiveness**!

LIVING WORD for TODAY—May 25:

LOADED with DAILY BLESSINGS (Ps. 68:19)-#146

FORGIVENESS—24

"And the Lord turned and looked at Peter. Then Peter remembered the word of the Lord, how He had said to him, 'Before the rooster crows, you will deny Me three times.' So Peter went out and wept bitterly." (Luke 22:61–62)

One of the worst sins one can commit against a loved one is to deny him or her publicly. This would even be more grievous when it is committed against the Lord to His face, at His most difficult time, going through trial in the enemy's courtroom. That's what Peter, the apostle of the Lord, did to his Master Jesus Christ.

Peter denied the Lord three times, not behind His back, but to His face, "I do not know Him."

But that was not the end of Peter's relationship with the Lord. The Lord's eye contact with him in that courtroom brought a deep conviction to Peter, which led to his repentance with tears. That was true godly sorrow that led Peter to deep contrition.

Fast forward to after the Lord's resurrection from the dead, He sought for Peter, forgave his sin, and restored him back to His fellowship and ministry (John 21:15–23).

The power of forgiveness by our Lord knows no limit to the contrite sinner. May the eye contact of the Lord connect with you today wherever you're in your compromise with sins.

Have a great day **loaded** with His **benefits** of **forgiveness**!

LIVING WORD for TODAY—May 26:

LOADED with DAILY BLESSINGS (Ps. 68:19)-#147

FORGIVENESS—25

"Then Jesus said, 'Father, forgive them, for they do not know what they do.' And they divided His garments and cast lots." (Luke 23:34)

The practice of forgiveness, as taught by the Lord in His preachings and practice, is not easy to be carried out by anyone without the Spirit of Christ. It takes His Spirit in us to turn the other cheek, His Spirit to bless those who curse us, and His Spirit to pray for our enemies when they are brutally killing us and we're going through severe pains.

The Lord of Glory exemplified all and more of these for us while He lived here in the flesh. While He was hanging on the painful cross with nails, before He died, He was able to pray forgiveness to the Father for His executioners.

What a perfect demonstration of the spirit of forgiveness.

Let us pray daily to live by His Spirit so that it would be easy for us to practice forgiveness to those we relate to in our day-to-day living. That's the Lord's requirement for the children of His kingdom.

Pray for those who don't see eye to eye with you in your circle of relationships and friendships.

Have a happy day/evening with His **loaded blessings!**

LIVING WORD for TODAY—May 27:

LOADED with DAILY BLESSINGS (Ps. 68:19)-#148

FORGIVENESS—26

"I appeal to you for my son Onesimus, whom I have begotten while in my chains, who once was unprofitable to you, but now is profitable to you and to me. I am sending him back. You therefore receive him, that is, my own heart..."(Phil. 10–12)

The practice of forgiveness in the early church knew no boundaries. It was practiced in homes, among families, and between friends and church members. In the atmosphere where the Holy Spirit is in action, forgiving one another is a common practice.

The small, one-chapter letter of Paul, the apostle, to his wealthy friend Philemon, demonstrates this fact. Philemon was one the disciples of Paul who had slaves. One of these slaves, Onesimus, stole some valuables from his master and ran away. He was caught and jailed to pay for his offense. While in prison, he came in touch with Paul, who was in the same prison with him. Paul and his ministry team were in jail for preaching the gospel. Paul led Onesimus to the Lord, discipled him, and when he was released from jail, Paul wrote a letter to Philemon, appealing to him to take his runaway slave back, not as a slave, but as a fellow brother in Christ.

Naturally, this was not possible, but in Christ, it was. We shall continue with the letter later in our devotional to learn more about the practice of forgiveness in our daily Christian living.

Never write anyone off as irredeemable, for the power of forgiveness of sins through Christ makes any penitent redeemable and profitable.

Have a great day **loaded** with His blessings!

LIVING WORD for TODAY—May 28:

LOADED with DAILY BLESSINGS (Ps. 68:19)-#149

FORGIVENESS—27

"For perhaps he departed for a while for this purpose, that you might receive him forever,
no longer as a slave but more than a slave—a beloved brother, especially to me but how much more to you, both in the flesh and in the Lord.
If then you count me as a partner, receive him as you would me." (Phil.15–17)

We see the beauty of the spirit of forgiveness as demonstrated in Paul's appeal to his honorable friend Philemon on behalf of a runaway slave. Paul's requests were unusual during his time. A slave had no legal rights but was the property of the owner.

But because of the grace of God in Christ Jesus, a slave could be considered a brother of equal rights with his owner. This was made possible by the forgiveness of sins through Jesus.

Philemon was not just to forgive his slave, Onesimus, but to receive him back with a new status in the household. He was to be treated as a brother and joint heir.

Thank God for this privilege we have in Christ. Let us practice this love in our day-to-day living and show to the world the power of forgiveness in Christ that breaks down all human barriers.

Our God is a God of second chances. Let us give people who fail to live up to our expectations more opportunities to rise through the power of forgiveness.

Have a great day **loaded** with God's **forgiveness**!

LIVING WORD for TODAY—May 29:

LOADED with DAILY BLESSINGS (Ps. 68:19)-#150

FORGIVENESS—28

"But if he has wronged you or owes anything, put that on my account. I, Paul, am writing with my own hand. I will repay—not to mention to you that you owe me even your own self besides." (Phil. 18–19)

Only those who have been forgiven know the value of forgiving others. "Just as we have been forgiven" is the Lord's requirement from us when it comes to forgiving others.

The aged Paul's request to his friend Philemon was hinged on the same grace of forgiveness Philemon had received from God through Paul in the past. Philemon was now required to return the same favor to his slave, Onesimus, who had wronged him.

May we be sensitive enough to return the same favor by which we were forgiven by the Lord to others who might have wronged us.

Have a happy day with His **loaded blessings!**

LIVING WORD for TODAY—May 30:

LOADED with DAILY BLESSINGS (Ps. 68:19)-#151

FORGIVENESS—29

"Yes, brother, let me have joy from you in the Lord; refresh my heart in the Lord. Having confidence in your obedience, I write to you, knowing that you will do even more than I say." (Phil. 20–21)

Our joy is from the Lord. However, having a trusted friend who can refresh us and meet our needs is a blessing from the Lord. Paul's need at this time was not for himself but for his convert, Onesimus, who needed forgiveness, restoration, affirmation, and acceptance from his master, Philemon.

Paul's joy was to see the power of the good news he preached working in building human relationships according to the will of Christ. His letter to his friend Philemon demonstrated this truth. Christianity is not a phony religion but a real, down-to-earth faith in a real world of human relationships. And without constant forgiving one another with love, which covers multitude of sins, this can not happen.

May God give us more friends like Philemon in the Christian communities around the world today. And I pray that you and I will be that trusted friend who displays love that covers a multitude of sins.

Have a lovely day with His **loaded blessings!**

LIVING WORD for TODAY—MAY 31:

LOADED with DAILY BLESSINGS (Ps. 68:19)-#152

FORGIVENESS—30

"'Take heed to yourselves. If your brother sins against you, rebuke him; and if he repents, forgive him...'" (Luke 17:3–4)

Forgiveness is the culture of the kingdom life:

The Christian life is the kingdom culture Jesus Christ founded. The culture is built on the foundation of forgiveness of sins. Sin separates us from the holy God, but when Christ forgives us, God does not see us any longer as sinners but as His beloved children.

The same love with which He receives us into His kingdom, He commands it to be extended to each other as we relate in His kingdom. Because it is impossible to relate together without offending one another, we must learn to rebuke the offending brother or sister in love. The offending ones must also be bumbled enough to accept their faults, repent, and heal.

As we emphasize forgiveness, let us not forget that our Lord also includes rebuke as part of the package. Let us learn how to exercise gentle rebuke in love as we try to reconcile with one another.

This may be difficult sometimes, but it is the Lord's requirement for reconciliation and healing.

"...bearing with one another, and forgiving one another. If anyone has a complaint against another, even as Christ forgave you, so you also must do" (Col. 3:13).

Have a lovely day!

Living Word for **today** with James E. Temidara

JUNE—FAVOR

LIVING WORD for TODAY—June 1:

LOADED with DAILY BLESSINGS (Ps. 68:19)-#153

FAVOR—1

"For You, O LORD, will bless the righteous;

With favor You will surround him as with a shield." (Ps. 5:12)

This is your month of **favor**!

With daily forgiveness and cleansing through the blood of Jesus Christ, we're declared righteous before God. Living daily, as forgiven and righteous persons, opens the floodgates of heaven to us for divine **favors**.

We are going to spend time during our daily devotional this month of June to meditate and apply God's principles of favor into our lives and situations.

Let us pray that we would not be distracted in the days ahead from what the Lord has for us in His Word on this subject of favor, which we all need from day to day.

May the **Lord** bless and surround you with **favor** as a shield now and always.

Have a happy month **loaded** with His **blessings** of **favor**!

LIVING WORD for TODAY—June 2:

LOADED with DAILY BLESSINGS (Ps. 68:19)-#154

FAVOR—2

"For His anger is but for a moment,

His favor is for life;

Weeping may endure for a night, But joy comes in the morning." (Ps. 30:5)

God's favor is for life. You and I need it to live a meaningful and fulfilled life here on earth. But what is favor?

Favor is a major key word in the Bible. It is unsolicited blessings, interventions, honors, promotions, and change of status orchestrated by God through human agents, institutions, or circumstances. It is obtaining success or rewards not worked for.

Sometimes we try to seek for favors from people or higher powers, but the truth is real favor finds us wherever we are, and once it finds us, it changes us for life.

May God's favor locate you in whatever situation you're in now and transform you to the person He wants you to be forever.

Have a happy day **loaded** with His **favor**!

LIVING WORD for TODAY—June 3:

LOADED with DAILY BLESSINGS (Ps. 68:19)-#155

FAVOR—3

"...Who crowns you with lovingkindness and tender mercies,

Who satisfies your mouth with good things, So that your youth is renewed like the eagle's." (Ps. 103:4–5)

There were many people in the Bible who were located by **favor** without soliciting for it.

- Abraham never prayed to become the father of many nations and a blessing to the world, but God chose him by His **favor**;
- The **favor** of God picked his grandson Jacob to become the father of the twelve tribes of Israel and gave him a new name, which became a name of a great nation;
- Joseph, a prisoner, was promoted to become the prime minister of a world empire and saved the world from famine;
- Moses was in his shepherding business when God's **favor** located him in a lonely desert to lead a new nation of Israel; and
- Ruth, David, Esther, and Mary are just a few people in the Bible whose statuses were changed by God's **favor** without solicitation.

May God's **favor** locate you today and change your status according to His will for you. You don't need to struggle for it, but keep believing for greater blessings ahead of you.

Have a great day/evening **loaded** with His **favor**!

LIVING WORD for TODAY—June 4:

LOADED with DAILY BLESSINGS (Ps. 68:19)-#156

FAVOR—4

"...to give you, large and beautiful cities which you did not build, houses full of all good things, which you did not fill, hewn-out wells which you did not dig, vineyards and olive trees which you did not plant..." (Deut. 6:10–11)

God's **favor** can find individuals or a community of people. This was the situation with the people of Israel. God gave them large and beautiful cities, which they did not build, houses full of good things, wells full of spring waters, farmlands full of vineyards and olive trees—all for free because of the favor bestowed upon their forefathers centuries before them.

They became the inheritors of favor, which their forefathers lived for.

In the days ahead, we shall meditate on:

(1) Favor and changes;

(2) Favor and challenges; and

(3) Favor and character.

So there's a lot to look forward to as we consider this subject.

May the favor of God find you and make you the inheritor of what those who had gone ahead of you labored, lived, and believed for.

Have a great day/evening **loaded** with His **favor**!

LIVING WORD for TODAY—June 5:

LOADED with DAILY BLESSINGS (Ps. 68:19)-#157

FAVOR—5

"Thus says the LORD:
'In an acceptable time I have heard You,
And in the day of salvation I have helped You;
I will preserve You and give You
As a covenant to the people,
To restore the earth,
To cause them to inherit the desolate heritages;
That You may say to the prisoners, 'Go forth,'
To those who are in darkness,
'Show yourselves.'" (Isa. 49:8–9)

It is important we clarify that God's favor is much more than material possessions or promotions. There is a spiritual component of divine favor that may be overlooked. God's unsolicited favor to the world is in the sending of Jesus Christ to change the world. The word "acceptable" in the above text is the same as favor. So the time of God's favor to the world was the coming of the Lord Jesus Christ.

If you're among the privileged few who have accepted the call of the gospel and received Jesus Christ as your personal Lord and Savior, know that divine favor has located you. You're already in the year of God's favor, and as your relationship with Him is developed from day to day, He changes and transforms you from glory to glory. God's **favor** lives in you!

May He lead and place you where He needs you in His vast kingdom and resources.

Have a happy day **loaded** with His **favor!**

LIVING WORD for TODAY—June 6:

LOADED with DAILY BLESSINGS (Ps. 68:19)-#158

FAVOR—6

"The Spirit of the LORD is upon Me,
Because He has anointed Me
To preach the gospel to the poor; He has sent Me to heal the brokenhearted, To
preach liberty to the captives
And recovery of sight to the blind, To set at liberty those who are oppressed;
To proclaim the acceptable year of the LORD." (Luke 4:18–19)

Since the appearance of the Lord Jesus Christ on earth, we have been living in the year of God's **favor**. Every time you write the date during this era, you're writing it with *AD*, which is the abbreviation of two Latin words, "anno Domini" meaning, in the year of our Lord. So today is June 6, in the year of our Lord.

The implication of this to us is that God's **favor** is revealed in the person of our Lord Jesus Christ daily as He proclaimed to be in the text above.

There are many blessings He brought to us as God's favor.

- Preaching the good news;
- Healing the brokenhearted;
- Liberty to the captives;
- Recovery of sight to the blind;
- Freedom to the oppressed; and
- Proclamation of the year of God's favor.

There are even more blessings from the original text where the Lord read from. Read it in Isaiah 61:1–3. Do you see all these as favors to you and the world?

So live and function with the Lord's favors if you know Him and He lives in you. You are **loaded** with **favor**!

Have a blessed day!

LIVING WORD for TODAY—June 7:

LOADED with DAILY BLESSINGS (Ps. 68:19)-#159

FAVOR—7

"And Jesus increased in wisdom and stature, and in favor with God and men."
(Luke 2:52)

As we continue in our foundational studies on the subject of favor, let us remember that though our Lord Jesus Christ is God's favor to us, yet, while He was here physically, He had to grow. He continued to increase mentally, physically, socially, and spiritually. He "increased in wisdom, in stature, in favor with God and men."

The same thing said about the Lord was said about Samuel (1 Sam. 2:26). The implication of this to us is that God expects us to continue to grow in His knowledge, wisdom, in relationships with Him, and the world around us for Him to commit His vast opportunities to us.

So there are degrees of favor.

If you studied the Bible rightly, you would observe that all those who God bestowed His special favors upon and who successfully carried out their assignments were people who advanced in their intimacy with Him.

Therefore, our prayers daily should be: "Lord, increase my closeness to you so I can know more of you and your love." God is waiting for as many of His children who are ready to be moved into the higher levels of His favor.

May the Lord increase His favor in your life today.

Have a beautiful day **loaded** with God's **favor!**

LIVING WORD for TODAY—June 8:

LOADED with DAILY BLESSINGS (Ps. 68:19)-#160:

FAVOR—8

"Now the LORD said to Samuel, 'How long will you mourn for Saul, seeing I have rejected him from reigning over Israel? Fill your horn with oil, and go; I am sending you to Jesse the Bethlehemite. For I have provided Myself a king among his sons.'" (1 Sam. 16:1)

Favor and Changes:

David, a man after God's heart, started life with many odds against him.

- He was the youngest in his family;
- As the youngest, he was the errand boy for his dad and seven older brothers;
- He was not visible to be known in the public;
- He was kept in a lonely shepherd field;
- He was exposed to the attacks of wild beasts; and
- He was not even invited to the family feast.

But:

God's favor was looking for him. David was faithful in his menial job until he was located by favor, which brought him to the limelight and changed everything about his life.

Let me encourage you in whatever you're doing now with this Scripture:

"And whatever you do, do it heartily, as to the Lord and not to men" (Col. 3:23).

Have a great day/evening **loaded** with His **favor!**

LIVING WORD for TODAY—June 9

LOADED with DAILY BLESSINGS (Ps. 68:19)-#161

FAVOR—9

"But the LORD said to Samuel, 'Do not look at his appearance or at his physical stature, because I have refused him. For the LORD does not see as man sees; for man looks at the outward appearance, but the LORD looks at the heart.'" (1 Sam. 16:7)

God's special favor is always specific. It is always designed for a specific person and without that person, no one else can fit in to fulfill God's desired purpose.

This concept is important in selecting a leader to govern a nation or lead an organization. Many nations or institutions today are suffering because of wrong leadership.

For the most part, humans' democratic methods of selecting leaders have been taken over by Satan, the prince of this world. This is even pathetically true of many Christian organizations. People's choices are not necessarily God's choice because humans decide on outward qualifications, achievements, and likeness.

God summoned a meeting in Jesse's house because of David, yet he was not invited to the meeting by his family because, to them, he was not qualified.

The people of Israel had made a costly mistake in choosing Saul as their king, and they were about to make another one due to outward appearance and qualifications. Thank God for His intervention in the process. The right choice would have been missed.

It is important that we pray with an open mind when it comes to choosing a leader to govern a nation or lead a Christian institution because it takes just a leader to derail a nation or an institution from God's plans. May God's special favor find you where you are, doing your normal job unnoticed regardless of the human bureaucracy involved.

Have a happy day LOADED with God's FAVOR!

LIVING WORD for TODAY—June 10:

LOADED with DAILY BLESSINGS (Ps. 68:19)-#162

FAVOR—10

"So he sent and brought him in. Now he was ruddy, with bright eyes, and good-looking.

And the LORD said, 'Arise, anoint him; for this is the one!'" (1 Sam. 16:12)

David was chosen to lead and govern as the king of a great nation, Israel. But David was young, obscured, and unrecognizable, though he was handsome. He was a pushed-over candidate in the human democratic selection into a leadership position. David himself would not have applied or prayed for the position he got, but God's favor found him in a lonely desert and chose and anointed him to be the king of His people.

All eyes were now on him.

Because God's favor chose and anointed David, he was preserved till his public recognition.

The people God uses are appointed and prepared in the private before their public recognition. They are always full of favor from the Lord.

Are you anxious about your time of manifestation? Just be patient and wait on His timing for you. God's assignment for you will never be given to someone else as long you're available and not making things happen in your own way (Prov. 3:5–6). Most successful leaders are not position seekers but God's favored people.

May the favor of God find and move you to where you belong in His vast kingdom according to your calling.

Have a blessed day **loaded** with His **favor**!

LIVING WORD for TODAY—June 11:

LOADED with DAILY BLESSINGS (Ps. 68:19)-#163

FAVOR—11

"Then Samuel took the horn of oil and anointed him in the midst of his brothers; and the Spirit of the LORD came upon David from that day forward. So Samuel arose and went to Ramah" (1 Sam. 16:13)

Favor, unsolicited, unmerited, has brought changes to David. "And the LORD said, 'Arise, anoint him; for this is the one!'" (1 Sam. 16:12)

This statement from the **Lord** changed David's life forever. A shepherd boy suddenly became a celebrity and the commander of the Lord's army, conquering nations and becoming the heir of eternal kingdom of Christ on earth! Can you imagine what's going on in David's mind?

David left the desert as a poor shepherd boy, but went back as the anointed king of his nation. His life was never the same again because the anointing brought the whole hosts of heaven around him wherever he was.

The favor of God, which located David, when he wasn't thinking about it, and changed his life forever; it will find you in your situation and change your status forever! That's my prayer for you.

Have a great day or evening with God's **loaded favor!**

LIVING WORD for TODAY—June 12:

LOADED with DAILY BLESSINGS (Ps. 68:19)-#164

FAVOR—12

"Then one of the servants answered and said, 'Look, I have seen a son of Jesse the Bethlehemite, who is skillful in playing, a mighty man of valor, a man of war, prudent in speech, and a handsome person; and the LORD is with him.'" (1 Sam. 16:18)

The favor of God, which found David when he was a poor shepherd boy, anointed him to be a king to shepherd God's people, Israel, was now promoting him to the king's palace to minister, though he hasn't taken the throne. But the anointing of the LORD was developing many skills in him. These were the skills that he would need later in years ahead to lead the nation of Israel into prominence.

Within time, news about him spread around, even to the king's palace. Here again is the unsolicited favor working in David's life. The Spirit of the LORD who was upon Saul, the rejected king, has now come upon David, transforming his life into God's glory. But the opposite was taking place in the king's palace. Whenever the Spirit of God leaves anyone's life, demons take over, and that life goes from bad to worst; so was Saul's life. No wonder David prayed later in his life when was caught in sin, "Do not cast me away from Your presence, and do not take Your Holy Spirit from me." (Ps. 51:11)

This prayer is relevant to all of us today when we reflect on what became of King Saul.

May the Holy Spirit who brings God's favor into our lives never be replaced in us in Jesus Christ's name. Every success in David's life and in our lives hangs on this: "and the LORD is with him" (1 Sam. 16:18).

Have a blessed day with His **loaded favor!**

LIVING WORD for TODAY—June 13:

LOADED with DAILY BLESSINGS (Ps. 68:19)-#165

FAVOR—13

"So David came to Saul and stood before him. And he loved him greatly, and he became his armor bearer.
Then Saul sent to Jesse, saying, 'Please let David stand before me, for he has found favor in my sight.'" (1 Sam. 16:21–22)

From a poor shepherd boy to the king's armor bearer, David was now incredibly increasing in favor, both with God and now with the king of the land.

But take note of this: David was sought for. God's favor and anointing were operating in his life that he couldn't be hidden. The news about him spread to King Saul, which made him request the services of David from his father. "Send me your son David, who is with the sheep" (1 Sam. 16:19).

David had been anointed the next king, but he was still in his job as a shepherd. He was not going around bragging about his anointing, but the favor and anointing of God upon him made him in demand, even by the king.

The Bible says: "A man's gift makes room for him, and brings him before great men" (Prov. 18:16).

When the favor and anointing of God are upon your life, you will not be the one seeking for recognition, but you will stand out among the crowd. Let us therefore learn to cultivate the presence of God in our lives for the growth of His favor upon us. The presence of God and favor go together.

Have a pleasant day **loaded** with His **favor**!

LIVING WORD for TODAY—June 14

LOADED with DAILY BLESSINGS (Ps. 68:19)-#166

FAVOR—14

"And so it was, whenever the spirit from God was upon Saul, that David would take a harp and play it with his hand. Then Saul would become refreshed and well, and the distressing spirit would depart from him." (1 Sam. 16:23)

God's favor in David's life changed his occupation from a shepherd boy to the king's spiritual care therapist. He was now visible to the whole nation of Israel.

Let's talk about the distressing spirit from God upon King Saul. God has absolute control over all His creations. Since demons are created beings, they are under the control of God. They were once holy angels, but became fallen angels by joining the rebellion of Satan (Isa. 14:12–17; Ezek. 28:12–19).

So once God's Spirit left Saul, they were allowed to take over his life. But the presence of God's Spirit in David's life and his music always drove them away. Where there's presence of the Holy Spirit, Satan or his demons cannot coexist with Him.

May the Holy Spirit of God never depart from our lives.

Have a happy day/evening **loaded** with His **favor!**

LIVING WORD for TODAY—June 15

LOADED with DAILY BLESSINGS (Ps. 68:19)-#167

FAVOR—15

"Now the Philistines gathered their armies together to battle, and were gathered at Sochoth, which belongs to Judah... And a champion went out from the camp of the Philistines, named Goliath, from Gath, whose height was six cubics and a span." (1 Sam. 17:1, 4)

Favor and Challenges:

If you're a person of favor, your life can never be stagnated.

Favor, high favor, leads to challenges. This is something many of us who pray for favor don't realize. And sometimes those challenges make our lives uncomfortable.

David had an easy and comfortable life tending his father's sheep. But with God's favor and anointing upon him, he had to move from his comfort zone to where the actions were. The Philistines had gathered their armies against Israel with a commander named Goliath. His name was just enough to strike fear on the hearers. But his appearance was more terrifying. He was nine foot nine inches tall. He was a champion who had never lost a battle. For forty days, he appeared on a mountain, challenging the armies of Israel, led by King Saul, and no one could confront him until the anointed man of favor showed up.

There are many challenges facing God's people all over the world today. Where are the God's anointed men and women of favor to respond?

May the Lord raise more people anointed with the Holy Spirit and power in our communities to respond with God's favor upon their lives to establish the rule of God over the destruction of truth and godly values. You and I are anointed with His favor to make the difference. Let us act now by faith.

Have a victorious day **loaded** with His **favor**!

LIVING WORD for TODAY—June 16:

LOADED with DAILY BLESSINGS (Ps. 68:19)-#168

FAVOR—16

"Then David said to Saul, 'Let no man's heart fail because of him; your servant will go and fight with this Philistine.'" (1 Sam. 17:32)

David, a man of favor and God's anointing, showed up at a national scene, confronted with a challenge of mission impossible! Saul and his trained armies were already terrorized and destroyed by the psychological warfare waged against them by Goliath of Gath for forty days.

But when David saw the challenge presented by Goliath, he saw an opportunity to glorify God with His victory. A person of faith and favor does not calculate the risks of taking up the enemy's challenge but is convicted of the Lord's victory in every battle. David approached the champion Goliath with a conviction of a done deal victory. But Saul, the captain of the Lord's armies, Israel, saw a different thing. They saw their defeat.

There are times in our lives, as we operate under the anointing of God's favor, that we don't have to wait for consensus advice or opinion to act in a challenging situation. As good and laudable expert advice and opinions could be, they are not a match for the supernatural faith, which God's anointing releases in us to confront any given situation. So let us be fully persuaded in our decisions as we face daily challenges that we are being led by His Spirit.

Have a great day **loaded** with His **favor!**

LIVING WORD for TODAY—June 17:

LOADED with DAILY BLESSINGS (Ps. 68:19)-#169

FAVOR—17

"'Your servant has killed both lion and bear; and this uncircumcised Philistine will be like one of them, seeing he has defied the armies of the living God.' Moreover David said, 'The LORD who delivered me from the paw of the lion and from the paw of the bear, He will deliver me from the hand of this Philistine.' And Saul said to David, 'Go, and the LORD be with you!'" (1 Sam. 17:36–37)

Becoming a national hero doesn't just happen overnight. The anointed people of favor have their private and domestic challenges, which God uses to train and prepare them for greater challenges in the future. Our past experiences of faith adventures prepare and give us testimonies to confront greater battles ahead, demanding an exercise of faith.

David had private experiences of divine interventions with God in his life with which he built his confidence in God's victory before confronting Goliath. By God's anointing, he had killed a lion and bear with his hands without any weapon. He sized up Goliath with those wild beasts he had killed and saw no difference. Faith sees God's victory in advance before the actual result.

So when God's special favor locates you, pray for the operations of His supernatural faith to be evident in your life because you're going to face many challenges demanding faith to succeed. I pray that as you increase in favor, the faith of God would also increase in your life to confront the enemy's challenges.

Have a victorious day or night **loaded** with God's **favor!**

LIVING WORD for TODAY—June 18:

LOADED with DAILY BLESSINGS (Ps. 68:19)-#170

FAVOR—18

"So Saul clothed David with his armor... And David said to Saul, 'I cannot walk with these, for I have not tested them.' So David took them off." (1 Sam. 17:38–39)

Doing spiritual warfare with the armor of the flesh is a spiritual suicide. David learned this truth quickly as King Saul, without God's anointing, tried to help David fight the battle that he himself could not fight. David, operating under God's anointing of faith and favor, rejected every human's help at this point and focused on the only weapon he was familiar with: the name of the **Lord**.

Our God does not depend on the fleshly armor to fight and win. Everyone of His children must also learn that our struggles are not against flesh and blood but against spiritual hosts of darkness and "the weapons of our warfare are not carnal but mighty in God for pulling down strongholds... " (2 Cor. 10:4–6).

May the Lord help us to be sensitive to the nature of the warfare we fight from time to time so we can use the right weapon.

Have a great day **loaded** with God's **favor**!

LIVING WORD for TODAY—June 19:

LOADED with DAILY BLESSINGS (Ps. 68:19)-#171

FAVOR—19

"So the Philistine said to David, 'Am I a dog, that you come to me with sticks?' And the Philistine cursed David by his gods... Then David said to the Philistine, 'You come to me with a sword, with a spear ,and with a javelin. But I come to you in the name of the LORD of hosts, the God of the armies of Israel, whom you have defied.'" (1 Sam. 17:43–45)

This was a battle of gods against God; the champion of the Philistine versus the underdog challenger from Israel. The champion had records of won battles, the underdog had never fought any battle except with the wild beasts. The champion Goliath was armed with destructive weapons and cultic spiritual power. But the challenger David was armed with the instruments to wade off wild beasts and faith in the **Lord** of hosts. Who is going to win?

If you're to bet the result, the champion Goliath would be the presumptive winner. But in the spiritual dimension, the anointed challenger with faith and favor wins. Each approached the battle with his proven weapons, but the Lord determined who won.

Please note that David was an expert in slingshots, which was his hidden weapon from Goliath. David was not just a lazy believer who expected God to do everything for him. He was always armed with his limited amateur weapon God anointed for the victory—faith in action!

Our faith in the Lord is not an excuse for us not to perfect our skills in whatever field of our calling and be ready for action. God loves to anoint what He finds in our hands for His victory. With Moses, it was his staff, and with David, his sling. But if He finds nothing, as long as we put our faith in Him into action, He would fight our battles, and victory would be won.

So let us learn the secret of giving our battles to the Lord by faith and letting Him fight for us regardless of our strengths. He has never lost any battle.

Have a happy day with His **loaded favor!**

Living word for **today** with James E. Temidara

LIVING WORD for TODAY—June 20:

LOADED with DAILY BLESSINGS (Ps. 68:19)-#172

FAVOR—20

"'This day the LORD will deliver you into my hand, and I will strike you and take your head from you... that all the earth may know that there is a God in Israel. Then all this Assembly shall know that the LORD does not save with sword and spear; for the battle is the LORD'S, and He will give you into our hands.'" (1 Sam. 17:46–47)

There comes a decisive moment when we have to stop praying in our spiritual warfare and start making faith declarations against the situation we're facing.

David got to that decisive moment in his battle with Goliath. His declaration was:

- Specific; "This day, the LORD will deliver you into my hand."
- Striking; "I will strike you and take your head from you."
- Sovereign; "that all the earth may know that there is a God in Israel."
- Supernatural; "the LORD does not save with sword and spear."
- Saving and secure; "the battle is the LORD's, and He will give you into our hands."

This kind of spiritually loaded public declaration in battle does not come from a person who has not been with the Lord. It takes the supernatural faith of a person hearing and seeing the invisible to make this explosive declaration. David was the man of the moment who rose to the challenging occasion with God's presence in his life.

May the Lord give us men and women who are willing to risk their lives and reputations to stand publicly and declare God's judgment against the hosts of darkness invading our communities with ungodly lifestyles. The battle belongs to the Lord, but He needs connecting agents on earth to bring the victory. Let us be His Davids today.

Have a great day **loaded** with His **favor**!

LIVING WORD for TODAY—June 21:

LOADED with DAILY BLESSINGS (Ps. 68:19)-#173

FAVOR—21

"So it was, when the Philistine arose and came and drew near to meet David, that David hurried and ran toward the army to meet the Philistine. Then David put his hand in his bag and took out a stone; and he slung it and struck the Philistine in his forehead, so that the stone sank into his forehead, and he fell on his face to the earth." (1 Sam. 17:48–49)

Favor, faith, fighting, and fulfillment go together. A person of favor is a person of faith, and a person of faith fights to see his or her dreams/visions come to fulfillment .

Mark David's predictions in verses forty-six to forty-seven; they all came to pass in the following verses.

But also notice that a person of faith is also a person of action. David took control of the fight without allowing the Philistine to strike first. Visualize his actions:

- He hurried;
- He ran toward the Philistine;
- He took a stone;
- He targeted the open space in the forehead of Goliath;
- He slung the stone;
- The stone sank into the Goliath's forehead, and he fell; and
- David ran, stood on top of the dead giant, and used his sword to cut off his head.

Through this victory, Israel regained the territories it had lost to the enemy.

Begin to put your faith into action; speak to your giant, declare God's judgment upon your enemy of progress, praise God for your victory, and move forward. The battle is the **Lord's**, and He will grant you the victory.

Have a lovely day **loaded** with His **favor**!

LIVING WORD for TODAY—June 22

LOADED with DAILY BLESSINGS (Ps. 68:19)-#174

FAVOR—22

"And Saul said to him, 'Whose son are you, young man?' So David answered, 'I am the son of your servant Jesse the Bethlehemite.'" (1 Sam. 17:58)

David came as a poor shepherd boy to the king's spiritual care minister and now to a national hero.

There's no limit to where God's favor can take us. David left home the day he killed Goliath to take lunch to his brothers in the battle front, but he was transformed by the Lord into a household name; not only in Israel but in the world forever.

Interestingly, David had been attending to King Saul for a while through his harp music to drive away distressing spirits from him. But at the time of doing a great exploit for the nation, Saul could not recognize David.

It takes just one of God's miracle in your life for you to be transformed into a different person, unrecognizable to those who once knew you.

This happened to the blind man Jesus healed in John 9:8–9. This also happened to our Lord Jesus Christ after His resurrection (Luke 24:14–32).

May the Lord perform a miracle of great favor in your life to transform you from an ordinary person into a supernatural powerhouse of God's glory in your community and globally.

Have a blessed day with Christ's **loaded favor!**

LIVING WORD for TODAY—June 23:

LOADED with DAILY BLESSINGS (Ps. 68:19)-#175

FAVOR—23

Now when he had finished speaking to Saul, the soul of Jonathan was knit to the soul of David, and Jonathan loved him as his own soul. Saul took him that day, and would not let him go home to his father's house anymore." (1 Sam. 18:1–2)

• Favor and Character:

While God's unsolicited favor opens doors of many opportunities to us, it takes character to keep those doors open and sustain us there.

Have you seen people who were privileged to graciously obtained positions of honor but couldn't hold them for a long time before messing up?

If you compared King Saul with David, you would see the difference.

At this point in David's life, all eyes were on him. He was the giant killer who singlehandedly brought a great victory to his nation. He was instantly promoted into the royal family and enjoyed tremendous accolades. Remember also that he had previously been secretly anointed by the king maker of the nation, Samuel, to be the next king, which was unknown to Saul.

In the midst of all these favorable honors, successes, and splendors, how should David behave himself in the royal palace, armies, and nation without letting his achievements get to his head?

It takes Christ-like character of humility to survive, when all eyes are on you with many expectations. May the Lord clothe us with His humility as He advances us into the positions of power, prosperity, and prominence in our chosen careers or His callings for us (Phil. 2:5).

Have a great day **loaded** with His **favor!**

LIVING WORD for TODAY—June 24:

LOADED with DAILY BLESSINGS (Ps. 68:19)-#176

FAVOR—24

"So David went out wherever Saul sent him, and behaved wisely. And Saul set him over the men of war, and he was accepted in the sight of all the people and also in the sight of Saul's servants." (1 Sam. 18:5)

Just as our Lord Jesus Christ increased in favor, David was accelerating in speed with God's favor. Everywhere Saul sent him, he was getting things done in and for the nation. He was the favorite of the king, loved by Crown Prince Jonathan, promoted as a military commander, and accepted by all. What a season of favor in David's life!

But in the midst of being highly favored by God and people, David behaved wisely.

This is a lesson all of us must learn regarding development of character in the midst of loud ovations. Favors, achievements, honors, and loud ovations are all seasonal and temporary, but the characters we develop will stick with us forever.

Jesus instructed us as His disciples in the world to be conscious that we're like "sheep in the midst of wolves." Therefore, we must "be wise as serpents and harmless as doves" (Matt. 10:16).

May the gentle Spirit of God, like the dove, continue to develop our inner characters as we climb the ladder of His high favor.

Have a lovely day **loaded** with God's **favor**!

LIVING WORD for TODAY—25:

LOADED with DAILY BLESSINGS (Ps. 68:19)-#177

FAVOR—25

"Now it happened as they were coming home, when David was returning from the slaughter of the Philistine, that the women had come out of all the cities of Israel, singing and dancing, to meet King Saul with tambourines, with joy, and with musical instruments. So the women sang as they danced, and said:
'Saul has slain his
thousands, And David his
ten thousands.'
Then Saul was very angry... So Saul eyed David from that day forward." (1 Sam. 18:6–9)

Many times, what leads to the fall of heroes and leaders is what people say about them. Fallen heroes let people's praises get into their heads while successful ones are not moved by them, but focus more on their tasks.

What the women of Israel did in this passage was a common triumphant procession in any community of people. It is normal to have victory parties, to praise leaders or people in any profession that excel. What is out of character is when those being praised love the praises of people and live by them.

Leaders who have not much result to show for their positions love to relish on vain glory and ignore the challenges ahead.

Let us learn a lesson from our Lord when He was being praised for the miracles.

"But Jesus did not commit Himself to them, because He knew all men, and had no need that anyone should testify of man, for He knew what was in man" (John 2:24–25).

David passed this character test by not dancing to the praises of the women, and so should we.

Let us live by the praise of God and not by the fickle praises of people who shout, "Hosanna" today, and "crucify Him" tomorrow.

Have a happy day **loaded** with God's **favor**!

LIVING WORD for TODAY—June 26:

LOADED with DAILY BLESSINGS (Ps. 68:19)-#178

FAVOR—26

"Then Saul was very angry, and the saying displeased him; and he said, 'They have ascribed to David ten thousands, and to me they have ascribed only thousands. Now what more can he have but the kingdom?' So Saul eyed David from that day forward" (1 Sam. 18:8–9)

One of the deadly diseases in leadership is the spirit of envy. Envy is usually predicated by insecurity. Wherever this spirit reigns, no noticeable progress can be realized. The spirit of envy says: "Every important achievement or innovation in the organization has to come from me or through me. If from someone else, I'm resentful and wish it should have come from me." What about the thought, "How I wish I was the one" in response to someone else's favor or attributes?

Envy, jealousy, and insecurity destroy progress and innovation in any organization, business, or ministry.

The spirit of envy builds up in leaders in subtle ways until it becomes a stronghold, which only the power of God can destroy.

Instead of seeing gifts and attributes in people working with us or under us as assets, envy sees them as threats and devises a means of putting them down or ignoring their contributions altogether.

This was a major problem with King Saul. Instead of embracing the anointing of God in David's life to expand his kingdom, he saw him as a rival rising to dethrone him. If not dealt with quickly, the spirit of envy could lead to outbursts of rage and murder.

There would always be people better than us in our careers or callings, so let us accept new talents and gifts in people who are being sent our ways with open arms, and grant them freedom and encouragement they need to flourish.

God's kingdom is big enough to accommodate every one of us with our gifts. His favor, matched with character, will always lead us to His destinies for us.

Have a beautiful day **loaded** with His **favor!**

LIVING WORD for TODAY—June 27

LOADED with DAILY BLESSINGS (Ps. 68:19)-#179

FAVOR—27

"And Saul cast the spear, for he said, 'I will pin David to the wall!' But David escaped his presence twice." (1 Sam. 18:11)

When you're a person of favor, be careful how you live because character counts. But it's not just your character that you should be aware of. What about the characters of the people around you? A person of favor has many friends and foes. In fact, many of the foes appear like friends, and they're those who plot to destroy either physically or by character assassination.

Saul was supposed to be David's mentor but ended up being his adversary who pursued him to his grave.

So beware when you're highly favored because not everyone around you is happy for you. There's little or nothing you can do about the character of people around you other than living with wisdom around them. May the Lord protect and keep us from destructive enemies who relate to us as friends.

Have a happy day **loaded** with God's **favor!**

LIVING WORD for TODAY—June 28

LOADED with DAILY BLESSINGS (Ps. 68:19)-#180

FAVOR—28

"Now Saul was afraid of David, because the LORD was with him, but had departed from Saul." (1 Sam. 18:12)

One of the ways in which the Lord fights our battles against our enemies is to put our fear upon them. The person who is afraid of you is already under your feet and cannot defeat you. Sometimes we don't know this and are still afraid of him or her.

Saul was afraid of David because he knew God was with him and protecting him from every attack that Saul was plotting against him. But David didn't know that the Lord had put His fear upon Saul; rather, he was running away from Saul out of fear.

Therefore, we need a constant reminder and assurance from the Lord through His Word of His protection so we can focus more on His assignments for us.

Jesus assures us: "Do not fear therefore, you are of more value than many sparrows" (Matt. 10:31).

May we live with the courage of knowing that, "no weapon formed against us shall prosper" (Isa. 54:17).

Have a great day with His **loaded favor!**

LIVING WORD for TODAY—June 29:

LOADED with DAILY BLESSINGS (Ps. 68:19)-#181

FAVOR—29

"And David behaved wisely in all his ways, and the LORD was with him." (1 Sam. 18:14)

The hallmark of a person of favor is the presence of the Lord. The presence of the Lord is the flow and channel of favor in our lives.

Because the **Lord** was with David, he was well behaved and well-received by all Israel and Judah. He was also victorious in the battles of the **Lord** against the enemies of God's people. The presence of the Lord also put His fear upon those who planned to harm him.

The same summary about David's life was recorded about Joseph, Moses, Joshua, and all God's champions in the Scriptures, through the ages and today.

What is the hallmark of your life? Are you pursuing favors and God's blessings, or the Lord Himself? As we conclude this series, it is my prayer for us that we will not miss the Lord while pursuing successes and blessings of life.

Have a happy day **loaded** with His **favor**!

LIVING WORD for TODAY—June 30:

LOADED with DAILY BLESSINGS (Ps. 68:19)-#182

FAVOR—30

Finally, as we end this thirty-day devotional meditations on favor, let me pronounce the apostolic prayer and benediction of the Lord's Apostle Paul on favor upon you and your loved ones.

"Now to Him who is able to do exceedingly abundantly above all that we ask or think, according to the power that works in us, to Him be glory in the church by Christ Jesus to all generations, forever and ever. Amen" (Eph. 3:20–21).

The Lord will grant you, your family, and loved ones favor; high and exceedingly abundantly above and beyond favor throughout your lifetimes. You will always serve the Lord and be channels of blessings to many. You shall leave great inheritance to the generations after you in Jesus Christ's name! Amen and amen.

Have a great day **loaded** with **favor**!

Living Word for **today** with James E. Temidara

JULY—FAMILY

LIVING WORD for TODAY—July 1:

LOADED with DAILY BLESSINGS (Ps. 68:19)-#183

FAMILY—1

"So God created man in His own image; in the image of God He created him; male and female He created them." (Gen. 1:27)

Thanks be to God, our Father, and to our Savior Jesus Christ, who endow us always with good things of life. We can all count our blessings in the last six months of the year and give glory to God for His sustaining grace abounding to us daily. I want to assure us that the same Lord who saw us through in the first half of the year will definitely see us through in the second half of the year.

We have also been blessed with many subjects in our daily devotional, and the last one on favor has been well-received by many through the testimonies received. In fact, a well-known international NGO adopted the messages as the Message of the Day on different days in their publications sent to about 100,000 leaders in over one hundred nations of the world during the month. To God be the glory!

As we continue with our daily devotional meditations, we are going to focus on the subject of **family**. Family is one of the daily blessings we receive from the Lord. In fact, family is the bedrock of every society of human existence on earth. Every one of us has been assigned a family unit we can identify with. So we cannot take this beautiful blessing for granted, but applaud and appreciate it as a gift from God our Creator.

Let us begin by thanking God, who demonstrates to us in His Word, His plans, and purposes for the human families on earth. To Him be the glory and honor, forever and ever. Amen. When God created mankind, He created them with family in mind; hence, the Bible says, "male and female He created them." This statement indicates God's origin in human families on

earth. May the Lord help us to preserve this beautiful foundation of human societies, institutions, governments, and nations.

Have a happy month **loaded** with His **blessings**!

LIVING WORD for TODAY—July 2:

LOADED with DAILY BLESSINGS (Ps. 68:19)-#184

FAMILY—2

"So God created man in His own image; in the image of God He created him; male and female He created them." (Gen. 1:27)

The idea of human family did not come from man but from God, the Creator of all things.

In His original plan to create Planet Earth, He designed to populate it with the human family. The first humans He created were male and female. That's all He needed to do to populate the earth.

The potentials of male and female are tremendously great.

- They have the image of God in them;
- They are like God;
- They can reproduce what God had already created; and
- They are incomplete without each other.

A healthy male and female are capable of producing the population of villages, towns, cities, and even nations.

So we cannot underestimate the creative power of a man and woman together. This is the biblical foundation of a human family on earth; "male and female He created them."

Therefore, any attempt to change this creative order is a rebellion against divine authority.

My prayer is for God to give us wisdom on how to be His agent of recreation and decently populate the earth in today's world.

Have a happy day **loaded** with His **blessings!**

LIVING WORD for TODAY—July 3:

LOADED with DAILY BLESSINGS (Ps. 68:19)-#185

FAMILY—3

"Then God blessed them, and God said to them, 'Be fruitful and multiply; fill the earth and subdue it; have dominion over the fish of the sea, over the birds of the air, and over every living thing that moves on the earth.'" (Gen. 1:28)

This verse is regarded as the cultural mandate by many theologians. But I would like to call it the family mandate.

Without the family, there can be no culture. Human cultures and traditions are derived from the family; hence, God instituted the home as the foundation of all cultures and traditions.

So God blessed the first couple He created with the mandate to be fruitful, multiply, fill the earth, and dominate it. If we fail to subdue and dominate the earth, other things like weeds, wild beasts, erosions, and water will take over.

Let us pray to the Lord to grant us knowledge and wisdom and to raise quality Christian families around the world, who can make productive use of the land and space around them for the benefit of all.

Have a fruitful day **loaded** with God's **blessings**!

LIVING WORD for TODAY—July 4:

LOADED with DAILY BLESSINGS (Ps. 68:19)-#186

FAMILY—4

"Then God said, 'Let Us make man in Our image, according to Our likeness; let them have dominion over the fish of the sea, over the birds of the air, and over the cattle, over all the earth and over every creeping thing that creeps on the earth.'" (Gen. 1:26)

There is the eternal family that exists in heaven before the creation of the earth. It is headed by God the Father. That's why we call Him, "Our Father who is in heaven."

In the creation of man, He summoned His family, the Triune God, the Holy Trinity, consisting of God the Father, God the Son, and God the Holy Spirit, into a conference. The only agenda of the meeting was the extension of the Family in heaven on earth. "Let Us make man in Our image, according to Our likeness..." Notice the plurality of the address: "Let Us" and "Our." From this address, we conclude that God is a family God, and His original plan was to replicate what He had in heaven here on earth through the creation of the first man.

There is also perfect unity in God's family in heaven, and His plan is the same for the family on earth. Though we don't see that in practice on earth since the Fall, but through Christ, God the Son, who is the Restorer of all things, it is going to happen. Until then, we will continue to pray: "Your kingdom come. Your will be done on earth as it is in heaven" (Matt. 6:10).

May our families today be the reflection of God's family.

Have a great day **loaded** with His **benefits!**

LIVING WORD for TODAY—July 5:

LOADED with DAILY BLESSINGS (Ps. 68:19)-#187

FAMILY—5

"And the LORD GOD said, 'It is not good that, man should be alone; I will make him a helper comparable to him." (Gen. 2:18)

God instituted marriage as the foundation of starting a family unit. In order to replicate the life of heaven on earth, God had to deal with the loneliness of the first man. In divine assessment of humans, nothing else is capable of meeting a man or woman's loneliness other than a comparable helper. Everything else will fail. Wealth, pleasure, and prestige accomplishments would fail. There is a void in each of us that only a comparable helper can meet.

So marriage is not just to raise a family but, primarily, to fill the void of loneliness in our hearts. The first man, Adam, didn't have to find that comparable helpmate; God created a perfect female helper who met that need. Today, each of us has to find his or her compatible helper to be fulfilled. Living and raising families with incompatible helpers is one of the major problems in the world today. For those thinking of starting families, the starting point is finding compatible helpers. Although this may be difficult in a complicated world of today, but with God's help, many are still finding their right helpers. Pray for wisdom and God's guidance.

Have a happy day **loaded** with God's **blessings**!

LIVING WORD for TODAY—July 6:

LOADED with DAILY BLESSINGS (Ps. 68:19)-#188

FAMILY—6

"Then the rib which the LORD God had taken from man He made into a woman, and He brought her to the man.
And Adam said:
'This is now, bone of my bones
And flesh of my flesh;
She shall be called Woman.
Because she was taken out of Man.'" (Gen. 2:22–23)

Finally, Adam found his missing link for fulfillment and completion. Nothing in the world could ever play the role of a woman in man's life. Woman is made for man. This truth is confirmed in 1 Corinthians 11:8–9.

But note that the same truth goes for man. While the first woman was taken from the man, every man thereafter has been coming into the world through the woman. Hence, we're made for each other. A man is not complete without a woman, and neither is a woman complete without a man. A man and woman of compatible mindset together is the foundation of a happy family, according to the Bible.

Let us pray that the Lord intervenes and brings proper understanding into our minds about the biblical truth of marriage in today's confusing world. A man and woman together is the foundation of spreading the family life.

Have a healthy day **loaded** with His **blessings!**

LIVING WORD for TODAY—July 7:

LOADED with DAILY BLESSINGS (Ps. 68:19)-#189

FAMILY—7

"Therefore a man shall leave his father and mother and be joined to his wife, and they shall become one flesh." (Gen. 2:24)

One Flesh Union

This is the beginning of marriage instituted by God.

Let us make some affirmations from our text:

1. Whenever a man and a woman agree to live together as husband and wife, there's a covenant between them, which God honors;
2. Marriage is to leave both parents and cleave (join) together with each other;
3. When a man and woman agree to live together as husband and wife, they're making a statement to their parents and friends that they are starting their own family unit. Hence, there's a shift of loyalty from their parents to one another. Parents have no business remotely guiding them in their new life;
4. Marriage is also for the grownups and not for the kids. Nothing matures a man and a woman faster than to be in a marriage relationship;
5. This one-flesh union was affirmed by our Lord Jesus Christ when He was answering a question about divorce in Matthew 19:4–6; and
6. Marriage is a divine institution established by God, primarily to solve the problem of loneliness, and secondarily, for the extension of family units on earth.

So let us do our best to protect this institution from various attacks in our world today.

Have a great day **loaded** with God's **blessings!**

LIVING WORD for TODAY—July 8:

LOADED with DAILY BLESSINGS (Ps. 68:19)-#190

FAMILY—8

"And they were both naked, the man and his wife, and were not ashamed."
(Gen. 2:25)

The story of God's institution of a blissful and perfect home ended with trust and openness. For any marital relationship to thrive, there must be complete trust and nothing concealing. The idea that Adam and his wife were both naked and not ashamed of each other is more than physical nudity. It means they were bare open and had nothing to hide from each other. Whenever sin enters a relationship, the first thing it does is destroy trust and create suspicion. Once there's doubt, there's hiding from each other. Nothing destroys any love relationship as quickly as lack of trust and openness. Once trust is destroyed, it takes time to be rebuilt and restored. Trust can also be earned over time.

Are you in a marriage relationship? Be sure you're both naked to each other, not only in the bedroom, but also in all areas of life. Are you thinking of getting married one day? Don't ever get into it with a person you cannot trust. Trust is the cord that holds any relationship together.

Have a lovely day with God's **loaded blessings!**

LIVING WORD for TODAY—July 9:

LOADED with DAILY BLESSINGS (Ps. 68:19)-#191

FAMILY—9

"Then the serpent said to the woman, 'You will not surely die. For God knows that in the day you eat of it your eyes will be opened, and you will be like God, knowing good and evil.'" (Gen. 3:4–5)

God founded the first family on the foundation of trust and loyalty to Himself and each other. Trust and loyalty in marriage flow from our trust in God and loyalty to His Word.

While Adam and his wife, Eve, were living in a happy and blissful marital life, one thing they were innocent of was another crafty creature living around them, who heard God's words to them and was ready to shift their loyalty from God to himself by deception. The devil came in through a familiar creature and deceived them into doubting their Maker. That was the end of a perfect home and family on earth.

Since then, the old serpent, the devil, has been busy to suck out life, joy, and happiness from every marriage, home, and family on earth. So watch out and protect what you have going well for you! Your happy life, marriage, home, and family are all out for grabs by the evil one. Saint Peter warns:

"Be sober, be vigilant, because your adversary the devil walks about like a roaring lion, seeking whom he may devour. Resist him, steadfast in the faith" (1 Pet. 5:8–9).

The good news is, if you resist him with steadfast faith and submission to God, he will flee from you (James 4:7).

Have a happy day **loaded** with His **blessings**!

LIVING WORD for TODAY—July 10:

LOADED with DAILY BLESSINGS (Ps. 68:19)-#192

FAMILY—10

"So when the woman saw that the tree was good for food, that it was pleasant to the eyes, and a tree desirable to make one wise, she took of its fruit and ate. She also gave to her husband with her, and he ate. Then the eyes of both of them were opened, and they knew that they were naked; and they sewed fig leaves together and made themselves coverings." (Gen. 3:6–7)

The fall of mankind into sin brought catastrophic disruption into the beautiful world God created and gave to the human race to manage. The disruption affected every good thing God created, including marriage and family.

Sometimes when people quote our Lord's statements in Matthew 19:4–6 as a kind of marriage to envisage, they forget that the Lord was referring to the pre-Fall marriage, which no longer exists in a sinful world. Since Adam and Eve were driven out of their perfect home in the Garden of Eden, marital life has been under attacks of the lust of the flesh, the lust of the eyes, and the pride of life (1 John 2:16).

It takes the grace of God through Jesus Christ to navigate through these challenges as they confront every marriage. Despite these challenges, marriage is still commendable to deal with loneliness and spread family units on earth.

So we constantly pray for the grace of God to abound in every given situation as we live, procreate, and spread godly families on earth.

Have a great day/night **loaded** with God's **blessings!**

LIVING WORD for TODAY—July 11:

LOADED with DAILY BLESSINGS (Ps. 68:19)-#193

FAMILY—11

"And Adam knew Eve his wife, and she conceived and bore Cain, and said, 'I have acquired a man from the LORD.' Then she bore again, this time his brother Abel. Now Abel was a keeper of sheep, but Cain was a tiller of the ground." (Gen. 4:1–2)

Starting a family without the presence of the Lord in the home is laying a foundation for endless troubles.

That's exactly the story of the first family on earth. Adam and Eve were driven from the presence of the **Lord**, and they settled down in their new home and started a family. The result produced an angry son who became the murderer of his own brother (Gen. 4:1–16). Cain murdered Abel and became a fugitive who ran away from the presence of the Lord to establish his family and then built a city without the presence of the Lord.

A family started without the presence of the Lord developed to become a city without the presence of the Lord. That accounts for where we are in the world today. Families, communities, cities, and states without the presence of the Lord produce people without the fear of God.

Let us pray for God's presence to be restored back to us and our families so that we become God's conscious wherever we are. Lord, fill our homes with Your holy presence in Jesus Christ's name! Amen.

Have a glorious day **loaded** with His **blessings**!

LIVING WORD for TODAY—July 12:

LOADED with DAILY BLESSINGS (Ps. 68:19)-#194

FAMILY—12

"And Adam knew his wife again, and she bore a son and named him Seth. 'For God has appointed another seed for me instead of Abel, whom Cain killed.' And as for Seth, to him also a son was born, and he named him Enosh. Then men began to call on the name of the LORD." (Gen. 4:25–26)

The ungodly families began to spread on earth through Cain and built cities with renowned men with many gifts. Despite their gifts and prosperity, God was out of their lives and thoughts. It is possible for people and nations to prosper in wealth and technology without God because God has already endowed human race with skills to develop the earth. But without the fear of the Lord, man is capable of using the same skills to destroy himself.

Thank God for not leaving mankind to his own desires but raised another family through Seth that took the place of godly Abel. In contrast to the ungodly linage of Cain, the family lineage of Seth became true worshipers of the **Lord**. It is written about them that: "Then men began to call on the name of the LORD."

May the Lord raise a new generation of true worshipers in each community of the world today.

People with passion for God's righteousness is to be established in all institutions around them. May you and I, with our families, be part of Seth generation.

Have a wonderful day **loaded** with God's **blessings**!

LIVING WORD for TODAY—July 13:

LOADED with DAILY BLESSINGS (Ps. 68:19)-#195

FAMILY—13

"But Noah found grace in the eyes of the LORD. This is the genealogy of Noah. Noah was a just man, perfect in his generations. Noah walked with God. And Noah begot three sons. Shem, Ham, and Japheth. The earth also was corrupt before God, and the earth was filled with violence." (Gen. 6:8–11)

As the world's population grew in number, so also the human's corruption and violence increased until God could not bear them anymore.

God's conclusion of mankind was: "every intent of the thoughts of his heart was only evil continually." God then decided to wipe out mankind and animals from the face of the earth by a flood.

But in the midst of corrupt practices and violence, there was a man with his family whom God preserved as His own, and would survive the judgment of God to carry on His purpose on earth. Noah and his family found grace in God's sight. They walked with God by faith and were perfect before God. The Lord was able to get Noah's attention to disclose to him,= His judgment and the plan of salvation through the ark.

No matter how corrupt our society could be, God will always preserve a remnant of people willing to believe and follow His plan of salvation. They are perfect, not in the sense of flawlessness, but because of their faith and the fear of God in their lives.

May we and our families be part of the remnant of the generations of His people who walk with Him and follow His plan of salvation by faith daily during our time and succeeding generations.

Have a beautiful day with His **loaded blessings** for you and your family!

LIVING WORD for TODAY—July 14:

LOADED with DAILY BLESSINGS (Ps. 68:19)-#196

FAMILY—14

"Now the LORD had said to Abram:
'Get out of your country,
From your family
And from your father's house,
To a land that I will show you.'" (Gen. 12:1)

The Model Family

God is a family God. He revealed this to us by His triune name: God the Father, God the Son, and God the Holy Spirit. This family unit is the model He intended for mankind.

We see throughout the Scriptures how He transferred His blessings through the family unit. From Adam to Seth to Enoch to Noah and Abraham, we saw how God's transferrable blessings were demonstrated through those family units.

Abram was specifically called out of his father's house to have his own identity and become a blessing to others. Abram was already established and comfortable within his extended family compound before God told him to get out. Living within the extended family may be okay for a while, but there comes a time when a man or woman has to leave the extended family to establish his or her own identity and start a family unit by which God's blessings can be pronounced over him or her, and through him or her to others. I've seen this happen in many lives, in my father's life, and even in my own life. There are some reserved blessings that one cannot realize within the extended family until a separate identity of a family unit is established. One of the major problems of the poor nations is the extended family system. God's model for the family is the establishment of the family unit of a father, mother, and child(ren).

May God open our eyes of understanding to grasp this concept.

Have a great day with His **loaded blessings!**

LIVING WORD for TODAY—July 15:

LOADED with DAILY BLESSINGS (Ps. 68:19)-#197

FAMILY—15

"I will make you a great nation; I will bless you
And make your name great;
And you shall be a blessing.
I will bless those who bless you.
And I will curse him who curses you;
And in you all the families of the earth shall be blessed."' (Gen. 12:2–3)

God promised a sevenfold blessing to Abram if he would obey and take a step of faith to get out of his father's house and establish a new identity of his own. This sevenfold blessing is total and unilateral covenant. God in His sovereignty initiated it as His ideal way to bless a family and use it to bless all the families of the earth.

All Abram needed to do in this covenant of blessings was to obey and move in God's direction. But what if he had stayed put with his family inheritance in Haran? God would have bypassed him to someone else. But Abram obeyed and moved. This was not an easy move for him, but because he obeyed, he was blessed, became great, and the whole world now benefits from his act of obedience and faith.

There are some painful decisions we may make today in response to God's convictions in our lives that would positively impact many generations to come. So whatever it takes to do the will of God, let's just do it for our sake, for the sake of our children, and for the generations yet to come.

Have a happy day **loaded** with God's **blessings** to you and your **family!**

LIVING WORD for TODAY—July 16:

LOADED with DAILY BLESSINGS (Ps. 68:19)-#198

FAMILY—16

"'...And in you all the families of the earth shall be blessed.'
So Abram departed as the LORD had spoken to him, and Lot went with him
..." (Gen. 12:3–4)

God's ideal family unit excludes the extended family, but that does not mean relatives who are in need of support cannot be helped within our means.

Abram was commissioned for blessings and to be a channel of blessings to others.

But he was not called with his nephew Lot, who later became a blockade to Abram's flow of blessings. Lot brought strife into Abram's family, and where there's strife, God's blessings are not sustainable (Gen. 13:7–13). It was not until Abram took a decisive move to separate himself from his relative Lot that God renewed His covenant of blessings to him and moved him to a new level of blessings (Gen. 13:14–17).

Later over the years, after both lived apart from each other, when Lot ran into a big problem, Abram came to his rescue without living together (Gen. 14:12–16).

Beware of the Lots in your family. Relatives cause strife and division in the family unit, and where there's strife, there can be no flow of fresh blessings. Use the wisdom of God as demonstrated by Abram to help relatives without yielding your space to them in your family unit.

I wish every one of us unrestricted flow of God's blessings in our families.

Have a happy day with His **loaded blessings!**

LOADED with DAILY BLESSINGS (Ps. 68:19)-#199

FAMILY—17

"For I have known him, in order that he may command his children and his household after him, that they keep the way of the LORD, to do righteousness and justice, that the LORD may bring to Abraham what He has spoken to him." (Gen. 18:19)

It is interesting to study Abraham's family life as we try to find principles to model a pragmatic family life in a fallen world full of sins. But before we summarize his family life, let us listen to God's testimony about Abraham's family life.

- Abraham was known by God,
- that he would command his children and household after him;
- to keep the way of the LORD;
- to do righteousness and justice, so that the LORD could fulfill all His promises through his family.

This testimony to Abraham's family commitment could be described as the Lord's mission statement to him, which he lived by and earned him the title: "A friend of God."

This mission statement of God to Abraham should be adopted by every serious-minded person that would like to raise a family unit in this sinful world. May the God of the whole universe, who sees through our motives, testify of us as He did for Abraham, as we live by faith and raise godly family units all over the world that will succeed us and carry on the life of faith, which we have practiced. The summary of Abraham's life will continue.

Have a great day/night with God's **loaded blessings!**

LIVING WORD for TODAY—July 18

LOADED with DAILY BLESSINGS (Ps. 68:19)-#200

FAMILY—18

"So Abram departed as the LORD had spoken to him... Then Abram took Sarai his wife and Lot his brother's son, and all their possessions that they had gathered, and the people whom they had acquired in Haran, and they departed to go to the land of Canaan. So they came to the land of Canaan." (Gen. 12:4–5)

When looking for a model family life in the Scriptures, Abraham and his family come first since they became the family foundation upon which the world's three monotheistic religions, Judaism, Christianity, and Islam, built their faiths. But Abraham's family life was far from perfect. In fact, it could be described as a dysfunctional family. Yet, God trusted him and his family with His way of life and blessings to all the families of the earth.

I have drawn up six principles from his family life to help us with our struggles to build godly families in the modern era:

    I.   Life of convictions;

    II. Life of contentions;

    III. Life of compromises;

    IV. Life of courage;

    V. Life of conflicts; and

    VI. Life of contentment.

We are going to examine these topics and learn some lessons from Abraham's family life in the remaining days of this month in our daily devotional meditations.

May the Lord open our inner eyes of understanding and grant us His wisdom as we apply some of these principles into our manifold family problems today.

Have a pleasant day as you enjoy His **loaded blessings** with your **family**!

LIVING WORD for TODAY—July 19

LOADED with DAILY BLESSINGS (Ps. 68:19)-#201

FAMILY—19

"Then the LORD appeared to Abram and said, 'To your descendants I will give this land.' And there he built an altar to the LORD, who had appeared to him." (Gen. 12:7)

Life of Convictions:

Abraham's conviction was predicated by his faith in the God of the whole universe. There was no doubt in his mind about who appeared and spoke to him. "He believed in the LORD and He accounted it to him for righteousness." (Gen. 15:6)

Throughout the Book of Genesis, there are many recorded appearances of the **Lord** to Abraham, and he responded by building altars of worship to the **Lord**. Let us remember that he lived in a confused world of polytheism. People around him, even his extended family, were idol worshipers. But in the midst of all the confusion and deities, Abraham had a clear conviction of who was the only true God, and he committed to serve Him. This conviction was foundational in raising his family. Therefore, God became his family-God. Till today, the true living God is known as the God of Abraham, God of Isaac, and God of Jacob. What a legacy!

This is the starting point of raising a godly family in a confused world: a clear conviction of the true and living God. That's why Jesus Christ came to show us the only true God. "And this is eternal life, that they may know You, the only true God, and Jesus Christ whom You have sent" (John 17:3).

This conviction must start with the parents before it can be passed onto the children. I used to tell my children when raising them that in my home, there's no freedom of worship. When it was time for the family devotion, everyone must be present, and when it's time for the church service, everyone must go. My God is their God. Thank God, it paid off. They're all serving the Lord today. So have a personal conviction, like Abraham, of who God is to you and pass it on to your household.

Have a great day with His **loaded blessing** of the **family**!

LIVING WORD for TODAY—July 20:

LOADED with DAILY BLESSINGS (Ps. 68:19)-#202

FAMILY—20

"By faith Abraham obeyed when he was called to go out to the place which he would receive as an inheritance. And he went out, not knowing where he was going." (Heb. 11:8)

Life of Convictions:

Abraham's conviction was not only demonstrated by his faith in knowing the only true God but also in clear discernment of His voice. The reason why he obeyed God was because he could distinguish between God's voice and other voices.

There are four major voices every child of God hears, and we need a clear understanding of the Bible and convictions of the Holy Spirit to know the difference.

1. The voice of God through the Scriptures and the presence of the Holy Spirit in us (Heb. 4:12; John 16:13–14);
2. The voice of Satan through his demons twisting the Bible (Luke 4:3–13; 1 Tim. 4:1–3);
3. The human voice through our spirits (Rom. 8:16); just as God can speak to us through our spirits, the devil can as well, or even our own spirits can mislead us (Jer. 17:9–10); and
4. The voices of people around us through their opinions, concerns, and advice (Matt. 16:22; Acts 21:10–15).

All these voices were heard by Abraham, but because his conviction in knowing God's voice was unambiguous, he obeyed the **Lord** by faith.

It will be difficult to raise a godly family in the internet world of today without being disciplined in teaching the Scriptures and praying together with the family at home. Remember, "faith comes by hearing, and hearing by the word of God." So have a family altar where the family can gather from time to time to praise and worship the Lord, read His Word, and pray together. The family that prays together stays together.

Have a lovely day/night **loaded** with His **blessings**!

LIVING WORD for TODAY—July 21:

LOADED with DAILY BLESSINGS (Ps. 68:19)-#203

FAMILY—21

"Now there was a famine in the land, and Abram went down to Egypt to dwell there, for the famine was severe in the land."(Gen. 12:10)

Life of Compromise:

Abraham was a man of faith and a friend of God! But why did he go to Egypt? With all the promises of Yahweh to give him the land where he had settled and built altars of worship where God talked to him—did he ask for God's permission before going down to Egypt because of famine?

Sometimes as committed people of faith in the Lord, we make mistakes by compromising our faith and godly values with our environmental situations without seeking God's direction. Abraham's decision to go down to Egypt made him compromise his eternal heritage because of temporary needs. His decision led him to the:

- Compromise of values;
- Compromise of fears; and
- Compromise of lies.

He also passed all of these to his family. What a legacy!

Thank God, His grace accommodated all and led Abraham back to where he began.

It is comforting to know that the Lord doesn't disown His own people because of their mistakes and compromises. Why? Because "He knows our frame. He remembers that we are dust" (Ps. 103:14). So stay faithful in your commitment to serve the Lord through whatever temptations you may be going through to compromise your Christian values. If your faith is real, the Lord will always lead you back to where you belong with His abundant love, even when you fail.

Have a great day/night **loaded** with His **blessings**!

LIVING WORD for TODAY—July 22

LOADED with DAILY BLESSINGS (Ps. 68:19)-#204

FAMILY—22

"Then Sarai, Abram's wife, took Hagar her maid, the Egyptian, and gave her to her husband Abram to be his wife, after Abram had dwelt ten years in the land of Canaan." (Gen. 16:3)

Life of Compromises:

There are many compromises we make out of common sense to help God in fulfilling His promises to us. As smart as we might be in our common-sense decisions, we could be circumventing God's ultimate best for our lives. Of course, there's a "theology of common sense," as my professor of philosophy in the seminary, Dr. Joseph Tong, would say during our class lectures; meaning, God is not going to teach us everything about life. But He has given us common sense to be our guide.

While there are some truths to this, not everything God does make sense to us. It didn't make human sense for Abram to be expecting a son through his menopausal wife Sarai, who would inherit all that God had promised him. So Sarai's advice to Abram in Genesis 16 made sense and agreed with the cultural practices of their time. But being culturally relevant doesn't mean being godly relevant. We settle for God's second-best when we compromise His words with our ideas, no matter how relevant they may be. There are always costly consequences whenever God's direct injunctions are comprised with our ideas. The unending conflicts in the Middle East today would have been avoided if Abram and his wife did not compromise God's promised son Isaac with their own culturally relevant son Ishmael. But we thank God for His accommodating grace in Christ Jesus. His grace overrides our mistakes and makes all things to work together for our good and His purpose.

Have a happy day **loaded** with His **blessings**!

LIVING WORD for TODAY—July 23

LOADED with DAILY BLESSINGS (Ps. 68:19)-#205

FAMILY—23

"And there was strife between the herdsmen of Abram's livestock and the herdsmen of Lot's livestock. The Canaanites and Perizzites then dwelt in the land. So Abram said to Lot, 'Please let there be no strife between you and me, and between my herdsmen and your herdsmen, for we are brethren...'" (Gen. 13:7–11)

Life of Contention:

Wealth can lead to family feuds if not handled well. The manifestation of God's presence in the family brings wealth. Abram's business was growing, and money was coming in. His nephew Lot was also benefiting from the flow of God's anointing of blessings in Abram's life. The head of a family unit, when properly related to God, has certain anointing of blessings, which flows from him into the family that even a relative living in the household can benefit from.

But the family business has many challenges. One of them is contention. Abram and his nephew Lot got into a heated argument and disagreement over their business interests. This was already creating strife in the family. A person whose life is not controlled by God would be ruled by the vanities of this world. Money got into Lot's head, and he forgot how he made it.

A person under the rule of God may not be immune from contention, but knows how to deal with it and restore peace into the family. Abram did that, and gave Lot the opportunity to take all he wanted in the real estate. Lot covetously took what he could not keep. It was just a question of time before he lost all.

Jesus warns us: "Take heed and beware of covetousness, for one's life does not consist in the abundance of the things he possesses" (Luke 12:15).

Keep contention out of your life and family, and enjoy God's **loaded blessings!**

Have a blessed day!

LIVING WORD for TODAY—July 24:

LOADED with DAILY BLESSINGS (Ps. 68:19)-#206

FAMILY—24

"Then Sarai said to Abram, 'My wrong be upon you! I gave my maid into your embrace and when she saw that she had conceived, I became despised in her eyes. The LORD judge between me and you.'" (Gen. 16:5)

Life of Contention:

There's nothing more capable to bring contention and strife into a family than to have two women married to the same man and living together. It's even worse when one of the women was once a housemaid and now promoted to the status of a second wife. Welcome to the contentious home of Father Abraham!

Abram and Sarai's compromise is now bearing fruits that would live long after them. Solving the problem of a contentious nephew Lot was much easier for Abram than staying at home and dealing with nagging, contentious, and fighting wives. What a dysfunctional family life!

While the Bible does not directly condemn polygamous marriage, we can, however, develop many biblical principles to support monogamy as God's ideal marriage. For example, if God knew that one wife would not meet Adam's needs, He would have created many women for him. But He created one and joined them together.

There could be many reasons why men marry more than one wife, but the plurality of wives in a man's life has many burdens than blessings. Since sin and the hardness of human hearts destroyed the beauty of monogamy, every man and woman has to deal with their problems in marriage under the grace of Jesus Christ and the power of the Holy Spirit to affirm the ideal marriage in a sinful world.

Have a happy day **loaded** with God's **blessings**!

LIVING WORD for TODAY—July 25:

LOADED with DAILY BLESSINGS (Ps. 68:19)-#207

FAMILY—25

"And Sarah saw the son of Hagar the Egyptian, whom she had borne to Abraham, scoffing.
Therefore she said to Abraham, 'Cast out this bondwoman and her son, for the son of this bondwoman shall not be heir with my son, namely with Isaac.'
And the matter was very displeasing in Abraham's sight because of his son."
(Gen. 21:9–11)

Life of Conflicts:

From compromise to contention, and now conflict—while there were many external conflicts in the life of Abraham, a man of faith and friend of God, none was more painful to him than the family conflict. God's promise of a seed to him through Sarah, his old wife, has now been fulfilled. But there's an older son at home, born to him by his younger wife Hagar, competing with the son of promise, Isaac. The home became a battleground between two women, their sons, and the father in the middle. The conflict became so severe that a painful decision had to be made. Mama Sarah decreed:

"Cast out the bondwoman and her son, for the son of the bondwoman shall not be heir with the son of the freewoman" (Gal. 4:30).

Sarah's decision was a bitter pill for Abraham to swallow since he was the father of both sons. But with God's intervention, he obeyed and did the right thing.

When there are conflicts at home, the head of the household cannot ignore them while fighting and winning the external battles.

If the internal battles are not won, our external victories would amount to nothing.

Later, Saint Paul used the conflict in Abraham's family to describe the Christian life of struggles between the flesh and the Spirit. The painful action of Abraham is recommended for us to have victory over the flesh (Gal. 4:29–31) and be free in Christ Jesus.

Have a victorious day with Christ's **loaded blessings!**

LIVING WORD for TODAY—July 26:

LOADED with DAILY BLESSINGS (Ps. 68:19)-#208

FAMILY—26

"'This is My covenant which you shall keep, between Me and you and your descendants after you. Every male child among you shall be circumcised; and you shall be circumcised in the flesh of your fore skins, and it shall be a sign of the covenant between Me and you...'" (Gen. 17:10–11)

Life of Conversion:

We cannot study the events in Abraham's family and overlook the institution of circumcision. This event marked a turning point and new level in Abraham's relationship with God. At ninety-nine years of age, God instructed Abraham to be circumcised first, and then every male in his household.

The spiritual significance of this rite is important to Abraham, the Jewish race, and Christians.

To Abraham and the Jewish race, circumcision is the outward sign of their conversion to serve Yahweh God as His covenant people. To the Christian, spiritual circumcision is the seal of genuine conversion to Christ.

God is not interested in our religion without being truly converted to Him. It is not enough to compel everyone in our household to go to church with us, but we must ensure that everyone has a true conversion experience by leading each person to invite Christ into his or her heart. That is the only way our faith in God can be transferred from generation to generation.

"...but he is a Jew who is one inwardly; and circumcision is that of the heart, in the Spirit, not in the letter; whose praise is not from men but from God" (1 Cor. 2:29).

So let us ensure that everyone in our household has a personal relationship with the Lord as a sign of true conversion to be in covenant relationship with Him.

Have a great day **loaded** with His **daily blessings!**

LIVING WORD for TODAY—July 27:

LOADED with DAILY BLESSINGS (Ps. 68:19)-#209

FAMILY—27

"Now when Abram heard that his brother was taken captive, he armed his three hundred and eighteen trained servants who were born in his own house, and went in pursuit as far as Dan... So he brought back all the goods, and also brought back his brother Lot and his goods, as well as the women and the people." (Gen. 14:14–16)

Life of Courage:

There were many events in Abraham's life that portrayed him as a man of courage. Due to time constraints, two will be examined: his military rescue mission of his nephew Lot, and the offering of his promised son Isaac for sacrifice.

The rescue of Lot and his family:

Remember Lot, how he greedily chose a greener pasture and separated himself from his uncle, Abram?

The area where he settled got in trouble with nine kings in warfare. The conquering kings captured Lot, his family, and all his goods. The news got to Abram, and the zeal of God came upon him to go into battle. With God's help and good strategy, he and his army overran the army of four conquering kings and rescued Lot, his family, and all their goods, as well as the cities.

Abraham's courage was not ordinary but rooted upon his faith in God. While the people of faith are supposed to be gentle and humble, there could be situations when they have to be bold and courageous in taking a stand against the ungodly attacks on the family foundation and defend their moral values in the society. Christians can do this without bearing arms, but be the conscience of the society/nation by speaking out against the destruction of family and moral values being perpetrated. May we be filled with the Holy Spirit's boldness as we speak out against the vises in our cultures and nations.

Have a lovely day **loaded** with godly **courage!**

LIVING WORD for TODAY—July 28:

LOADED with DAILY BLESSINGS (Ps. 68:19)-#210

FAMILY—28

Now it came to pass after these things that God tested Abraham, and said to him, 'Abraham!' And he said, 'Here I am.'
Then He said, 'Take now your son, your only son Isaac, whom you love, and go to the land of Moriah, and offer him there as a burnt offering on one of the mountains of which I shall tell you.'" (Gen. 22:1–2)

Life of Courage:

This event in Abraham's life leaves us with many unanswered questions.

- Is God interested in human sacrifices like the pagan deities;
- Why didn't Abraham ask God any questions to be sure He was the one speaking to him;
- Where was Sarah who was protecting Isaac as the apple of her eyes in all this; and
- Why didn't Isaac resist his father's irrational behavior and cry out for help?

These and many more questions should be asked as we read this episode. One key word in the story, however, is *tested*. God knows how to interrupt our busy schedules to get our attention. Abraham's family life was busy at this time. God was blessing him and making him great as a force to be reckoned with in the area. God had fulfilled the promise of an heir in his old age. But it was at this prosperous time that God interrupted with a test. It takes a lot of courage and trust to pass this kind of test. Why did Abraham pass the test? The writer of the epistle to the Hebrews answers this question.

"By faith Abraham, when he was tested, offered up Isaac and he who had received the promises offered up his only begotten son... concluding that God was able to raise him up, even from the dead, from which he also received him in a figurative sense" (Heb. 11:17–19).

Faith in God can give us courage to do anything for God regardless of the cost. Centuries later, our Heavenly Father offered up His only begotten Son as a sacrifice for our sins on this same mountain.

Have a great day **loaded** with His **blessings**!

LIVING WORD for TODAY—July 29:

LOADED with DAILY BLESSINGS (Ps. 68:19)-#211

FAMILY—29

"Now Abraham was old, well advanced in age, and the Lord had blessed Abraham in all things." (Gen. 24:1)
"This is the sum of the years of Abraham's life which he lived; one hundred and seventy-five years. Then Abraham breathed his last and died in a good old age, an old man and full of years, and was gathered to his people. And his sons Isaac and Ishmael buried him in the cave of Machpelah..." (Gen. 25:7–10)

Life of Contentment and Fulfillment:

With all the ups and downs in Abraham's life and family, it is encouraging to know that he ended well, blessed in all things, united his children, gave each his inheritance, and passed on the legacy of faith to the next generation that succeeded him. He lived by faith in God throughout, and this became his hallmark. When he was being inaugurated into the hall of faith heroes in Hebrews 11, the phrase that runs through all he did is, "by faith."

Abraham's family life, with wives and concubines, may not be a model family in the twenty-first century, but we can all learn some principles from him on how to raise a godly family in a sinful world. We shall recap some of these principles in our closing thoughts.

May we all solidly build our faith upon the solid rock of our Lord and Savior Jesus Christ, who is the Author and Finisher of our faith and family.

Have a refreshing day/night **loaded** with God's **blessings!**

LIVING WORD for TODAY—July 30:

LOADED with DAILY BLESSINGS (Ps. 68:19)-#212

FAMILY—30

"Blessed is every one who fears the LORD, Who walks in His ways... Your wife shall be like a fruitful vine In the very heart of your house. Your children like olive plants all around your table. Behold, thus shall the man be blessed Who fears the LORD." (Ps. 128:1–4)

Family is one of the blessings we receive from God. It is the oldest institution founded by God to replicate Himself on earth. Though God's original plan for the family was distorted by the Fall, yet, God has never given up to help anyone who trusted Him for help to raise a godly family in a sinful world.

We see from the Scriptures how He helped Abraham raise a family of faith who passed on the baton from generation to generation till our Lord Jesus Christ showed up in his family lineage. Some principles we can learn from him are timeless and eternal.

We shall summarize them next.

Have a blessed day with His **loaded blessings** in your **family**!

LIVING WORD for TODAY—July 31:

LOADED with DAILY BLESSINGS (Ps. 68:19)-#213

FAMILY—31

Let us summarize some timeless principles we have studied so far in the family life of the father of faith and friend of God, Abraham.

Life of conviction: He knew God enough to be convinced of His voice always;

Life of contention: Abraham's family was not perfect, but he handled contentions well with working solutions;

Life of compromise: Trying to help God fulfill His promise, Abraham almost settled for God's second-best;

Life of conversion: The institution of circumcision was God's sign of ownership of Abraham and his seeds. The Christian's born-again experience is a mark of spiritual circumcision;

Life of conflict: As Abraham fought many battles for his family, so are we to speak out and be the conscience of our nations to protect Christian family values;

Life of courage: Just as his courage was rooted in his faith in God, so are we to firmly build our faith and courage upon Jesus Christ; and

Life of contentment: Abraham lived long enough to see God's promises of blessings fulfilled. We are to completely trust the Lord and know He will bring to pass His promises to us.

With all these lessons, let us believe God to help us raise godly families all over the world today.

"Unless the LORD builds the house, They labor in vain who builds it."

"Behold, children are the heritage from the LORD, The fruit of the womb is a reward" (Ps. 127:1, 3).

Have a lovely day/night **loaded** with His **blessings!**

AUGUST—FRIENDS

LIVING WORD for TODAY—August 1:

LOADED with DAILY BLESSINGS (Ps. 68:19)-#214

FRIENDS—1

"A friend loves at all times,
And a brother is born for adversity." (Prov. 17:17)

Happy National Friendship Month!

The United Nations declared August as the month to celebrate friendship.

To us as Christians, we don't need to be directed by the US Congress or United Nations Assembly before celebrating God's blessings to us. Friends are God's gift to us, and it's better to have more friends than more enemies. True and trusted friends are priceless. They are not easy to find, and whenever we're blessed with them by divine connection or other means, we treasure them like priceless jewels.

If we're well familiar with the Bible, we will identify many blessings we're **loaded** with by the Lord. We've identified a specific blessing for each of the months in the year, such as life, love, health, redemption, forgiveness, favor, family, and now, friends. The Bible has so much to say about this subject, and it is my hope we will unveil some components about it during the month.

As we celebrate this month as a National Friendship Month, may the Lord give each of us friends who love at all times and become more to us than our blood brothers and sisters.

"A friend loves at all times."

Have a happy day **loaded** with His **blessing** of **friends!**

LIVING WORD for TODAY—August 2:

LOADED with DAILY BLESSINGS (Ps. 68:19)-#215

FRIENDS—2

"A friend loves at all times,
And a brother is born for adversity." (Prov. 17:17)

National Friendship Day

Historical Background:

What started as a business marketing strategy in the early 1930s by Joyce Hall, the founder of Hallmark Cards, to celebrate people closest to us and send them cards, soon became a movement of celebration of important people in our lives. In 1935, the United States Congress pronounced the first Sunday in August as a National Friendship Day holiday.

In 2011, during the 65th season, the United Nations designated July 30 as the International Friendship Day (Google).

Friends are part of God's blessings to us, and they can make a lot of difference in our social, emotional, psychological, and spiritual well-being.

Google Dictionary defines a friend as "a person whom one knows and with whom one has a bond of mutual affection, typically exclusive of sexual or family relations" (Google Dictionary).

I like this definition and will explore it more biblically during our daily devotions this month.

I was careful in the selection of word used for the title. Instead of "Friendship," which is more generic, I have selected "Friends," which is more personal. Every one of us needs at least one true friend whom we can identify and relate to in our lives. If you don't have one, I pray that the Lord will lead you to one during our meditations on the subject matter during this month.

Have a lovely day/night **loaded** with God's **blessings**!

LIVING WORD for TODAY—August 3:

LOADED with DAILY BLESSINGS (Ps. 68:19)-#216

FRIENDS—3

"A friend loves at all times,
And a brother is born for adversity." (Prov. 17:17)

There are different levels of friendship we keep with people. There's platonic friendship, there are common friends, distant friends, family friends, closest friends, and covenant friends.

The last two on this list will attract more of our attention during our devotional time. But before we go too far, let me ask you some personal questions:

1. Do you have friends;
2. Do you know them, and do they know you;
3. How well do you know each other;
4. How long have you known each other;
5. How much time do you spend together;
6. What are the common things that bind you together; and
7. Do you mutually accept each other regardless of your differences?

These seven checklist, and you can add more of your own, will help evaluate the levels of the current friends in your life and guide you in finding new ones. Above all, pray constantly for the Lord to expand your horizons and connect you with potential friends.

Have a great day **loaded** with God's **blessings!**

LIVING WORD for TODAY—August 4:

LOADED with DAILY BLESSINGS (Ps. 68:19)-#217

FRIENDS—4

"A man who has friends must himself be friendly.
But there is a friend who sticks closer than a brother." (Prov. 18:24)

Who is your friend?

Finding and keeping a true friend in the world of sins and adversities is almost impossible. But with God's grace, all things are possible.

The starting point, however, before seeking friendship with others, is yourself. Know who you are.

A lot of what shapes our personalities and characters in life come from others. People whose formations are weak and shake are easily swayed by peer pressure or the influence of others. Hence, developing and redefining your personal core values are foundational to associating with people and allowing certain individuals into your circle of friendship.

The Bible says, "A person who has friends must first be friendly." So love yourself and be your own friend first by defining who you are or want to be. If not, others will shape your characters for the good or bad.

Since only God knows us more than we know ourselves, pray constantly like David in Psalm 139.

"Search me, O God, and know my heart; Try me, and know my anxieties; And see if there is any wicked way in me, And lead me in the way everlasting" (Ps. 139:23–24).

Have a great day **loaded** with His **blessings!**

LIVING WORD for TODAY—August 5:

LOADED with DAILY BLESSINGS (Ps. 68:19)-#218

FRIENDS—5

"A man who has friends must himself be friendly.
But there is a friend who sticks closer than a brother." (Prov. 18:24)

Finding and Keeping a True Friend:

There are some guidelines to help us as we seek friendship with others or individuals who try to connect with and befriend us.

1. Know who you are;
2. Develop core values for yourself;
3. Have non-compromising values. While there are some of our core values that can blend with others, there should, however, be certain lines to drawn that cannot be crossed as we develop friendship with others. There's a difference between sheep and dogs. Both are domesticated animals and may live together in the same compound. But they don't eat the same food. Dogs will never eat grass, and sheep will never eat dung. So be known for who you are, both in private and in public; and
4. Make yourself friendly. Don't wear a sanctimonious or sad mask in your outlook that repels people away from you. Though you should have non-compromising core values, that should never stop you from being friendly and interact with people in various settings.

Jesus Christ, our Lord and Model, was known as a friend of winebibbers, tax collectors, and sinners (Matt.11:19). He freely mixed with sinners without practicing their sins. So let Him be our example as we develop a friendship with people.

Have a happy day/evening with His **loaded blessings!**

LIVING WORD for TODAY—August 6:

LOADED with DAILY BLESSINGS (Ps. 68:19)-#219

FRIENDS—6

"Then all the tax collectors and the sinners drew near to Him to hear Him. And the Pharisees and scribes complained, saying, 'This Man receives sinners and eats with them.'" (Luke 15:1–2)

Finding and Keeping a True Friend:

Friendship with people is costly. It may cost us our status and prestige. It may open us up to criticism. So the fifth guideline is important:

Be vulnerable.

If we're afraid of being bitten and taken advantage of, we're not going to attract potential friends into our lives. Although not all who want to befriend us have pure motives, many are takers than givers; yet, we must keep our doors of friendship open to all. If we carefully follow the first three guidelines: (1) Know who you are, (2) Develop core values for yourself, and (3) Have non-compromising core values, we would be confident as our Lord to welcome people without discrimination.

Let us follow our Savior's example by receiving those He sends us as we pray to Him to enlarge our horizons. Some of them may be like us, while many may be totally different and strangers. Let us take the risk and be vulnerable.

Have a great day **loaded** with His **blessings!**

LIVING WORD for TODAY—August 7:

LOADED with DAILY BLESSINGS (Ps. 68:19)-#220

FRIENDS—7

Finding and Keeping a True Friend:

True friends are hard to find; if you found one, do your best to keep him or her.

The sixth guideline in finding a true friend is open-mindedness.

Some of us have already built walls in our minds that block potential friends from getting close to us. Prejudices based on skin color, accent, race, tribe, ethnicity, gender, and class could limit our effectiveness to expand our circles of influence.

Friendship with people enables us to exert a tremendous influence and build bridges, especially in our mission for Christ in a world plagued with tensions, hostilities, and divisions.

Let us learn from Apostle Paul as we expand our influence and build bridges.

"For though I am free from all men, I have made myself a servant to all, that I might win the more; and to the Jews I became as a Jew, that I might win Jews; to those who are under the law, as under the law, that I might win those who are under the law; to those who are without law, as without law (not being without law toward God, but under law toward Christ), that I might win those who are without law; to the weak I became as weak, that I might win the weak. I have become all things to all men that I might by all means save some" (1 Cor. 9:19–22).

May we be humble enough to allow Christ to break down the walls of hostility, prejudice, and separation in our minds toward others.

Have a happy day **loaded** with His **blessings!**

LIVING WORD for TODAY—August 8:

LOADED with DAILY BLESSINGS (Ps. 68:19)-#221

FRIENDS—8

"But He gives more grace. Therefore He says:
'God resists the proud,
But gives grace to the Humble." (James 4:6)

Finding and Keeping a True Friend:

The seventh and last guideline in finding true friends and keeping them is to be simple-minded. Being high-minded and wearing it in our outlook drives people away from us. Avoid being too class-oriented. It is natural for professionals to attract their professional colleagues to their circles. But the purpose of Christ's coming to the world was to bring people together without class distinction.

We see this model in the selection of the twelve apostles by our Lord. There were fishermen, a tax collector hated by the Jews, a zealot from a terrorist group plotting revolutionary attacks against the government, religious pietists, an accountant, a proof-producing scientist, and a diplomat. What a group of friends to work with.

The same simple mindset ran through the early Christian community in Jerusalem. Listen to the summary of the community:

"Now the multitude of those who believed were of one heart and one soul; neither did anyone say that any of the things he possessed was his own, but they had all things in common" (Acts 4:32).

May we learn these lessons from our root and let them grow and spread through our friendship with others.

Have a fruitful day/evening with God's **loaded blessings!**

LIVING WORD for TODAY—August 9:

LOADED with DAILY BLESSINGS (Ps. 68:19)-#222

FRIENDS—9

"Blessed is the man Who walks not in the counsel of the ungodly,
Nor stands in the path of sinners,
Nor sits in the seat of the scornful..." (Ps. 1:1)

Friends to Avoid:

While it is good and beneficial to do our best in welcoming potential friends into the circles of our relationships, it is also important for us to ensure they fit into the values we embrace.

Jesus Christ is a friend of sinners. But He receives sinners into His friendship to change them. He did not come to find the righteous but sinners into repentance. We can come to Jesus just as we are, but He never leaves us the same. He transforms us from glory to glory.

The Bible is full of warnings for us to examine those whom we associate with. We are to avoid:

- Walking in the counsels of the ungodly;
- Standing in the paths of sinners; and
- Sitting in the seats of the scornful.

These are the general characteristics of the unbelievers who refused to be changed by the grace of God.

Why should we avoid them?

Because God's Word says so.

If the grace of God cannot change them, they will, with time, change us into their lifestyles. So avoid them as your closest friends, but love them and keep praying for their conversion.

Your destiny cannot be sacrificed on the altar of friendship.

Have a blessed day with His **loaded blessings!**

LIVING WORD for TODAY—August 10:

LOADED with DAILY BLESSINGS (Ps. 68:19)-#223

FRIENDS—10

"My son, if sinners entice you,
Do not consent.
If they say, 'Come with us,

Let us lie in wait to shed blood; Let us lurk secretly for the innocent without
cause... Cast in your lot among us, Let us all have one pause'—
My son, do not walk in the way with them, Keep your foot from their path."
(Prov. 1:10–15)

Friends to Avoid:

The Book of Proverbs is full of certain characters to avoid in our association
of friends.

We shall go through some of them without doing exegetical studies on them
since they are self-explanatory. I encourage everyone to read the Bible references for better understanding.

Avoid friendship with:

- Sinners who entice and lure you to join their sinful company to make
  easy wealth (Prov. 1:10–18);
- Greedy people looking for easy gains (Prov. 1:19);
- Immoral people who seduce and flatter with their words for sexual
  affairs. (Prov. 2:16–19; 5:3–20; 6:24–29);
- The oppressors who are perverse and under the curse of God
  (Prov. 3:31–35);
- The wicked who delight in wicked acts (Prov. 4:14–17);
- The talebearers who reveal secrets (Prov. 11:13; 26:20–22); and
- The perverse and whisperers who sow strife and divide the best of
  friends (Prov. 16:28).

To be continued.

So the godly counsel is summed up in Proverbs 12:26: "The righteous should choose his friends carefully..."

May God's wisdom prevail in our choice of friends.

Have a happy day/evening with God's **loaded blessings!**

LIVING WORD for TODAY—August 11:

LOADED with DAILY BLESSINGS (Ps. 68:19)-#224

FRIENDS—11

"The righteous should choose his friends carefully,
For the way of the wicked leads them astray." (Prov. 12:26)

Friends to Avoid:

We continue with the list of friends we're instructed to stay away from if we're going to fulfill our God's given destinies here on earth and make it to our eternal home.

Avoid friendship with:

- Those who flatter with their words. Beware of sweet talks (Prov. 20:19);
- Contentious and angry women. It is better to live in a corner of a housetop or even dwell in the wilderness alone than to live with them (Prov. 21:9, 19);
- Fools in general. Their companions will be destroyed (Prov. 13:20);
- The scoffers—cast them out to end strife and reproach (Prov. 22:10);
- The angry and furious people. You can easily learn their ways and set a snare for your soul (Prov. 22:24–25);
- The winebibbers and gluttonous eaters (Prov. 23:20–21); and
- Wine and drunkards in general (Prov. 23:29–35).

To be continued.

May the Lord grant us His discernment to choose our friends wisely without discrimination.

Have a great day **loaded** with God's **blessings**!

LIVING WORD for TODAY—August 12:

LOADED with DAILY BLESSINGS (Ps. 68:19)-#225

FRIENDS—12

"The righteous should choose his friends carefully,
For the way of the wicked leads them astray." (Prov. 12:26)

Friends to Avoid:

While the Book of Proverbs is loaded with daily wisdom of God to live by, I have carefully selected a few passages that deal with toxic friends to avoid in our relationships:

- The unstable who are easily given to changes (Prov. 24:21, 22). The Bible affirms this in James 1:6-8: "...he is a double-minded man, unstable in all his ways";
- Lazy people (Prov. 24:30–34). The Bible says: "...if anyone will not work, neither shall he eat" (2 Thess. 3:10);
- Those who disrespect their parents and steal from them (Prov. 28:24). If you still have a parent or both of them, remember this: "Honor your father and mother, which is the first commandment with promise: that it may be well with you and you may live long on the earth" (Eph. 6:2–3); and

Those who aid and abet thieves (Prov. 29:24). Avoid friendship with them regardless of what you stand to gain from them.

I urge everyone again, to read the Book of Proverbs. The book is divided into thirty-one chapters, so we can read one chapter a day in every month of the year.

Have a great day/evening **loaded** with His **blessings!**

LIVING WORD for TODAY—August 13:

LOADED with DAILY BLESSINGS (Ps. 68:19)-#226

FRIENDS—13

"If anyone comes to you and does not bring this doctrine, do not receive him into your house nor greet him; for he who greets him shares in his evil deeds." (2 John 10–11)

Friends to Avoid:

The New Testament is full of warnings from the Lord and His apostles about certain people to avoid in our friendships. We will limit our meditations to the Epistles:

- Those who suppress the truth in unrighteousness (Rom. 1:18);
- People of vile passions and perversion of humans natural orientations (Rom. 1:26–32);
- Evil people and impostors (1 Tim. 3:13);
- Profane and idle babblers who lead people astray from the faith in Christ (2 Tim. 2:14, 16–18);
- People who live in sins of the last days (2 Tim. 3:1–9);
- False teachers (1 Tim. 4:1–5; 6:3–11); and
- Deceivers through philosophy and traditions of men and legalistic teaching (Col. 2:8; Gal. 3:1–6).

To be continued.

The command of the Lord's apostles is to not welcome such people into your homes nor even greet them. Avoid them like the plague. This is not about hate crime but obedience to the Spirit of love in Christ Jesus.

Have a lovely day/evening with God's **loaded blessings!**

LIVING WORD for TODAY—August 14:

LOADED with DAILY BLESSINGS (Ps. 68:19)-#227

FRIENDS—14

"But avoid foolish disputes, genealogies, contentions, and strivings about the law;
for they are unprofitable and useless.
Reject a divisive man after the first and second admonition,
Knowing that such a person is warped and sinning, being self condemned."
(Titus 3:9–11)

Friends to Avoid:

Warnings from the apostles of the Lord continued:

- Divisive people and foolish disputers who appear as friends but look for allies (Titus 3:9–11);
- Abusers of the grace of God into lawless living (Jude 4);
- Grumbling, rebellious, complaining, lustful, bigmouth, flattering people for personal gains (Jude 8, 10–15);
- Exploiters, blasphemers, and deceivers (2 Pet. 2:2–3); and
- Adulterers and adulteresses (James 4:4–5).

Going through the lists and studying them creates spiritual awareness and sensitivity in us as we seek to have fellowship and befriend people. Watch out and keep a distance from the wrong allies, or else, you may be contaminated!

Have a lovely day **loaded** with God's **blessings!**

LIVING WORD for TODAY—August 15:

LOADED with DAILY BLESSINGS (Ps. 68:19)-#228

FRIENDS—15

"Ointment and perfume delight the heart,
And the sweetness of a man's friend gives delight by hearty counsel." (Prov. 27:9)

The Sweetness and Strength of a Friend:

Do you have a close friend you can turn to in times of adversity and need? What is the quality of your relationship with each other? Do you have a friend or friends whose presence lifts up your countenance and strengthens you when you're cast down?

Just as sweet-smelling perfume or air freshener transforms the odors of an environment into a sweet-smelling fragrance, so is the presence of a good friend. It changes everything in your life when he or she is around.

That's what our Bible text is talking about. "The sweetness of a man's friend gives delight by hearty counsel."

May the Lord give us true and indispensable friends.

Have a great day/night **loaded** with His **blessings!**

LIVING WORD for TODAY—August 16:

LOADED with DAILY BLESSINGS (Ps. 68:19)-#229

FRIENDS—16

"Do not forsake your own friend or your father's friend,
Nor go to your brother's house in the day of your calamity;
Better is a neighbor nearby than a brother far away." (Prov. 27:10)

The Sweetness and Strength of a Friend:

If we keep our minds open and make ourselves friendly, we would discover that there are potential friends all around us, especially in our neighborhoods. Many of them may not be like us nor in the same faith with us. But there are some good people around us. As much as we have emphasized avoiding bad influences of bad friends, we must also be careful not to be caught up in the spirit of exclusiveness, thinking that we are the best.

So let us learn a couple of lessons from our text:

- Keep your old friends and be in touch with them from time to time, no matter how far they are from you. Old friends are better than new ones, they say; and
- Make yourself friendly to your neighbors, no matter how different they are from you. Christians are to be light and salt in their communities. Be part of the social clubs as long they're not secret cults.

Remember, a friend nearby is better to you than a brother far away in the time of calamity when you need help (Prov. 17:17).

Have a bright day **loaded** with God's **blessings**!

LIVING WORD for TODAY—August 17:

LOADED with DAILY BLESSINGS (Ps. 68:19)-#230

FRIENDS—17

"As iron sharpens iron,
So a man sharpens the countenance of his friend." (Prov. 27:17)

The Sweetness and Strength of a Friend:

True friends are a blessing from God. So if you have one, please cherish, keep, and protect him or her.

The Bible says, "As iron sharpens iron, So a man sharpens the countenance of his friend" (Prov. 27:17).

There are many examples of this sharpening ministry in the Bible. Think of Job and his friends, Jonathan and David, and the Lord Jesus Christ and His circles of friends.

Job and his three friends:

Job was a real man who lived a godly life in the ancient world. He feared God and shunned evil. God, in turn, blessed him with the good things of life, such as wealth, a great family, great security, and good health. But suddenly, by one disaster after the other, he lost everything. Finally, Satan, who brought the disasters, got permission from God and afflicted Job with painful boils all over his body.

The only person left with Job was his wife, who was clueless of the source of their calamities and helpless.

But Job had some friends. Three of them who lived far apart made an appointment with each other to meet at Job's home. These were Job's inner circle of friends who had come to mourn and comfort him (Job 1–2)

We all need friends like these who can be with us in the time of great need of comfort, even when we differ in our opinions. Pray for connection to a true friend if you have none, and God will direct you.

Have a great day with God's **loaded blessings!**

LIVING WORD for TODAY—August 18:

LOADED with DAILY BLESSINGS (Ps. 68:19)-#231

FRIENDS—18

"As iron sharpens iron,
So a man sharpens the countenance of his friend." (Prov. 27:17)

The Sweetness and Strength of a Friend:

How do you minister comfort and strength to a friend in distress who is going through physical, spiritual, and emotional pains or a loss?

We can learn some lessons from Job's three friends (Job 2:11–13).

- Empathy-Dictionary defines empathy as "the ability to understand and share the feelings of another" (Google).

Job's three friends made plans to visit him, and when they saw him in ashes, they lifted their voices and wept. Weeping in public in response to pains or loss is not a sign of weakness but a release of the emotional reaction to the event. Our Lord Jesus wept at the graveside of His friend Lazarus (John 11:35).

Notice also that they tore their robes, which was their cultural way of expressing deep grief. Their next action was also cultural. They sprinkled dust on their heads.

Their actions reflected the expression of deep empathy in connecting with the feelings of their friend (to be continued).

Do you have a friend or friends going through a loss or losses? These could be the loss of a loved one, job, business, finances, home, divorce, or health. Though it may be impossible, at this time of COVID 19, to visit them in person, but you can express your feelings by sending them gifts, cards with comforting words, phone calls, and let them know that your thoughts and prayers are with them. "And if one member suffers, all the members suffer with it..." (1 Cor. 12:26).

May we be filled with the Spirit of compassion to minister comfort and strength to our friends when they need us to be there for them.

Have a bright day **loaded** with God's **blessings!**

LIVING WORD for TODAY—August 19:

LOADED with DAILY BLESSINGS (Ps. 68:19)-#232

FRIENDS—19

"So they sat down with him on the ground seven days and seven nights, and no one spoke a word to him, for they saw that his grief was very great." (Job 2:13)

The Sweetness and Strength of a Friend:

There are many things we can do positively or negatively when we visit those who are in grief, pain, or distress. What we do or say can either minister comfort and strength to them or aggravate their feelings of pain and distress. So watch what you say. Most of the time, people in distress don't need our preaching. Preaching can be so offensive and turn them off during pain and distress. We can learn this lesson from Job's three friends.

- Presence: They sat down with him on the ground for seven days without saying a word. Nothing is more powerful than the ministry of presence to those who are in pain, grief, or distress.

I've learned this lesson with my patients and their families over the years in my involvements as a spiritual care counselor in some busy healthcare industries in the United States. Sitting by the bedside of dying or recovering patients or standing by the side of families during trauma and grief as a spiritual person and how calming and soothing my presence meant to them taught me the power of spiritual presence in healing.

This was also demonstrated by our Lord in His earthly ministry.

In our busy world today, we don't have to be in our friend's house for seven days. But our presence and prayers mean a lot to them in times of loss, trauma, and distress. Remember: "As iron sharpens iron, so a man sharpens the countenance of his friend" (Prov. 27:17).

Have a pleasant day **loaded** with His **blessings!**

LIVING WORD for TODAY—August 20:

LOADED with DAILY BLESSINGS (Ps. 68:19)-#233

FRIENDS—20

"As iron sharpens iron,
So a man sharpens the countenance of his friend." (Prov. 27:17)

The Sweetness and Strength of a Friend:

The third component of the strength Job's friends brought to him in his time of crisis was:

- Expression. Job's friends' silent presence empowered him to express his feelings. When people are sick, grieving, or going through a crisis, they are humbled, confused, and powerless. The only power left for them is expressing their feelings. Sometimes they could be agitated in their expressions, sobbing, or groaning. And other times, they even express anger.

The understanding friends, caregivers, or counselors would not contend nor correct them because they were exercising the only power left to them. The best support friends can provide to them is active listening.

Notice that Job's friends did not stop him from talking, even when some of the things he was saying did not make sense. They actively listened to him, and each took his turn to respond. This cycle of expressions helped Job process his feelings into expressions of acceptance and hope.

Let us be patient with people going through hurts and crises to assist them to connect with the realities of life in the hope of light after darkness.

Be a listening friend and not just a proponent of solutions. None of Job's friends, including Job and his wife, knew the source of Job's crisis. Only God knew, and His solution restored Job and blessed him twice more than all that Satan had taken away from him.

Whatever crisis you may be going through today, I pray for God's interventions into your situations for comfort, peace, joy, and hope for a better tomorrow.

Have a lovely day **loaded** with His **blessings!**

LIVING WORD for TODAY—August 21:

LOADED with DAILY BLESSINGS (Ps. 68:19)-#234

FRIENDS—21

"Now when he had finished speaking to Saul, the soul of Jonathan was knit to the soul of David, and Jonathan loved him as his own soul." (1 Sam. 18:1)

The Sweetness and Strength of a Friend:

There are many more lessons we can learn from Job and his friends on how they approached Job's crisis and God's interventions, but because of time, we have to shift to the other side of the smile and strength friends can bring to each other's life in times of victory.

David had just done a heroic act no one could do in Israel. He had just killed the giant warrior Goliath, who was terrorizing the army of Israel and had defied Yahweh God.

King Saul and his son had every human reason to be jealous because the nation's attention was moving from them to a young hero David.

But Jonathan, the crown prince to the throne, did the unusual. Instead of being jealous of David, he drew closer to him, and both became covenant friends, even when his father, King Saul warned him against it.

True friends are not only known in trials but in triumph.

Distance yourself from friends who sympathize with you when you're suffering but are not eager to celebrate your success with you. It's okay to lend their feeble support when you're down in a pitiable condition, but as soon as God turns your situation around and you're promoted above them, they are not so excited to celebrate you. Why? Envy.

We saw this spirit in Saul, but not in his son, Jonathan, who saw David's victory as his own victory. True friends suffer when one friend suffers, and feel honored when a friend is honored (1 Cor. 12:26).

Have a great day honored with His **loaded blessings!**

LIVING WORD for TODAY—August 22:

LOADED with DAILY BLESSINGS (Ps. 68:19)-#235

FRIENDS—22

"Then Jonathan and David made a covenant, because he loved him as his own soul.

And Jonathan took off the robe that was on him and gave it to David, with his armor, even to his sword and his bow and his belt." (1 Sam. 18:3–4)

The Sweetness and Strength of a Friend:

True friends are not only known in suffering but are eager to celebrate each other's success.

Jonathan and David are a model example of true and sincere friendship.

Observe Jonathan's actions after David's victory:

- He immediately identified with David's victory (1 Sam. 18:1);
- He loved David as his own soul (1 Sam. 18:1, 3);
- He entered into a covenant of friendship with David (1 Sam. 18:3);
- He gave his royal authority to David, promoting him to the same royal status as himself (1 Sam. 18:4); and
- He equipped David with more effective weapons for victory in battles (1 Sam. 18:4).

Jonathan was a true and selfless friend to David.

The Bible says:

"Be kindly affectionate to one another with brotherly love, in honor giving preference to one another" (Rom. 12:10).

May the Lord give you your own covenant friend.

Have a happy day **loaded** with His **blessings!**

LIVING WORD for TODAY—August 23:

LOADED with DAILY BLESSINGS (Ps. 68:19)-#236

FRIENDS—23

"Now Saul spoke to Jonathan his son and to all his servants that they should kill David; but Jonathan, Saul's son, delighted greatly in David.
So Jonathan told David, saying, 'My father Saul seeks to kill you. Therefore please be on your guard until morning, and stay in a secret place and hide...'" (1 Sam. 19:1–2)

The Sweetness and Strength of a Friend:

True friends watch for each other's backs. They advocate and protect each other. Take time to read 1 Samuel chapters nineteen and twenty. It makes a good read. You will see how Jonathan and David's friendship developed and how Jonathan saved David from untimely death, even when it meant losing the right to the throne by Jonathan.

Covenant friends are rare, but when found, they last forever and from one generation to another.

Do you have anyone out there watching for your back and advocating for you even in your absence? We all need selfless friends in our lives, and we can also be one in someone else's life in our circle of friendship with others.

May the Lord connect your heart together with someone who can be your own covenant friend.

Have a glorious day **loaded** with God's **blessings**!

LIVING WORD for TODAY—August 24:

LOADED with DAILY BLESSINGS (Ps. 68:19)-#237

FRIENDS—24

"Now David said, 'Is there still anyone who is left of the house of Saul, that I may show him kindness for Jonathan's sake?'" (2 Sam. 9:1)

The Sweetness and Strength of a Friend:

The good deeds and kindness done to a friend will never be forgotten but will, one way or the other, be rewarded.

Jonathan and his father, King Saul, were killed in the battle with the Philistines, and the kingdom of Israel was in disarray for some time until the leaders of Israel sought out David from the exile where he had been hiding from his enemy Saul and crowned him as the king. Though anointed by God, it took a long time with a lot of warfare to realize what the Lord had ordained for him. Sounds like the Christian life?

But years later, after David had been fully established in his throne as the king of a united Israel, he remembered the covenant between him and his friend Jonathan. Jonathan might be dead, but the covenant lived on. At this time, the beneficiary was a poor, unworthy, feeble, and lame son of Jonathan called, Mephibosheth, who was living and hiding in a slum of the city.

David sought him out, elevated him back into the royal class, restored all the property and wealth of his grandfather, Saul, being encroached by others back to him, and sat him on the royal banqueting table to dine with King David and his family daily. What an amazing grace!

That's what a covenant friendship does. That's what our covenant relationship with our eternal covenant Friend, Jesus Christ, did for us. Praise His holy name!

Maybe you don't have anyone you can refer to on earth as your covenant friend; know that you have a trusted covenant Friend. His name is Jesus Christ.

"...But there is a friend who sticks closer than a brother" (Prov. 18:24).

Have a lovely day **loaded** with His **blessings**!

LOADED with DAILY BLESSINGS (Ps. 68:19)-#248

FRIENDS—25

"Greater love has no one than this, than to lay down one's life for his friends. You are My friends if you do whatever I command you." (John 15:13, 14)

The Sweetness and Strength of a Friend:

We now come to the last part of our topic on friends. No matter how good our friends could be, they will never be a match to our good and perfect Friend, Jesus Christ. He is the perfect Model by whom we measure all our friends in the world.

Our relationship with Him can be experienced in four stages:

Stage 1: We are His children by adoption into His family (John 1:12–13);

Stage 2: We are His brothers and sisters by listening to His Word and doing it (Luke 8:21);

Stage 3: We are His servants as we obey His commands, and He commits His riches to our care (Mark 3:13–15; John 15:15); and

Stage 4: We are His friends. This is a deeper and intimate stage of trust in our relationship with Christ (John 15:13–15).

At this stage of friendship with Him, we also have different circles. I have identified seven circles of friendship with the Lord in my studies and meditations of the Gospels. We shall look into these circles and see where we belong in our friendship with the Lord.

No matter where you and I belong, however, we must know for sure that we have a Friend who loves us more than any earthly friend to the point of laying down His life for us. Let us embrace Him as our eternal covenant Friend.

Enjoy His love with His **loaded blessings** daily!

LIVING WORD for TODAY—August 26:

LOADED with DAILY BLESSINGS (Ps. 68:19)-#239

FRIENDS—26

"No longer do I call you servants, for a servant does not know what his master is doing; but I have called you friends, for all things that I heard from My Father I have made known to you." (John 15:15)

The Sweetness and Strength of a Friend:

○   The first circle of the Lord's friends during His earthly ministry consisted of Peter, James, and John. These three disciples were in His inner circle that He took with Him to events, which were so private and close to His heart, such as the Mount of Transfiguration, where He met with Moses and Elijah (Matt. 17:1–8) and the Garden of Gethsemane, where He travailed in prayer to His Father (Matt. 26:36–37).

While the twelve apostles were close to Him, these three could be described as His right-hand friends who knew all about Him.

May our relationship with the Lord be so close that He could reveal what He's doing and wants to do to us. This level of friendship requires living in His presence regularly with unbroken fellowship. Are you in that group? May He count us worthy to be in His inner circle.

Have a great day with His **loaded blessings!**

LIVING WORD for TODAY—August 27

LOADED with DAILY BLESSINGS (Ps. 68:19)-#240

FRIENDS—27

"And He went up on the mountain and called to Him those He Himself wanted. And they came to Him.

Then He appointed twelve, that they might be with Him and that He might send them out to preach, and to have power to heal sicknesses and to cast out demons." (Mark 3:13–15)

Jesus's Circle of Friends:

The second circle of the Lord's friends is the Twelve. The twelve apostles were special servants who later became Christ's friends. But notice that the primary purpose of choosing them from among the crowd was not to send them out to preach and heal. The Lord went to the mountain and prayed all night to choose the friends who would be with Him. They were appointed, first and foremost, to be with Him. Only those who are with Him in His presence as His friends have a special privilege of taking His presence to the sick, afflicted, and the needy. Real Christian ministry flows from being in Christ's presence as His friend.

Are you His friend? Does He know you to be one of His inner circle friends? May He, by His magnetic grace and power, draw us closer to His circle of friendship, where we can enjoy sweet communion with Him and other like-minded disciples always.

Have a gracious day **loaded** with His **blessings!**

LIVING WORD for TODAY—August 28:

LOADED with DAILY BLESSINGS (Ps. 68:19)-#241

FRIENDS—28

"Therefore the sisters sent for Him, saying, 'Lord, behold, he whom You love is sick...
Now Jesus loved Martha and her sister and Lazarus." (John 11:3, 5)

Jesus's Circle of Friends:

Our Lord Jesus Christ is a model example of making friends. He carefully and prayerfully picked His inner circle of friends, though He was a friend to all who came to Him.

There was a family of three siblings in a small town of Bethany near Jerusalem that was dear to our Lord. He and His disciples lodged in their home frequently as their retreat home during their ministry trips. I found this family of Martha, Mary, and Lazarus to be the third circle of friends to our Lord.

Find time to read about them and their hospitality to the Lord and His ministry team in the Gospels. Besides John the Beloved, no one else earned the same title of "whom Jesus loved" in the New Testament other than Martha, Mary, and Lazarus. Note also that Mary was a well-known, high-society sinner in town that no religious leader would ever associate with. But the Lord did (Luke 7:36–39).

The Lord who sees the heart saw beyond her outward appearance and befriended her and her siblings. Remember how she sat at the Lord's feet and took in every word of the Lord while her sister was serving the Lord (Luke 10:38–42)?

May the Lord choose your home and my home as His retreat place where He is comfortable enough to relax and refresh. Let's make Him comfortable to dwell in our hearts.

Have a lovely day/evening **loaded** with His **blessings!**

LIVING WORD for TODAY—August 29:

LOADED with DAILY BLESSINGS (Ps. 68:19)-#242

FRIENDS—29

"After these things the Lord appointed seventy others also, and sent them two by two before His face into every city and place where He Himself was about to go." *(Luke 10:1)*

Jesus's Circle of Friends:

The fourth group of our Lord's circle of friends consisted of seventy disciples. They were His ambassadors, sent out to prepare the hearts of people in the cities He was to visit. They were sent out two by two to exercise His authority and power as they announced the arrival of the kingdom of God.

Because of their friendship and closeness with the Lord, they flowed with His anointing everywhere they went, which made the demons subject to them.

If the Christian church today could be so close in her friendship and relationship with the Lord, our mission in the world would be more productive with the harvest of souls into Christ's kingdom. Ministry becomes easy when it is carried out in obedience to the Lord's command.

"You are My friends if you do whatever I command you" (John 15:14).

This circle of friendship with the Lord is open-ended, so whosoever will may come in and be accepted in the Savior's open arms.

You're most welcome to the circle of His disciples' friendship.

Have a great day **loaded** with His **blessings**!

LIVING WORD for TODAY—August 30:

LOADED with DAILY BLESSINGS (Ps. 68:19)-#243

FRIENDS—30

"...and certain women who had been healed of evil spirits and infirmities—Mary called Magdalene, out of whom had come seven demons, and Joanna the wife of Chuza, Herod's steward, and Susanna, and many others who provided for Him from their substance." (Luke 8:1–3)

Jesus's Circle of Friends:

Women played prominent roles in Jesus's life and ministry, just as they do in Christian ministries all over the world today.

Certain prominent women, like Mary Magdalene, Joanna, the wife of King Herod's steward, Susanna, and many other women, were those I named the fifth circle of Jesus's closest friends. These women were well-to-do, and they provided for His ministry needs, including His special clothing, food, and provisions for Him and His disciples. Throughout His earthly ministry, our Lord and His disciples, who left their occupations to follow Him, lacked nothing because of these ladies' financial support.

People who are genuinely called into the Christian ministry flow better with God's anointing when they are not distracted by worldly affairs, such as working to fend for themselves and their families.

Christian men and women around such who are called into the ministry owe it as a duty to God to provide for their necessities. This is a scriptural principle practiced throughout the Bible.

When you take care of God's messengers, He, in turn, takes a better care of you.

Have a happy day **loaded** with His **blessings**!

LIVING WORD for TODAY—August 31:

LOADED with DAILY BLESSINGS (Ps. 68:19)-#244

FRIENDS—31

"Ointment and perfume delight the heart.
And the sweetness of a man's friend gives delight by hearty counsel." (Prov. 27:9)

Jesus's Circle of Friends:

As we conclude our meditations on friends, let me quickly identify the last two groups in the circle of Jesus's friends.

- The secret disciples—there were some Pharisees, like Nicodemus (John 3:1–2), and some Jewish government council members, such as Joseph of Arimathea (Luke 23:50–53), who believed and followed Jesus Christ secretly because of fear of losing their positions. They were His distant friends. We need influential friends, like them too, in our circles of friendship; and
- The 120 disciples who saw His ascension to heaven and tarried in the Upper Room to receive His promise of the Holy Spirit (Acts 1:14–15). They were His true friends.

Which of Jesus's friendship circle do you belong to? Are you a friend, fan, or foe?

Be the Lord's friend and His follower.

Also, I invite you to be my friend if you're not yet. The fact that I'm personally sending this devotional to you shows that I've chosen you as my friend. Some of you are even my brothers, sisters, sons, or daughters. Let's continue to strengthen our ties of friendship in communication, fellowship, and love.

Have a lovely day/night **loaded** with God's **blessing** of **friends**!

Living Word for **today** with James E. Temidara

SEPTEMBER
————-FOOD

LIVING WORD for TODAY—September 1:

LOADED with DAILY BLESSINGS (Ps. 68:19)-#245

FOOD—1

"Bless the LORD, O my soul;
And all that is within me, bless His holy name...
Who satisfies your mouth with good things,
So that your youth is renewed like the eagle's." (Ps. 103:1,5)

We have crossed another milestone in our journeys of life by stepping into the last four months of the year. The same Lord who has always navigated us through the thin and thick of life will be our Shepherd and Guide for the rest of the year.

Our subject focus for the month of September is food.

Food is so common that we take it for granted. However, food is indispensable that no life, whether it be a plant, tree, animal, or human can survive without.

Some indispensable gifts of life, such as, air, oxygen, water, and food are taken for granted that we don't even think of them when using until they are taken from us.

Most of the time, we don't think of food until we're hungry. If we don't think of the gift, how then can we even think of the giver?

Let us spend some time in our meditations this month to celebrate the Giver of food, and to connect with Him to fill our lands and mouths with good things.

"Who satisfies your mouth with good things, so that your youth is renewed like the eagles" (Ps. 103:5).

Have a happy month **loaded** with God's **blessings**!

Food is a major blessing of life from God to us. Let us receive it daily with thanksgiving to Him.

LIVING WORD for TODAY—September 2:

LOADED with DAILY BLESSINGS (Ps. 68:19)-#246

FOOD—2

"And God said, 'See, I have given you every herb that yields seed which is on the face of all the earth, and every tree whose fruit yields seed: to you it shall be for food...'" (Gen. 1:29)

Food as a Blessing:

Food is a major blessing God gave to mankind, the beasts, and the birds at creation. It is so important that we cannot live for too long without it.

But as important as it is, we hear very little about it compared to how much we hear about other spiritual matters. Let me ask you, how many times have you heard a sermon from the pulpit on food since you became a Christian? Yet, the Bible is full of references on food from Genesis to Revelation.

Please note that food was the first blessing God gave to His creatures for their survival on earth (Gen. 1:29–30). He could have given something else, but He chose food. If God speaks so much about a subject in His Word, why then do we speak less of it in our teachings? It is time we develop a proper theology about food in our Christian understanding. Hopefully, we'll do a little of that in our meditations this month.

May you never lack good things in your mouth all the days of your life.

Have a great day **loaded** with God's **blessings!**

LIVING WORD for TODAY—September 3:

LOADED with DAILY BLESSINGS (Ps. 68:19)-#247

FOOD—3

"Every moving thing that lives shall be food for you. I have given you all things, even as the green herbs." (Gen. 9:3)

Food as a Blessing:

Food is good and a blessing from God. Everyone loves food except people dealing with the disease of anorexia, which makes them lose appetite for food. Food is the most popular friend all over the world. Events of human gatherings are more exciting and attractive when food is included.

Food and eating are mentioned more frequently in the Bible and in the ministry of our Lord. It is important that we see food as the necessity of life next to life itself. We must also correct the misconception that only vegetables were given to us for food by God. While eating vegetables is a healthy diet, God has, however, given mankind, "Every moving thing that lives" for food. That includes vegetables, fruits, nuts, fish, birds, reptiles, beasts, and even insects.

So let us enjoy God's blessing of food and glorify Him in our eating and dining here on earth before we join Him and the saints in heaven at His banqueting table.

Have a happy day **loaded** with His **blessings!**

LIVING WORD for TODAY—September 4:

LOADED with DAILY BLESSINGS (Ps. 68:19)-248

FOOD—4

"Who gives food to all flesh...
For His mercy endures forever." (Ps. 136:25)

Food as a Blessing:

Just a quick reminder, our broad theme of meditations for the year is: **loaded** with **daily blessings** taken from Psalm 68:19: "Blessed be the LORD, Who daily loads us with benefits. The God of our salvation! Selah."

Since January, we've meditated on God's benefits of life, love, health, redemption, forgiveness, favor, family, friends, and now food. It is my belief that we've all been experiencing these blessings from the God of our salvation in different dimensions. The Lord is always eager to load us with His benefits.

Food is one of those blessings we enjoy from Him. Hence, the Bible commands us to "give thanks to the Lord, for He is good! For His mercy endures forever... Who gives food to all flesh" (Ps. 136:1, 25).

Let us do that and appreciate God every time we eat or drink. May we never take His blessings for granted but always remember that He gives them to us out of His mercy.

Have a great day/ evening **loaded** with His **blessings!**

LIVING WORD for TODAY—September 5:

LOADED with DAILY BLESSINGS (Ps. 68:19)-#249

FOOD—5

"So when the woman saw that the tree was good for food, that it was pleasant to the eyes, and a tree desirable to make one wise, she took of its fruit and ate. She also gave to her husband with her, and he ate." (Gen. 3:6)

Food as a Bait:

Our basic theology is to view God as the provider of food, which is a blessing to all the living. Yes, He is because every good and perfect gift comes from Him. But we must also understand that every good gift God made can also become a snare to trap and stop us from our God-given purpose in life if used wrongly.

Just as we use food as a blessing, it can also become a bait. Just as we use food as a bait to lure and catch animals, the devil, the enemy of our souls, can also use food to lure and imprison us from reaching our God-assigned destinies.

It was food the devil used to lure our first parents, Adam and Eve, into sin, which disconnected them from God and brought miseries to the human race. They ate the forbidden fruit through the devil's deception.

May we not be controlled by our appetites for food, but put our desires under the sovereign Lordship of Him who created food for our enjoyment.

Have a blessed day/evening **loaded** with His **blessings!**

LIVING WORD for TODAY—September 6:

LOADED with DAILY BLESSINGS (Ps. 68:19)-#250

FOOD—6

"But Jacob said, 'Sell me your birthright as of this day.' And Esau said, 'Look, I am about to die; so what is this birthright to me?'
Then Jacob said, 'Swear to me as of this day.' So he swore to him, and sold his birthright to Jacob.
And Jacob gave Esau bread and stew of lentils; then he ate and drank, arose, and went his way. Thus Esau despised his birthright. (Gen. 25:31–34)

Food as a Bait:

It was food that made our first parents lose their paradise on earth. Now food has done it again! It made Esau lose his birthright inheritance to his younger brother Jacob.

The birthright was a transfer of the family authority, right, and inheritance to the oldest son in the family. This was important in the ancient world. Esau and Jacob knew this, but Esau, the oldest son, took it for granted, while Jacob cherished it and looked for an opportunity to get it from his brother. He found the opportunity in Esau's desire for food. Jacob wasted no time to exploit Esau's hunger to satisfy his momentary need, and grabbed his brother's eternal blessings from him.

Jacob used food as a bait to steal his brother's birthright.

If this didn't happen, maybe today, we would be calling God as the God of Abraham, Isaac, and Esau. But Esau despised his birthright, so it shifted to Jacob.

So be careful how you go about sacrificing your eternal inheritance on the altar of temporary blessing. More on this later.

Have a beautiful day/evening with God's **loaded blessings!**

LIVING WORD for TODAY—September 7:

LOADED with DAILY BLESSINGS (Ps. 68:19)-#251

FOOD—7

"Now therefore, please take your weapons, your quiver and your bow, and go out to the field and hunt game for me. And make me savory food, such as I love, and bring it to me that I may eat, that my soul may bless you before I die." (Gen. 27:3–4)

Food as a Bait:

Like father like son. Isaac loved to eat good food, just like his son Esau. It seemed that both of them had this trait in common. But there's another son at home who knew this about them and was always ready to use their weakness against them.

Jacob used food to steal his brother's birthright, and now he's using the same weapon of food to deceive his father and finally get his brother's blessings.

Too much love for food can dull our spiritual sensitivity to the realities of our eternal inheritance in Christ. At the time when Esau should have cried for repentance when his birthright was stolen from him, he found no time for repentance but for food. He "despised his birthright" (Gen. 25:34).

The Bible warns us never to be like Esau, "who for one morsel of food sold his birthright. For you know that afterward, when he wanted to inherit the blessing, he was rejected, for he found no place for repentance, though he sought it diligently with tears" (Heb. 12:16–17). Read Genesis 25 and 27 to learn more about Esau's painful experience due to lack of self control.

May the Holy Spirit of God restrain us daily from being addicted to our appetites for fleshly pleasures.

Have a great day/ evening with His **loaded blessings!**

LIVING WORD for TODAY—September 8:

LOADED with DAILY BLESSINGS (Ps. 68:19)-#252

FOOD—8

"Now when the tempter came to Him, he said, 'If You are the Son of God, command that these stones become bread.'
But He answered and said, 'It is written, Man shall not live by bread alone, but by every word that proceeds from the mouth of God.'" (Matt. 4:3–4)

Food as a Bait:

Like our first parents, Adam and Eve, who failed and took the bait of food from the devil and brought sin and misery to the world, our Savior Jesus Christ, when He came to redeem us, the same tempter came to Him with the bait of food. But instead of taking the bait and becoming trapped into the snare of the devil, our Lord flipped it around and rejected the bait of food from Satan. This was the beginning of our victory over Satan, sin, sickness, and other miseries.

Although the Lord was hungry and needed to eat food, the source of the food was wrong and must be rejected.

Our fleshly needs will always scream at us for gratification, but they must be put under control by the power of God's spoken Word in us.

Food is good, but "Man shall not live by (food) alone, but by every word that proceeds from the mouth of God" (Matt. 4:4).

Make His victory yours today in the midst of temptations!

Have a victorious day **loaded** with His **blessings**!

LIVING WORD for TODAY—September 9

LOADED with DAILY BLESSINGS (Ps. 68:19)-#253

FOOD—9

"Therefore when Jesus perceived that they were about to come and take Him by force to make Him king, He departed again to the mountain by Himself alone." *(John 6:15)*

Food as a Bait:

Is your church or ministry struggling to attract the crowd to come to your meetings? Introduce free feeding and see the result. Feeding people and giving away free food attracts the crowd, and if not well monitored, it may become the enemy's bait to distract attention from the real objectives of the church or ministry.

Jesus's ministry was already attracting the crowd due to the miraculous signs. But as soon as He added another dimension to the miracles, multiplying food to feed the crowd, (John 6:1–14), His approval rating went so high that people wanted to forcefully crown Him as the king. Food that was intended for the good of the crowd has now turned into a weapon of the enemy to change the mission of Christ.

From that moment, the Lord had to retreat and refocus. His message changed from meeting the temporary needs of the multitude to addressing their eternal need of salvation.

So be careful when using food to attract people, and beware how you're attracted by food into a meeting. The eternal need of salvation is greater than the temporal need of the stomach.

Food is a blessing, but don't let it become a bait.

Have a happy day **loaded** with God's **blessings**!

LIVING WORD for TODAY—September 10:

LOADED with DAILY BLESSINGS (Ps. 68:19)-#254

FOOD—10

"Then the twelve summoned the multitude of the disciples and said, 'It is not desirable that we should leave the word of God and serve tables.'" (Acts 6:2)

Food as a Bait

Ministry of food is good and desirable in the church or in the community of God's people.

After the church was inaugurated by the Holy Spirit on the Day of Pentecost, the number of Jesus's disciples grew in Jerusalem as many worshipers who had come from various regions thought the world would end, and Jesus was about to come back and establish His kingdom in Jerusalem. Hence, they refused to go back to their regions and stayed in Jerusalem. This large crowd of disciples became a management burden to the twelve apostles, especially in the distribution of food. Earlier, they were eating "their food with gladness and simplicity of heart" (Acts 2:46). But it didn't take too long before the enemy used food distribution to divert their minds from the eternal Lord to their temporal need. A happy, Spirit-filled, and loving community of disciples soon became a contentious community.

If food was strong enough to turn the attention of the early disciples of Christ, under the leadership of the twelve apostles from their common goal, then we need to handle food and its ministry with a great care and under the power of the Holy Spirit.

That's what the apostles did. They appointed ministers with apostolic gifts to be in charge of food ministry.

Let us see food as God's blessing to us and use it to advance the gospel of Jesus Christ instead of allowing the enemy to use it as his bait to distract people from the Lord.

Have a nice day/evening LOADED with His BLESSINGS!

LIVING WORD for TODAY—September 11:

LOADED with DAILY BLESSINGS (Ps. 68:19)-#255

FOOD—11

"But food does not commend us to God; for neither if we eat are we the better, nor if we do not eat are we the worse." (1 Cor. 8:8)

Food as a Bait:

God gave us food to sustain us; hence, good nutrition is essential to the health of the body.

But foods are being used as a spiritual bait by the devil to connect people with idols. Every cultic religion serves foods in their worship meetings. Some even have certain types of foods they freely share in a particular day of the week. This was the backdrop of the epistle to the Corinthian Christians by Paul. The question whether to eat foods offered to idols was asked since the converts were surrounded by idol shrines.

Paul's answer was to downplay the importance of food in the Christian relationship to God. Unlike the pagan gods, our God does not use food to entice and draw us closer to Him. Food is good for our health, but does not draw us closer to God. Our faith and contrition draw us closer to Him. So we don't use food as baits to entice people to worship Jesus Christ, but as a necessity for physical health as we eat in moderation.

Have a great day/evening **loaded** with God's **blessings!**

LIVING WORD for TODAY—September 12:

LOADED with DAILY BLESSINGS (Ps. 68:19)-#256

FOOD—12

"Therefore concerning the eating of things offered to idols, we know that an idol is nothing in the world, and that there is no other God but one.
For even if there are so-called gods, whether in heaven or on earth (as there are many gods and many lords),
yet for us there is one God, the Father, of whom are all things, and we for Him; and one Lord Jesus Christ, through whom are all things, and through whom we live." (1 Cor. 8:4–6)

Food as a Bait:

Food is good and a blessing from God. But what about foods being offered to idols? Can Christians eat them?

These questions may not be relevant to the Christians who live in the United States and some parts of the Western world. But there are many Christians living in communities around the world where idol worship is still predominant and foods are always offered as part of worshiping them.

Here are some scriptural principles to guide Christians living in the Gentile societies.

Principle of:

- Knowledge-idols are nothing;
- Love-God and our neighbors;
- Worship- only one God;
- Faith in the Lordship of Jesus;
- Avoiding demonic influences;
- Witnessing Christ to others;
- Edification to weak believers;
- Non-compromising our faith with demon worship;
- Eating with a clear conscience; and
- Eating to glorify God.

These principles are taken from 1 Corinthians 8 and 10. Please read the two chapters for more understanding on the topic.

Have a happy day **loaded** with His **blessings**!

LIVING WORD for TODAY—September 13

LOADED with DAILY BLESSINGS (Ps. 68:19)-#257

FOOD—13

"Eat whatever is sold in the meat market, asking no questions for conscience' sake; for 'the earth is the LORD's and all its fullness.'" (1 Cor. 10:25–26)

Food as a Bait:

In his final instructions to the believers in Corinth, Apostle Paul gave a freedom to buy and eat the meat being sold in their market, whether it was offered to idols or not, because all the earth and its fullness belong to the **Lord**.

There is, however, a difference between sitting in the idol temple to wine and dine with the pagans and buying meat offered to idols in the meat market for food. Christians in Corinth were to avoid the former but freed to do the latter.

The implication to us is the same. Let us use caution in exercising our freedom in Christ in whatever we do and how we gather together in parties with our unbelieving families and friends. Our presence among them should represent Christ as a light in darkness.

May the Lord help us to shine brighter in the midst of darkness around us.

Have a lovely day/night **loaded** with His **blessings!**

LIVING WORD for TODAY—September 14:

LOADED with DAILY BLESSINGS (Ps. 68:19)-#258

FOOD—14

*"...forbidding to marry, and commanding to abstain from foods which God cre-
ated to be received with thanksgiving by those who believe and know the truth.
For every creature of God is good, and nothing is to be refused if it is received with
thanksgiving; for it is sanctified by the word of God and prayer." (1 Tim. 4:1–5)*

Our Attitudes toward Food:

1. All foods are to be received with thanksgiving.

One of the signs of the last days is the rising of many false religions. Many
of these are with Christian roots and came out of the church. The devil has
never ceased to destroy the church from within. Hence, his religious demons
are busy day and night to mix the Christian truths with some heretical poi-
sonous doctrines.

Consider it a doctrine of demons in any teaching or ministry, which:

- Is in biblical words but not in practice;
- Forbids anyone to get married;
- Sets forms and rituals in worship meetings;
- Sets rules for garments and dress with certain colors to be worn;
- Uses extra-biblical materials for doctrines;
- Sets works above the grace of God to be saved;
- Idolizes and worships its leaders; and
- Sets laws to abstain from certain foods.

The Christian attitude toward food is to accept them with thanksgiving as
God's creation and enjoy the ones we love to eat in moderation.

To be continued.

Have a great day/night with His **loaded blessings!**

LIVING WORD for TODAY—September 15:

LOADED with DAILY BLESSINGS (Ps. 68:19)-#259

FOOD—15

"For every creature of God is good, and nothing is to be refused if it is received with thanksgiving; for it is sanctified by the word of God and prayer." (1 Tim. 4:4–5)

Our Attitudes toward Food:

2. Foods grown naturally are good because they are God's creation given to mankind's sustenance on earth. But foods are being mass produced by genetic mutations in our world today to meet the nutritional needs of the vast growing human populations. The implications of this to our health will be left to the nutritional experts to determine.

But ethically speaking, all natural foods are clean, sanctified, and approved by God. What about certain meats and fishes considered to be unclean in the Old Testament Bible? Are these dietary laws bidding on Christians? The answer to these questions is well answered by our Lord in the Gospels and His apostle, Paul, in the Epistles. We shall consider this in the next study.

Our attitudes toward foods in general, however, as Christians, should be positive.

All natural foods are created by God and good for consumption. Let us receive foods we're accustomed to in our different cultures with prayer and thanksgiving to God who is the Giver.

Have a pleasant day/evening **loaded** with His **blessings!**

LIVING WORD for TODAY—September 16:

LOADED with DAILY BLESSINGS (Ps. 68:19)-#260

FOOD—16

"However, you may slaughter and eat meat within all your gates, whatever your heart desires, according to the blessing of the LORD your God which He has given you; the unclean and the clean may eat of it, of the gazelle and the deer alike." (Deut. 12:15)

Our Attitudes toward Food:

1. All foods are to be received with thanksgiving;
2. Foods grown naturally are good because they are God's creation; and
3. All meats are clean and none should be declared unclean by Christians.

Leviticus chapter 11 contains all the clean and unclean meats, fishes, and insects to be eaten and forbidden by God to the Israelites while they were in the desert on their way to the Promised Land. God gave these dietary rules because of the poor hygienic condition of their environment. However, these rules were to be abolished after they might have settled in the Promised Land. But for some reason, the Jewish religious leaders continued to impose these dietary laws upon their adherents and turned them to be part of their religious laws.

Jesus did not support them as He declared all foods clean (Mark 7:14–23).

Peter, the apostle, was rebuked by the Lord in his vision for holding on to the Jewish dietary laws.

Paul, the apostle, commanded Christians in Corinth to eat whatever is sold in the meat market (1 Cor. 10:25).

So Christians are free to eat any food they enjoy eating without guilt or condemnation.

Have a great day/night **loaded** with God's **blessings**!

LIVING WORD for TODAY—September 17:

LOADED with DAILY BLESSINGS (Ps. 68:19)-#261

FOOD—17

"Therefore let us not judge one another anymore, but rather resolve this, not to put a stumbling block or a cause to fall in our brother's way.

I know and am convinced by the Lord Jesus that there is nothing unclean of itself, but to him who considers anything to be unclean, to him it is unclean." (Rom. 14:13–14)

Our Attitudes toward Food:

4. Christians should live with a non-judgmental attitude toward others who live with dietary rules.

This is important because not everyone we relate to has the same conviction as we do regarding foods. Hence, we should consider dietary rules as non-essential in our Christian beliefs and don't allow it to cause division in the body, Apostle Paul deals with "doubtful things" in 1 Corinthians 14, and food is one of them. Please read the chapter.

We must be convinced and stand on a solid foundation of our faith and salvation in Christ Jesus. But we should also leave rooms for people to grow in faith and knowledge at their own pace. Christ died and rose for all; He is also coming back to judge all. Let us leave the judgment to Him but continue to grow in His love for others.

Have a beautiful day **loaded** with His **blessings!**

LIVING WORD for TODAY—September 18:

LOADED with DAILY BLESSINGS (Ps. 68:19)-#262

FOOD—18

"Therefore I say to you, do not worry about your life, what you will eat or what you will drink; nor about your body, what you will put on. Is not life more than food and the body more than clothing?" (Matt. 6:25)

Our Attitudes toward Food:

5. Worry-free life; the Lord was concerned about humans' well-being by creating food. Therefore, He commands us to live a worry-free life about food.

One of the marks that distinguishes Christians from Gentiles is Christians trust the Lord to take care of them and their needs, while the Gentiles struggle with their efforts to meet their own needs.

If we worry about our lives and needs, we're living like the Gentiles, and the Lord is saying to us, "Stop worrying and start living." All the provisions we need in life had already been created by God before we were born. We, as the crown of His creation, have no cause to lack. So live a worry-free life and let the Creator of the universe take care of you.

Worry leads to anxiety, anxiety leads to stress, and stress leads to premature aging and an early grave. You can live better by trusting the Lord.

Life is more than food.

Have a peaceful day **loaded** with His **blessings**!

LIVING WORD for TODAY—September 19:

LOADED with DAILY BLESSINGS (Ps. 68:19)-#263

FOOD—19

"Do not mix with winebibbers,
Or with gluttonous eaters of meat, For the drunkard and the glutton will come
to poverty, And drowsiness will clothe a man with rags." (Prov. 23:20–21)

Our Attitudes toward Food:

    6.   Avoid overeating, but eat to satisfaction.

The Bible says much to warn us of the sin of glutton. Sometimes when we've been very hungry and found the food we love to eat, we could be tempted to eat too much, which might not be good for the body. So the rule is self control in eating food. "Have you found honey? Eat only as much as you need. Lest you be filled with it and vomit" (Prov. 25:16).

Food is good and a blessing from the Lord to satisfy our hunger and make our bodies function, but overindulging in it is sinful with adverse health consequences.

So let us heed God's warnings and eat moderately to be healthy and live long.

"The righteous eats to the satisfying of his soul,

But the stomach of the wicked shall be in want" (Prov. 13:25).

Have a great day **loaded** with God's **blessings!**

LOADED with DAILY BLESSINGS (Ps. 68:19)-#264

FOOD—20

"So He said to them, 'When you pray, say,
Our Father in heaven,
Hallowed be Your name.
Your kingdom come.
Your will be done
On earth as it is in heaven.
Give us day by day our daily bread." (Luke 11:2–3)

Our Attitudes toward Food:

7. Pray for God's provisions of food. We must not take food for granted when we see it available. We need to appreciate its source. Since our Heavenly Father God is the Provider of food, our Lord taught us to pray daily for His provisions of food to us.

It's also worth noting how our Lord viewed daily provision of food as a priority on the scale of human needs. It is the first request to be made in prayer after adoration and praying for the Kingdom and the will of God on earth.

God wants us to have food in abundance, so He urges us to ask Him for our daily supply. If you lack food, maybe it's because you're not praying for it.

The Lord urges you to "ask, and it will be given to you; seek, and you will find; knock and it will be opened to you" (Luke 11:9–13).

May God, the Giver of all good things, provide for your daily supplies of food and all the necessities of life throughout your earthly journey.

Have a lovely day/night **loaded** with His **blessings**!

LIVING WORD for TODAY—September 21:

LOADED with DAILY BLESSINGS (Ps. 68:19)-#265

FOOD—21

"But He answered and said, 'It is written, 'Man shall not live by bread alone, but by every word that proceeds from the mouth of God.'" (Matt. 4:4)

Our Attitudes toward Food:

8. Do not live to eat, but eat to live. Food is an essential necessity for life, but it is not all about living. There are times when we ought to deny ourselves of food to focus on God and listen to His directions for our lives.

That's what Jesus Christ did before He started His public redemptive ministry. He fasted without food for forty days and forty nights. The devil saw His need for food and came to tempt Him to perform a miracle of food to satisfy His fleshly need. The Lord simply answered the devil with the Word of God as it is written in Deuteronomy 8:3. Note that the Lord used the same context of the Scripture with which the devil used to tempt Him for the miracle of manna to answer him. That was the power of the spoken word of God quoted from the written Word.

If we're going to succeed in overcoming the devil in our lives, we must learn to use this secret weapon of the specific spoken word of God as our Lord did.

But as He said to His disciples, "This kind can come out by nothing but prayer and fasting" (Mark 9:29). He is saying the same to us today.

So eat food for physical strength, but there are times when we deny ourselves of food for spiritual strength. Let us apply this principle to our spiritual warfare against the enemy.

Have a victorious day **loaded** with God's **blessings!**

LIVING WORD for TODAY—September 22:

LOADED with DAILY BLESSINGS (Ps. 68:19)-#266

FOOD—22

"Do not labor for the food which perishes, but for the food which endures to everlasting life, which the Son of Man will give you, because God the Father has set His seal on Him." (John 6:27)

Our Attitudes toward Food:

9.   Don't work all your life just for food and the necessities of life, but make living for Jesus Christ your priority in life.

Our lives would be totally different positively if the same energy and effort we spent in seeking for wealth were directed in serving the Lord and His kingdom. That doesn't mean we all quit our jobs and go into the full-time preaching ministry. But it means representing the Lord and His kingdom in our various vocational callings. Love God with His Word to control our thoughts and actions, and demonstrate His love to others around us.

When the Lord's priority becomes our priority, we'll never lack any of His blessings, including food.

"But seek first the kingdom of God and His righteousness, and all these things shall be added to you" (Matt. 6:33).

"Do not overwork to be rich; because of your own understanding, cease!" (Prov. 23:4-5).

Have a great day/evening **loaded** with God's **blessings**!

LIVING WORD for TODAY—September 24:

LOADED with DAILY BLESSINGS (Ps. 68:19)-#267

FOOD—23

"Foods for the stomach and the stomach for foods, but God will destroy both it and them. Now the body is not for sexual immorality but for the Lord, and the Lord for the body." (1 Cor. 6:13)

Our Attitudes toward Food:

    10. Foods and the stomach are not eternal but will come to an end.

Whatever physical pleasures we derive from foods now should be regarded as temporal and must not rule our lives. In the biblical text above, Paul compares foods with sex as physical pleasures and draws a conclusion of the sanctity of the Christian's body as belonging to the Lord. While food and sex are good and blessings from the Lord, they must be enjoyed within the framework of His control. Because He owns us, we have no freedom to use His blessings and our bodies anyway we like.

The bottom line is whatever we do or enjoy in our physical bodies, we must do them to glorify the Lord and not our flesh (1Cor. 10:31), knowing that this body of flesh that we live in now will be destroyed one day. But our souls live on.

Let us live with the eternity of our souls in view.

These ten rules should guide our attitudes toward food and physical pleasures in general.

Have a beautiful day/night **loaded** with His **blessings**!

LIVING WORD for TODAY—September 24:

LOADED with DAILY BLESSINGS (Ps. 68:19)-#268

FOOD—24

"I have heard the complaints of the children of Israel. Speak to them, saying, 'At twilight you shall eat meat, and in the morning you shall be filled with bread. And you shall know that I am the LORD your God.'" (Exod. 16:12)

What about Supernatural Foods?

The Bible is full of lists of different kinds of food people of old ate. In fact, many of the food items we eat today were mentioned in the Bible. But there were some foods that were supernaturally provided by God that are no longer in existence.

For example, where is the fruit of the knowledge of good and evil that Adam and Eve ate and brought sins into the world? And what about the fruit of the tree of life? These are some of the supernatural foods out of our reach today.

There are also foods of the angels God Himself provided divinely for His people in times of need. Manna was rained down from heaven for forty years, the bread of heaven and the food of the angels. It was supernaturally provided to feed His people in their wilderness journey. (Ps. 78:23–25). They ate this heavenly bread for forty years, and none of them was feeble nor sick. This bread was fully loaded with all the nutrition to keep them healthy. God even added meat to the bread by raining quails from the wind (Exod. 16:13; Ps. 78:26–29).

The food God divinely provides are healthy, satisfying, and prolong life. While we cannot get His supernatural food today, we can, however, invoke His presence into our food and water daily at mealtime so He can fill them with His nutritional blessings as He promised in His Word.

May we be fed daily by the Bread of heaven and be healthy all the days of our lives here on earth.

Have a great day **loaded** with His **blessings!**

LIVING WORD for TODAY—September 25:

LOADED with DAILY BLESSINGS (Ps. 68:19)-#269

FOOD—25

"Get away from here and turn eastward, and hide by the Brook Cherith, which flows into the Jordan.

And it will be that you shall drink from the brook, and I have commanded the ravens to feed you there."(1 Kings 17:3–4)

What about Supernatural Foods?

God is real and intervenes in humans' affairs. He provides natural foods, and when humans' disobedience disrupts His natural orders to produce the resources needed for our survival, He miraculously comes to the aid of His people.

That was the situation in Israel during the time of Elijah, the prophet. King Ahab and Jezebel, his queen, had turned the nation away from Yahweh God to serve a pagan god Baal. God sent His prophet Elijah to pronounce a judgment of drought, which ravaged the land for three years. But during the famine, the Lord sustained Elijah by supernatural means.

First, he was sent to a brook where he could drink water, and while there, God used the ravens to feed him with bread and meat for breakfast and dinner. These were supernatural meals from God's kitchen to feed His servant for many days during the severe famine.

Are you worried about your daily provisions during the economic hardships brought about due to the current pandemic? Have faith in the Lord. You're covered by His divine providence. He will sustain and nourish you by whatever it takes.

"You shall drink from the brook, and I have commanded the ravens to feed you there" (1 Kings 17:4).

Have a pleasant day **loaded** with His **blessings**!

LIVING WORD for TODAY—September 26:

LOADED with DAILY BLESSINGS (Ps. 68:19)-#270

FOOD—26

"Arise, go to Zarephath, which belongs to Sidon, and dwell there. See, I have commanded a widow there to provide for you."(1 Kings 17:9)

What about Supernatural Foods?

From the ravens to the widow of Zarephath, notice that these were the unthinkable poor agents God used to supernaturally provide for His servant Elijah in the time of famine in Israel.

While the ravens brought prepared hot meals from the unknown kitchen of God, the widow's faith was united with Elijah's faith to produce a miracle of surplus food for their daily provisions throughout the famine.

"For thus says the LORD God of Israel: 'The bin of flour shall not be used up, nor shall the jar of oil run dry, until the day the LORD sends rain on earth.' So she went away and did according to the word of Elijah; and she, and he and her household ate for many days. The bin of flour was not used up, nor did the jar of oil run dry, according to the word of the LORD which He spoke by Elijah" (1 Kings 17:14–16).

Whatever it takes, God will always take care of His own, regardless of the world's economy. Only believe in His unlimited reservoirs of provisions; trust and obey His Word wherever you are and whatever your needs may be. The Lord will supernaturally make a way for you. He is Jehovah Jireh, the **Lord** who provides.

Have a refreshing day **loaded** with His **blessings**!

LIVING WORD for TODAY—September 27:

LOADED with DAILY BLESSINGS (Ps. 68:19)-#271

FOOD—27

"Then as he lay and slept under a broom tree, suddenly an angel touched him, and said to him, 'Arise and eat.'
Then he looked, and there by his head was a cake baked on coals, and a jar of water. So he ate and drank, and lay down again.
And the angel of the LORD came back the second time, and touched him and said, 'Arise and eat, because the journey is too great for you.'
So he arose, and ate and drank; and he went in the strength of that food forty days and forty nights as far as Horeb, the mountain of God. (1 Kings 19:5–8)

What about Supernatural Foods?

The life of Elijah, the prophet, exemplified the Christian life—a life of conflicts and conquests. He was called to lead a backslidden nation back to God. In his attempt to do this, he faced much opposition from the government of the day. In the midst of the judgment God brought upon the nation, Elijah had to be protected.

Note that in three instances, God had to feed and sustain him by supernatural food; first, by the ravens with hot meals, morning and evening, and second, by the miraculous supplies of food in a widow's house for days. In each of these cases, it was God who directed Elijah to where he was to be taken care of.

But in the third time, God did not direct Elijah to go where the angel fed him. It was out of fear for his life because of the threat of a woman, Jezebel, who wanted to kill him. With all his anointing to bring fire down from heaven, and the execution of 450 Baal prophets, Elijah was afraid of a woman and ran for his life. But while he was tired and resting under the tree, God sent an angel to attend to his physical needs. God provided for his refreshments through the angel's cake and water. This cake was loaded with divine nutritional ingredients that it energized Elijah to walk for forty days and forty nights.

God knows how to take care of us, even when our faith is weak and we're about to give up. God is faithful, and He will sustain us till the end through His presence and provisions in our journeys of faith. So don't ever give up.

Have a beautiful day **loaded** with His **blessings!**

LIVING WORD for TODAY—September 28:

LOADED with DAILY BLESSINGS (Ps. 68:19)-#272

FOOD—28

"But the servant said, 'What? Shall I set this before one hundred men?'
He said again, 'Give it to the people, that they may eat, for thus says the LORD:
'They shall eat and have some left over.'
So he set it before them; and they ate and had some left over, according to the
word of the LORD." (2 Kings 4:43–44)

What about Supernatural Foods?

One of the miracles common to the men of God in the Bible was the supernatural provision of foods.

We see this with Moses leading Israelites through the wilderness for forty years to the Promised Land. This also occurred in the ministries of Elijah, Elisha, Daniel, John the Baptist, and our Lord Jesus Christ.

In 2 Kings 4, the chapter starts with the miracle of divine provision of oil to pay off a widow's debt, and ends with divine multiplication of twenty loaves of bread to feed one hundred men with leftovers.

The abiding lesson we learn from each of these events is the inexhaustive provisions of God through all the seasons of life in which we may find ourselves. God is never limited by famines, crisis, little, or nothing. He controls cattle on a thousand hills, and nothing is impossible for Him.

Are you in need, in debt, or in a crisis and about to lose everything you have? Cry to the Lord in faith, believing that He loves you and will never leave you devastated. He says: "I will never leave you nor forsake you" (Hebrews 13:5).

So put your trust in the Lord and He will sustain you.

Have a great day **loaded** with God's **blessings!**

LIVING WORD for TODAY—September 29:

LOADED with DAILY BLESSINGS (Ps. 68:19)-#273

FOOD—29

"Now John himself was clothed in camels hair, with a leather belt around his waist; and his food was locust and wild honey." (Matt. 3:4)

What about Supernatural Foods?

John the Baptist was an unusual man. He was strong, rugged, and fearless. He lived in the wilderness among the wild beasts. He clothed himself with camel's hair and a leather belt around his waist.

His food? Locusts and wild honey. This man was born into a wealthy priestly family and had access to all the food and luxuries of his time. Yet, he chose a lonely and solitude life. He was used by God as the only prophet who was privileged to baptize our Lord Jesus Christ and introduce Him to the public as the Redeemer of mankind.

The food he ate in the desert to be so healthy and strong was not ordinary but supernatural. Locusts and wild honey could not have made him so strong without divine ingredients.

So our staple meals may be full of various cuisines or just a simple diet, but the Lord's blessing on them makes all the difference to keep us healthy, nourished, and strong. May the Lord bless your food and water to make them supply all the nutrients you need to be healthy and strong through life on earth.

Have a healthy day **loaded** with God's **blessings**!

LIVING WORD for TODAY—September 30:

LOADED with DAILY BLESSINGS (Ps. 68:19)-#274

FOOD—30

"And as they were eating, Jesus took bread, blessed and broke it , and gave it to them and said, 'Take, eat; this is My body.' Then He took the cup, and when He had given thanks He gave it to them, and they all drank from it.
And He said to them, 'This is My blood of the new covenant, which is shed for many. Assuredly, I say to you, I will no longer drink of the fruit of the vine until that day when I drink it new in the kingdom of God.'" (Mark 14:22–25)

Eating and Drinking with the Lord:

As we conclude our meditations on food, let us be reminded that our eating and drinking will not end here on earth but continue in heaven. The Bible says, "the kingdom of God is not eating and drinking, but righteousness and peace and joy in the Holy Spirit." However, there are many references that also indicate the redeemed of the Lord will eat and dine with Him in heaven.

Here are some references:

- Jesus statement at the Last Supper (Mark 14:22–26);
- Jesus ate breakfast with His disciples by the sea after His resurrection (John 21:12–15);
- The marriage supper of the Lamb (Rev. 19:9); and
- Eating from the fruit of the tree of life (Rev. 22:1–2, 14).

So always remember that while we cannot limit the kingdom of God to just eating and drinking, they are going to be an important part of our functions with the Lord in heaven.

So eat and live now with this perspective, and be ready for His return to take us home to be with Him at the end of our journey on earth. We shall live and eat with Christ forever!

Have a glorious day **loaded** with His **blessings**!

Living Word for **today** with James E. Temidara

OCTOBER —FREEDOM

LIVING WORD for TODAY—OCTOBER 1:

LOADED with DAILY BLESSINGS (Ps. 68:19)-#275

FREEDOM—1

"Therefore if the Son makes you free, you shall be free indeed." (John 8:36)

You are welcome to the last quarter of the year. While we must always thank God for all the daily blessings received so far, we are also eager to unpack His manifold blessings still ahead of us.

The package of blessings of God for us to open in this month of October is **freedom**. Freedom is one of the great blessings of life God has given to all creatures. Life is never the same in captivity. All creatures want to be free to live, free to act the ways they want to act, speak the ways they want to speak, think freely, associate with others they're comfortable with, eat what they want to eat, live where they want to live, and worship who they want to adore.

While freedom is a gift of the Creator to all creations, not all are free, and some who were once free have lost their freedoms and are now in bondage due to abuses.

Since this is a broad subject affecting all areas of life, we would limit our thoughts to the biblical principles and draw some applications for our benefits.

Fundamentally, our freedom as Christians is rooted in biblical truths and in Christ Jesus. He makes us free by the power of His Word. Hence, He says: "And you shall know the truth, and the truth shall make you free" (John 8:32).

May Christ, by His power, set us free from all hindrances to enjoy the true freedom that is inherent in us.

Have a great day **loaded** with His **blessings!**

LIVING WORD for TODAY—OCTOBER 2:

LOADED with DAILY BLESSINGS (Ps. 68:19)-#276

FREEDOM—2

"Therefore if the Son makes you free, you shall be free indeed." (John 8:36)

Freedom of Choice:

Only those who have been through bondage and knew it understand and appreciate freedom. There are many people in the world in bondage without knowing. They rejoice and glory in their ignorance and remain in bondage.

There are many areas in which people are in bondage. Some don't know they're in bondage, and others who know don't know how to be free or seek deliverance from the wrong sources.

When does bondage really begin?

Generally speaking, humans' bondage started with the Fall in the Garden of Eden (Gen. 3).

Everything that manifests in the physical has a spiritual root; hence, it is important to understand cause and effect of human bondages.

Bondage started with the choice our first parents (Adam and Eve) made by willingly disobeying God, their Maker, and choosing to obey the deceiver, the devil. Since then, everyone born into the world is born with spiritual bondage to the devil (John 8:44). Therefore, humans' bondage is spiritual, and true freedom must be spiritual to start with.

So Jesus Christ went into the root of the problems of His audience by proclaiming: "Therefore if the Son makes you free, you shall be free indeed" (John 8:36). This is not a religious statement but relational and spiritual.

May the Son of God set us free from all bondages, known and unknown.

Have a happy day **loaded** with God's **blessings**!

LIVING WORD for TODAY—OCTOBER 3:

LOADED with DAILY BLESSINGS (Ps. 68:19-#277

FREEDOM—3

"And the LORD God commanded the man, saying, 'Of every tree of the garden you may freely eat;
'but of the tree of the knowledge of good and evil you shall not eat, for in the day that you eat of it you shall surely die.'" (Gen. 2:16–17)

Freedom of Choice:

Humans are created as free moral agents, capable to determine their own fates. This power of choice makes us distinct from other living creatures.

In the creation narrative, God planted a beautiful garden without man's efforts and placed him in it to take care of it, and eat all the beautiful fruits there, except one: the fruit of the knowledge of good and evil. With a specific command, man was allowed to choose. But when temptation came, man used his power of choice to disobey his Maker and obey his enemy, the devil.

If there's one thing that is capable of causing humans trouble in the world, it's the ability to make right choices.

Because human's will power has been captured by the enemy and is distracted from the right directions, it needs the liberating power of the Son of God.

There's no substitute to the proclamation of the gospel of Jesus Christ to set mankind free and redirect the will to make right choices.

"For I am not ashamed of the gospel of Christ, for it is the power of God to salvation for everyone who believes..." (Rom. 1:16).

So our hope for freedom to make right choices is in the gospel of Christ. Let us proclaim it to all mankind without fear or favor.

Have a great day/night with His **loaded blessings!**

LIVING WORD for TODAY—OCTOBER 4:

LOADED with DAILY BLESSINGS (Ps. 68:19)-#278

FREEDOM—4

"I call heaven and earth as witnesses today against you, that I have set before you life and death, blessing and cursing, therefore choose life, that both you and your descendants may live;

'that you may love the LORD your God, that you may obey His voice and that you may cling to Him, for He is your life and the length of your days...'" *(Deut. 30:19–30)*

Freedom of Choice:

The power to make choices is part of the human makeup.

Children may be raised in the same home and by the same parents, yet, each of them would make a different choice or go a different path. This was the case with Cain and Abel (Gen. 4). Both were raised by the same parents and in the same environment, but Abel chose to be a righteous worshiper of God, while his brother Cain chose to be a murderer and fugitive.

Therefore, the constant scriptural appeal to us to make the right choices. The best choice to make in life is to love the Lord our God, obey His words, and hang onto Him. "For He is your life and length of days" (Deut. 30:20).

May the Lord, by His Spirit, empower us to use our freedom to love Him and follow His pathway, all the days of our life.

Have a beautiful day **loaded** with His **blessings**!

LIVING WORD for TODAY—OCTOBER 5:

LOADED with DAILY BLESSINGS (Ps. 68:19)-#279

FREEDOM—5

"And if it seems evil to you to serve the LORD, choose for yourselves this day whom you will serve, whether the gods which your fathers served that were on the other side of the River, or the gods of the Amorites, in whose land you dwell. But as for me and my house, we will serve the LORD." (*Josh. 24:15*)

Freedom of Choice:

God is not an imposter who forces Himself upon the mankind He created. He is the God of love, and love does not impose itself on others.

After settling the Israelites in their Promised Land, He allowed them to exercise their newfound freedom to choose who would be their Lord. Joshua 24 gives a summary of all that God had done for them by fighting their battles and giving them freely the prosperity others had labored for. Joshua, their leader, seeing the propensity of their hearts to go the wrong way, gave them the freedom to choose whom they would serve. Unfortunately, after Joshua's generation, the people used their God-given prosperity to worship other gods.

Exercising freedom wrongly has its consequences. It leads to losing the freedom and being enslaved by internal and external forces contrary to our wellbeing.

God's command to the Israelites is true to us today as it was to them: "Now therefore, fear the LORD, serve Him in sincerity and truth..." (Josh. 24:14).

I pray we will use all the blessings and freedom given to us by the Lord to love and serve Him with all our strength.

Have a lovely day **loaded** with His **blessings**!

LIVING WORD for TODAY—OCTOBER 6

LOADED with DAILY BLESSINGS (Ps. 68:19)-#280

FREEDOM—6

"'You shall fear the LORD your God, and serve Him, and shall take oaths in His name. You shall not go after other gods, the gods of the peoples who are all around you...'" (Deut. 6:13–15)

Freedom with Restriction:

Unrestricted freedom can be dangerous. God is the Giver of human freedom, but with restrictions. Freedom without restraints is like driving a vehicle without a wheel control and brakes. The end result would be disastrous.

So God blessed mankind with freedom, but with boundaries.

The problem with our human nature is we don't want control. We like to use our freedoms to do whatever we want to do. But the Giver of our freedoms says, "No."

The Bible says, "The LORD your God is a jealous God among you" (Deut. 6:15).

He doesn't want to compete with idols in our lives. He alone deserves the first place in our lives. As long we let Him pilot our lives, we are safe with our freedoms.

Do you have an idol taking the place of God in your life? Whatever or whoever you love most could become a competing god trying to dominate your life. Say to that idol the living Word that Jesus uttered to Satan: "...For it is written, 'You shall worship the LORD your God, and Him only you shall serve'" (Luke 4:8).

This is foundational to enjoying your freedom.

Have a great day **loaded** with His **blessings**!

LIVING WORD for TODAY—OCTOBER 7:

LOADED with DAILY BLESSINGS (Ps. 68:19)-#281

FREEDOM—7

"He has shown you, O man, what is good;
And what does the LORD require of you.
But to do justly,
To love mercy,
And to walk humbly with your God?" (Mic. 6:8)

Freedom with Responsibility:

Privileges come with responsibilities. There are requirements the Lord set for us as individuals, families, communities, and as nations as He endows us with freedom. When we begin to violate these requirements, we start abusing our freedom.

Micah, a prophet in Israel centuries before Christ, sums up God's requirements attached to human freedom and blessings in three statements:

- "But to do justly" (justice);
- "To love mercy" (mercy); and
- "...walk humbly before God" (lovingkindness).

When people, families, communities, and nations live carefree of these requirements, there are breakdowns of law and order leading to chaos.

•Human freedom is wrapped up in equal treatments to all (justice);

•Tempering justice with mercy (mercy); and

•Loving others as we love ourselves (humility and love).

There's no law, divine or human, against these standards anywhere.

May God help us to constantly uphold these standard requirements as we exercise and enjoy our freedom daily in whatever position of responsibilities we may find ourselves.

Have a happy day/evening **loaded** with God's **blessing** of freedom!

LIVING WORD for TODAY—OCTOBER 8:

LOADED with DAILY BLESSINGS (Ps. 68:19)-#282

FREEDOM—8

"Who are you to judge another's servant? To his own master he stands or falls. Indeed, he will be made to stand, for God is able to make him stand." (Rom. 14:4)

Freedom with Respect:

One of the problems in the world is imposing our freedoms on others. While there are fundamental rules of human freedom applicable universally, there are, however, some aspects of freedom limited to each person without interfering with others' freedom. For example, one person may enjoy loud music, while this could be a nuisance to someone else. There are tons of similar non-essential issues relating to personal freedom from place to place and from person to person, which are causing frictions all over.

The rule of thumb in dealing with these issues is respect. We need to respect individual's freedom and leave room for growth in people's lives, and also accommodate their peculiarities while affirming our own freedom.

The Christian non-judgmental attitude is admonished in the Bible to sustain peaceful coexistence everywhere we may find ourselves.

Let us bear in mind that we're called as Christians to: "Pursue peace with all people, and holiness, without which no one will see the Lord" (Heb. 12:14). Let us use our freedom to foster peace and respect with others who may differ from us in many areas.

Have a pleasant day/night with God's **loaded blessings!**

LIVING WORD for TODAY—OCTOBER 9:

LOADED with DAILY BLESSINGS (Ps. 68:19)-#283

FREEDOM—9

"Therefore if the Son makes you free, you shall be free indeed." (John 8:36)

Freedom in Relationship:

The power to be set free from slavery and enjoy the benefits of freedom is not within those who are enslaved but external. A person who falls into a deep well needs someone outside the well on a solid ground to get him or her out.

That is where the Son of God comes into the rescue. All humans were trapped in a deep well of sins, struggling to get out but couldn't. Religions tried, but could not. Rather, they were digging the well deeper. But when Christ came, He did for us what we couldn't do by human effort. He threw the rope down and pulled us out of the deep well of sin and its consequences.

"Christ has redeemed us from the curse of the law, having become a curse for us (for it is written, 'Cursed is everyone who hangs on a tree'), that the blessings of Abraham might come upon the Gentiles in Christ Jesus..." (Gal. 3:13–14).

So it takes being in a relationship with the Son of God to be free and stay free indeed.

Have you received the power of Christ's Sonship to be free? Be in relationship with Him and stay free indeed.

Have a happy day **loaded** with His **blessings!**

LIVING WORD for TODAY—OCTOBER 10:

LOADED with DAILY BLESSINGS (Ps. 68:19)-#284

FREEDOM—10

"That which is born of the flesh is flesh, and that which is born of the Spirit is spirit. 'Do not marvel that I said to you, 'You must be born again.''" (John 3:6–7)

Freedom in Relationship:

• With Christ—

Every person born into this world is born with spiritual bondage that manifests later in life. No matter how cultured, moral, religious, and educated, the chains of spiritual bondage bind and blind us from understanding the realities of spiritual freedom in Christ to function in the kingdom of God.

It takes the miracle of the spiritual birth to break the chains and release us into the kingdom of God. That was why Christ said to a religious teacher Nicodemus that "You must be born again." This miracle occurs when we wholeheartedly accept Christ's sacrifice on the Cross for our sins and by faith, invite Him to rule our hearts as the Savior and Lord.

Our relationship with Him starts the process of deliverance from the bondage of Satan in our lives.

"He has delivered us from the power of darkness and conveyed us into the kingdom of the Son of His love" (Col. 1:13).

Pray that the Holy Spirit of God would initiate you into the relationship with Jesus Christ if you're not sure of being related to Him; receive His gift of eternal life and believe in His promise that He would come into your heart if you invited Him. Thank Him for giving birth to you into His family.

Have a lovely day **loaded** with His **blessings**!

LIVING WORD for TODAY—OCTOBER 11:

LOADED with DAILY BLESSINGS (Ps. 68:19)-#285

FREEDOM—11

"The Spirit of the LORD is upon Me, Because He has anointed Me, To preach the gospel to the poor: He has sent Me to heal the brokenhearted, To proclaim liberty to the captives And recovery of sight to the blind,

To set at liberty those who are oppressed; To proclaim the acceptable year of the LORD." (Luke 4:18–19)

Freedom in Relationship:

• With the Anointed Lord—

Who is Jesus Christ to you?

Just a gentle Savior who came as the Lamb of God to take away your sins and the sins of the world? Yes, He is.

Just a Holy One of God? Yes, He is. A good man who lived to help others? Yes, He was. We can assign many titles to Jesus Christ to make Him our hero. But our Lord is much more than all the titles we may attribute to Him.

He came to the world with a mission.

Isaiah, a prophet in Israel, predicted Christ's mission centuries before He revealed Himself in a small Jewish synagogue in Nazareth to affirm Himself as the fulfillment of Isaiah's prophecy (Isa. 61:1–3; Luke 4:18–19).

The primary purpose of Christ in the world is to set the captive free. Our relationship with Him must always be focused on the freedom He came to give us.

There's nothing more deceptive than the thought of "once free, always free." We're free when we accept the Lord as our Lord and Savior. But we must live in the consciousness of that freedom and affirm it regularly in our lives and situations, or else, the enemy could take advantage of our complacency to enslave us again. "And from the days of John the Baptist until now the kingdom of heaven suffers violence, and the violent take it by force" (Matt. 11:12).

His anointing sets us free. So be free and stay free!

Have a great day/evening **loaded** with His **blessings**!

LIVING WORD for TODAY—OCTOBER 12:

LOADED with DAILY BLESSINGS (Ps. 68:19)-#286

FREEDOM—12

"Then Jesus, being filled with the Holy Spirit, returned from the Jordan and was led by the Spirit into the wilderness..." (Luke 4:1)

Freedom in Relationship:

- With the Holy Spirit
  To live and enjoy the total freedom the Lord gives, one has to be in a constant right relationship with the Holy Spirit.
  Take note of the levels of the operation of the Holy Spirit in the adult life of Jesus Christ our Lord and apply this to the Christian life.

- At His baptism, the Holy Spirit descended upon Him and a voice from heaven confirmed He's the Son of God (Luke 3:22).
  For us, to be children of God, we have to be born by the Spirit and constantly hear His confirmation in our spirit that we're children of God (John 3:6; Rom. 8:16).

- The Lord was filled and led by the Holy Spirit in His temptations by the devil.

For us, "as many as are led by the Spirit of God, these are sons of God" (Rom. 8:14).

Being filled and led by the Holy Spirit is the antidote to being carnally minded.

To be continued.

Be filled and live by the Holy Spirit, and enjoy a life of true freedom!

Have a happy day/evening **loaded** with His **blessings!**

LIVING WORD for TODAY—OCTOBER 13:

LOADED with DAILY BLESSINGS (Ps. 68:19)-#287

FREEDOM—13

"Then Jesus returned in the power of the Spirit to Galilee, and news of Him went out through all the surrounding region." (Luke 4:14)

Freedom in Relationship:

- With the power of the Holy Spirit.
  Knowing and being in relationship with the Person of the Holy Spirit is one thing, and that's where many Christians stop. But moving in the power of the Holy Spirit in our lives and services is a whole different thing.

- After being filled with and led by the Spirit to overcome the devil's temptations, the Lord was filled and moved by the power or anointing of the Holy Spirit in His ministry of deliverance. It was then He could say: "The Spirit of the LORD is upon Me, Because He has anointed Me, To..." (Luke 4:18–19).

The implication of this to us as Christians is the same. We must constantly be sensitive in our relationship with the person of the Holy Spirit in us as He leads and directs our behaviors. But we must also allow Him to flood and move us with His power and fresh anointing in our daily walks and operations to destroy the yokes and bondages of the devil in our lives, as well as through us to others we may encounter (Acts 1:8; 2:1–4; 4:8, 31, 33).

Since it is the anointing that destroys the yoke, we must live under the power and anointing of the Holy Spirit to experience God's total freedom.

May His anointing destroy every yoke of the enemy in your life!

Have a pleasant day **loaded** with His **blessings**!

LIVING WORD for TODAY—OCTOBER 14:

LOADED with DAILY BLESSINGS (Ps. 68:19)-#288

FREEDOM—14

"But if the Spirit of Him who raised Jesus from the dead dwells in you, He who raised Christ from the dead will also give life to your mortal bodies through His Spirit who dwells in you."(Rom. 8:11)

Freedom in Relationship:

- With the quickening power of the Holy Spirit.
  Understanding our true relationship with the Great Comforter and living by it secures our total freedom from all the yokes that bind us with the enemies of our spiritual and physical well-being.
- It was the Holy Spirit who raised Jesus Christ from the dead on the third day after He was buried.
- The same Spirit who lives and operates His power in us as Christians will give liberating life to our mortal bodies and raise us up from the dead to live with Christ in the resurrection bodies forever (1 Cor. 6:14; Rom. 8:11, 18–25).

The Holy Spirit who joins us with Christ is the same Spirit who directs us in our daily journeys of faith and fights our battles through life to eternity.

Only those who are born by the Spirit can be filled and led by the Spirit, and only those who are being led by the Spirit are anointed by the same Spirit, and those who are truly anointed by the Spirit are free from the bondages of the devil.

So live by the Spirit and be totally free!

Have a joyful day **loaded** with God's **blessings**!

LIVING WORD for TODAY—OCTOBER 15:

LOADED with DAILY BLESSINGS (Ps. 68:19)-#289

FREEDOM—15

"How God anointed Jesus of Nazareth with the Holy Spirit and with power, who went about doing good and healing all who were oppressed by the devil, for God was with Him." (Acts 10:38)

Freedom From Bondages:

- Bondage of poverty.

The primary mission of Jesus Christ in the world is to set people free from the yokes of the devil. Since the fall of mankind into sin, the devil has taken over control of humans' minds. He rules and binds them to different things.

Poverty is one of the bondages plaguing mankind everywhere. The first effect of the proclamation of the gospel of Jesus Christ is opening the eyes of the poor. This has to do with their spiritual eyes of understanding, and not just the physical eyes, to see the riches of God all around them. (Eph. 1:18)

Anywhere the gospel is preached and people are receptive to the message, there's always a liberating power that transforms their lives for the better.

The first thing Jesus was anointed to do in the world was: "To preach the gospel to the poor" (Luke 4:18).

Let the message of Christ be firmly established in your heart and live by it day by day. I assure you that, you will see the transformation effect in your life in all dimensions.

May the anointed power of Christ destroy the yoke of poverty in your life and family!

Have a happy day/evening **loaded** with His **blessings**!

LIVING WORD for TODAY—October 16:

LOADED with DAILY BLESSINGS (Ps. 68:19)-#290

FREEDOM—16

"'The Spirit of the LORD is upon Me, Because He has anointed Me, To preach the gospel to the poor;
He has sent Me to heal the brokenhearted,
To proclaim liberty to the captives
And recovery of sight to the blind, To set at liberty those who are oppressed;
To proclaim the acceptable year of the LORD.'" (Luke 4:18–19)

Freedom from Bondages:

- Bondage of poverty.

The gospel of Jesus Christ is the liberating force to deliver people from the bondage of poverty. Poverty accounts for most of the protests going on in the world today. Poverty is more than lack but a mentality; a mentality of accumulation without release or distribution, of keeping people in a state of perpetual servitude. Anywhere there's gross poverty, the people groan for release and deliverance. That is the place for the proclamation of the gospel. That was the condition of the world in which Christ came in to proclaim **freedom**!

That is the world He sent His early disciples to witness and proclaim the same message. That is the world He sends us as Christians today.

Every church or Christian ministry must be measured by the standard of Christ's proclamation of freedom in Luke 4:18–19. Any gospel that does not meet or fulfill this standard is a different or diluted gospel.

Why is there gross poverty in the nations where there's proliferation of churches? Something must be wrong. What is the message of the Christian church to the world?

Let us go back to the basics of the gospel of Jesus Christ.

The good news of Christ is the power of deliverance in any society. Let us proclaim and practice the principles of Christ's gospel and witness its liberating force in people's lives.

Have a peaceful day/night with His **loaded blessings**!

LIVING WORD for TODAY—October 17:

LOADED with DAILY BLESSINGS (Ps. 68:19)-#291

FREEDOM—17

"'The Spirit of the LORD is upon Me,
Because He has anointed Me,
To preach the gospel to the poor;
He has sent Me to heal the brokenhearted...'" (Luke 4:18)

Freedom from Bondages:

- Brokenhearted
  The proclamation of the gospel of Jesus Christ produces results when it is proclaimed with the anointing of the Holy Spirit. It sets people free from the yokes the devil and his agents have bound them with. True Christianity addresses and brings solutions to humans' spiritual bondages, which reflect through their physical felt needs.
- Felt needs of the poor are numerous and unending.
- Poverty in the midst of God's abundance everywhere
- Brokenheartedness, which makes people sigh for relief hopelessly. To be brokenhearted affects human dignity, which is lost through sins, pains, and sufferings physiologically, emotionally, psychologically, and spiritually. Brokenheartedness affects the whole person, and the cure must be holistic, which is only possible through the gospel of Jesus Christ.

It is amazing to note in Psalm 69:20–21 that our Lord was brokenhearted for us on the Cross as part of the price He paid for our deliverance. Therefore, "He heals the brokenhearted And binds up their wounds" (Ps. 147:3).

Let us come to Him daily to be healed and set free from all the wounds inflicted upon us by the world, sin, and Satan.

May the anointing of the Holy Spirit touch every area of pain, grief, and suffering in your life today.

Have a great day **loaded** with His **blessings**!

LIVING WORD for TODAY—OCTOBER 18:

LOADED with DAILY BLESSINGS (Ps. 68:19)-#292

FREEDOM—18

"'The Spirit of the LORD is upon Me,
Because He has anointed Me,
To preach the gospel to the poor;
He has sent Me to heal the brokenhearted,
To proclaim liberty to the captives...'" (Luke 4:18)

Freedom from Bondages:

- Liberty to the captives

The preaching of the gospel is the communication of the truth of God's Word declared through proclamation, teaching, announcement, application, and impartation.

Wherever it is fully preached with the Holy Spirit's anointing, people are liberated and set free from the yokes of sin, self, and Satan with all their products, which manifest openly.

Are you in captivity of anything that is hindering you from enjoying the freedom of God in your life? Let the anointed truth of the gospel of Jesus Christ set you completely free to be who He has made you to be.

"And you shall know the truth, and the truth shall make you free" (John 8:32).

To know the truth, you must commit yourself to listen to the gospel truths being communicated through the Holy Spirit's anointed ministers. Believe and live by the truth and you shall be free from all the snares and chains that hold you captive in the enemy's prison cells.

Have a victorious day **loaded** with His **blessings!**

LIVING WORD for TODAY—OCTOBER 19:

LOADED with DAILY BLESSINGS (Ps. 68:19)-#293

FREEDOM—19

"'The Spirit of the LORD is upon Me,
Because He has anointed Me,
To preach the gospel to the poor;
He has sent Me to heal the brokenhearted,
To proclaim liberty to the captives
And recovery of sight to the blind...'" (Luke 4:18)

Freedom from Bondages:

- Recovery of sight to the blind

People who are physically blind would be willing to pay any price to receive their sights to see. Likewise, those who are spiritually blind know it.

Because everyone born into this world through a woman, beside our Lord Jesus Christ, is born spiritually blind, they cannot see the present realities of the kingdom of God (John 3:3).

Spiritual blindness accounts for cultic practices and religious beliefs all over the world because people are afraid and trying to find their ways to the higher power or the God of heaven for protection. Nothing else can open humans' spiritual eyes other than the power of the gospel, preached under the anointing of the Holy Spirit.

Without the scale being removed, no one can know the Savior and Redeemer of mankind.

So we make it our constant prayers to God for Him to remove the scales from people's spiritual eyes so they can see the Lord, accept Him as their Savior, and be set free. Christianity is an eye-opener to anyone who believes and lives by the truth of the gospel. Opening of spiritual eyes is a necessity to being free, staying free, and continuing to receive the revelation knowledge of Jesus Christ (Eph. 1:17–21).

May the anointing of the Holy Spirit keep your spiritual eyes open to the benefits of your freedom in Christ.

Have a glorious day/night **loaded** with His **blessings!**

"'The Spirit of the LORD is upon Me,
Because He has anointed Me,
To preach the gospel to the poor;
He has sent Me to heal the brokenhearted,
To proclaim liberty to the captives
And recovery of sight to the blind...'" (Luke 4:18)

Freedom from Bondages:

- Freedom to the oppressed

The world is witnessing the rise to power of oppressors and the manifestations of evil rulers everywhere to prepare the stage for the revelation of the evil one called the antichrist.

What has been happening in some parts of the world where the armed military personnel were being ordered by the government to gun down unarmed civilian peaceful protesters and demanding an end to the rule of oppression in their countries could be regarded as barbaric to the core. But this act is a tip of the iceberg on what lies ahead in the world before the second coming of Jesus Christ to end this present political evil age and usher in the eternal reign of righteousness, peace, justice, and love to all mankind.

But while we're still here, awaiting that glorious era, the Lord has commissioned us to proclaim His good news to the oppressed. People who are oppressed are looking up to the civil authorities to deliver them to no avail. When I woke up this morning, I felt like living in the days of Habakkuk, the prophet, in ancient Israel (Hab. 1:2–4).

What is the role of the Christian church in the world of oppression today?

The Christian church should take Christ's commission more seriously. He says, "As the Father has sent Me, I also send you" (John 20:21).

Send us to do what? Form a political party or be in alliance with one around us?

Freedom for the oppressed was why our Lord came and what He died for. Let us not distort nor dilute His message but be empowered by it to proclaim total freedom to those who are oppressed around us.

Have a victorious day **loaded** with His **blessings!**

LIVING WORD for TODAY—OCTOBER 21:

LOADED with DAILY BLESSINGS (Ps. 68:19)-#295

FREEDOM—21

"'The Spirit of the LORD is upon Me,
Because He has anointed Me,
To preach the gospel to the poor;
He has sent Me to heal the brokenhearted,
To proclaim liberty to the captives
And recovery of sight to the blind...'" (Luke 4:18)

Freedom from Bondages:

- Deliverance from oppression

What is oppression?

Oppression can be defined as "the exercise of authority or power in a burdensome, cruel, or unjust manner, an act or instance of oppressing or subjecting to cruel or unjust impositions or restraints...the feeling of being heavily burdened, mentally or physically by troubles, adverse conditions, anxiety, etc." (Google).

This was the condition of the children of Israel in Egypt before God heard their cry and sent Moses to deliver them from the bondage of Pharaoh (Exod. 3:7–10)

It was in this situation of life that people found themselves during the time of Christ, and when He saw their burdens, He was moved with compassion. "But when He saw the multitudes, He was moved with compassion for them, because they were weary, and scattered, like sheep having no shepherd" (Matt. 9:36).

The situation of the world around us today hasn't changed that much but is getting worse. People around us are crying for freedom from oppression. Our answer as Christ's disciples is not political but the power of the gospel, preached under the anointing of the Holy Spirit, to set captives free. The spirit of oppression must be dealt with in the heart before the result can manifest outwardly.

This was how the early church changed their world, and the same power is available to us today. Let us apply the gospel, with the power of the Holy Spirit, to release Christ's freedom to those who are burdened with oppression.

There's a spiritual force that must be dealt with from time to time before any material support can be productive.

May the anointing of the Holy Spirit destroy every yoke of oppression in your life and family and release His freedom upon you today!

Have a great day **loaded** with His **blessings!**

LIVING WORD for TODAY—OCTOBER 22:

LOADED with DAILY BLESSINGS (Ps. 68:19)-#296

FREEDOM—22

"To proclaim the acceptable year of the LORD." (Luke 4:19)

Freedom from Bondages:

- The acceptable year of the **Lord**

The acceptable year of the **Lord** was the year of Jubilee, which God commanded through Moses to be observed every fifty years throughout the land of Israel.

Read about it in Leviticus 25.

It was a proclamation of freedom that was to affect everything, from land to humans in Israel. The year was usually announced with the sound of a trumpet.

In the year of Jubilee, all Israelites who had lost their possessions through debts and were in servitude to others were totally released from debts and servitude to return to their possessions.

This decree was to remind God's people of His redemptive deliverance to them.

"...I have broken the bands of your yoke and make you walk upright" (Lev. 26:13).

So when our Lord read the Scripture in Isaiah 61 about this decree, His audience knew that only God's Messiah was capable to set them free from all their yokes. And Jesus told them, "I am your Messiah."

The acceptable year of the **Lord**, which Christ announced to His people in Nazareth then, is still in force today to all who accept His Lordship into their lives—freedom from everything that causes distress and suffering to the whole person. That is the proclamation He decreed for us. Let us enforce and apply it to our situations in life today through the anointing of the Holy Spirit to enjoy His freedom.

Have a happy day of Jubilee **loaded** with God's **benefits.!**

LIVING WORD for TODAY—OCTOBER 23:

LOADED with DAILY BLESSINGS (Ps. 68:19)-#297

FREEDOM—23

"I am the LORD your God, who brought you out of the land of Egypt, that you should not be their slaves; I have broken the bands of your yoke and made you walk upright. (Lev. 26:13)

Freedom from Bondages:

• The bands of yoke of Egypt

God's deliverance of the Israelites from slavery in Egypt could be likened to Christ's deliverance of believers in Him from the yokes of the world represented by Satan, sin, and self.

Just as God demonstrated His power in Egypt over the hosts of spiritual and physical wickedness represented by Pharaoh and his deities, Jesus Christ, our Lord, exercised His victory over the devil and all his cohorts when He rose triumphantly from the dead.

So He has broken and destroyed the bands of our yoke and proclaimed our year of Jubilee! The only yoke we need to put on to remain free from the yokes He has destroyed for us is His yoke, which is very easy. He says:

"Come to Me, all you who labor and are heavy laden, and I will give you rest. Take My yoke upon you and learn from Me, for I am gentle and lowly in heart, and you will find rest for your souls. For My yoke is easy and My burden is light" (Matt. 11:28–30).

Love Christ, live in Him, learn from Him, and enjoy His freedom in your life forever.

Have a happy day/night **loaded** with His **blessings!**

LIVING WORD for TODAY—OCTOBER 24:

LOADED with DAILY BLESSINGS (Ps. 68:19)-#298

FREEDOM—24

"Grace to you and peace from God the Father and our Lord Jesus Christ, who gave Himself for our sins, that He might deliver us from this present evil age, according to the will of our God and Father, to whom be glory forever and ever. Amen."

Freedom from Bondages:

- Deliverance from this present evil age

We are living in an age full of evil. This truth is visible to us daily as we witness the devastating effects of many diseases, including the pandemic virus, COVID-19. Alongside these, we are also seeing protests all over the world against the powers that be for social injustices. Some of these protests might start with peaceful demonstrations, only to degenerate into violence, resulting in the destruction of lives and properties.

Living in this kind of world requires God's grace and peace. Knowing that we live in the world of evils, Jesus Christ gave Himself for our sins and replaced them with His grace and peace so we can live without fear in this present evil age.

Those who believe in Jesus Christ have been delivered from this present evil age, that is, forces of evil and systems operating in this world. Though they are living in it, they are protected from the turbulent waves of the evil one in this world. The Lord prayed for us before He left the world, and His prayer still has effect upon us who belong to Him.

"I do not pray that You should take them out of the world, but that You should keep them from the evil one" (John 17:15).

So be confident and know that you're insured by God and have the benefit of living in freedom from the evils of this world.

Have a peaceful day/night **loaded** with His **blessings**!

LIVING WORD for TODAY—OCTOBER 25:

LOADED with DAILY BLESSINGS (Ps. 68:19)-299

FREEDOM—25

"He has delivered us from the power of darkness and conveyed us into the kingdom of the Son of His love..." (Col. 1:13)

Freedom from Bondages:

- Deliverance from the power of darkness: Christians have been delivered from the power of darkness. Ephesians 2:1-3 described what the power of darkness in our lives looked like;
- Dead in trespassers and sins: We sinned without guilty conscience and gloried in sins;
- Walking in the polluted system of the world in ignorance;
- The prince of the power of darkness was directing our lives and affairs because we were prisoners in his kingdom;
- We were possessed by demonic spirits working in the children of disobedience;
- We were living according to the lusts of our flesh, fulfilling the desires of our flesh and minds; and
- We were condemned and lost, living in God's wrath.

With this picture of who we were and what God delivered us from, we can appreciate the power of His grace that conveyed us from the power of darkness into the kingdom of Christ, who is the Light of the world

Since we're in the kingdom of light, no power of darkness has power over us anymore because wherever there's light, darkness cannot exist. So turn on the light of Jesus Christ in you to overcome the power of darkness around you. Christ is in you!

Have a glorious day/night **loaded** with His **blessing** of **freedom**!

LIVING WORD for TODAY—OCTOBER 26:

LOADED with DAILY BLESSINGS (Ps. 68:19)-#300

FREEDOM—26

"Inasmuch then as the children have partake of flesh and blood, He Himself like-wise shared in the same, that through death He might destroy him who had the power of death, that is, the devil,
and release those who through fear of death were all their lifetime subject to bondage." (Heb. 2:14–15)

Freedom from Bondages:

- Deliverance from the fear of death

Everyone who is not born again by the Holy Spirit and filled by Him is in bondage to fear. There are different kinds of fear-plaguing humans. Fear itself is a demonic spirit that Satan is using to keep people in bondage to Him. People who are not delivered from the bondage of fear and die in it will find themselves in hell-fire with Satan (Rev. 21:8).

The most powerful of all fears is the fear of death. Every flesh and blood is afraid of death. But believers in Christ Jesus don't have to fear death anymore because our Lord tasted death for us and destroyed its power from domi-nating us with fear. Christ destroyed death, the destroyer, and made it the gateway to the glorious eternal life for those who believe in Him.

So just as He delivered us from the power of darkness and conveyed us into the kingdom of the Son of His love, He has also delivered us from bondage of the fear of death.

Let us not be afraid of death anymore because for the children of God, "to live is Christ, and to die is gain" (Phil. 1:21).

Let us continue to live for Christ with His freedom over death till He calls us home to be with Him.

Have a glorious day/night!

LIVING WORD for TODAY—OCTOBER 27:

LOADED with DAILY BLESSINGS (Ps. 68:19)-#301

FREEDOM—27

"The fear of man brings a snare,
But whoever trusts in the LORD shall be safe." (Prov. 29:25)

Freedom from Bondages:

- Deliverance from fear

The Spirit of fear is one of the greatest enemies the devil binds humans with after the fall into sin. There's no one who does not fear. We're afraid of things that are real and unreal.

But what about the fears in our imaginations? These fears ensnare us and prevent us from reaching our desirable destinies. Fear is powerful, but faith is much more powerful. Hence, while man's fear brings a snare, "But whoever trusts in the LORD shall be safe."

So the antidote to fear is trust; trusting in the Lord who is the God of love. This is something we must learn to do daily if we're going to be free and enjoy our freedom in the Lord.

Give your fears to God and stay totally free from snares of the evil one.

Have a beautiful day **loaded** with His **blessings!**

LIVING WORD for TODAY—OCTOBER 28:

LOADED with DAILY BLESSINGS (Ps. 68:19)-#302

FREEDOM—28

"And do not fear those who kill the body but cannot kill the soul. But rather fear Him who is able to destroy both soul and body in hell." (Matt. 10:28)

Freedom from Bondages:

- Deliverance from the fear of men

What about the fear of men, those who have authority over us or capable to do us harm?

Many people are afraid of others more than God.

Our Lord had to deal with this fear in His disciples as He sent them out to preach the gospel. The spirit of fear will prevent us from sharing our faith with people around us who need to hear about the power of the gospel of Jesus Christ. We may be so free to talk about other subjects but too shy or inhibited to share our faith.

The deliverance medicine our Lord prescribed to destroy the fear of men is twofold.

(1) The fear of God: Hate what God hates, and love what He loves. That's my simple definition of the fear of God in our lives, which would override the fear of people. We are to respect and honor people and obey those who have authority over us, according to the will of God; and

(2) The second part of the medicine to destroy the fear of men is being filled with the Holy Spirit. Jesus told His disciples: "But you shall receive power when the Holy Spirit has come upon you; and you shall be witnesses to Me..." (Acts 1:8).

If you're having problems standing firm and doing the will of God, check your relationship with the Lord and pray for the fear of God and the power of the Holy Spirit to fill you.

Have a fearless day **loaded** with His **blessings!**

LIVING WORD for TODAY—OCTOBER 29:

LOADED with DAILY BLESSINGS (Ps. 68:19)-#303

FREEDOM—29

"For God has not given us a spirit of fear, but of power and of love and of a sound mind." (2 Tim. 1:7)

Freedom from Bondages:

- Deliverance from the spirit of fear

Fear is a spirit attached to us by the devil and not from God.

St. Paul had to deal with this spirit in his protégé, Timothy, who had been called and appointed to be a circuit pastor to the churches in the region of Ephesus. Despite all the spiritual gifts bestowed upon Timothy by Christ and his mentor Paul, Timothy was still shy and afraid to preach, teach, and apply the Word with all boldness.

Paul had to remind his mentee of what he had in him. God's gifts of grace in Timothy and in every one of His children are:

- Power—of the Holy Spirit (Acts 1:8);
- Love—which is the fruit of the Spirit (Gal. 5:22; 1 John 4:18); "perfect love casts out fear"; and
- Sound mind—wisdom and self control in the exercise of spiritual gifts (1 Cor. 12:1–3; James 1:5).

Just as Timothy was reminded to stir up the gifts in him, the Holy Spirit is reminding you today, wherever you are and whatever situation you may be facing that is intimidating you. You have God's gifts of grace in you. Stir up the power of the Holy Spirit in you through prayer; start loving the unlovable in your life, and pray for God's wisdom and sound mind as you live among the crooked and perverse generation where you're to shine with the light of Jesus Christ.

Never allow the spirit of fear to override what you have in you, but get rid of your fear with the gifts of God in you and be **free!**

Have a bold day **loaded** with His **blessings!**

LIVING WORD for TODAY—OCTOBER 30:

LOADED with DAILY BLESSINGS (Ps. 68:19)-#304

FREEDOM—30

"There is no fear in love; but perfect love casts out fear, because fear involves torment. But he who fears has not been made perfect in love." (1 John 3:18)

Freedom from Bondages:

- Bondage of fear

As we round up our devotional meditations for this month on the subject of freedom, let me say this, freedom and deliverance from bondages is a broad subject in the Bible. We have only scratched the surface or the subject.

There are many areas of bondage people must be delivered from. Even Christians need deliverance from the oppression of the enemy from time to time. People need to be delivered from spiritual bondage, social bondage, economic bondage, religious bondage, cultural/traditions, emotional, sinful habits, sicknesses, and diseases represented by the spirit of infirmity, root issues, and so on. These are areas people must be ministered to by the power and anointing of the Holy Spirit, with regular and consistent teachings of God's Word by anointed ministers. Jesus Christ came to set us free from the yokes with which we might have found ourselves. He is the perfect Love who lived among people to demonstrate God's total freedom.

So we must continue to grow in Him and allow His love to fill our hearts so that fear will not have room there to torment us. Growing in grace and love is the antidote to fear. That's only possible when we submit to a thorough discipleship process in the Christian church and ministry. If you're not active in a well-established church, find one around you that is teaching the Word and commit yourself to the fellowship of the Spirit-filled believers to be discipled.

Have a happy day **loaded** with the **blessings** of **freedom**!

LIVING WORD for TODAY—OCTOBER 31:

LOADED with DAILY BLESSINGS (Ps. 68:19)-#305

FREEDOM—31

"Stand fast therefore in the liberty by which Christ has made us free, and do not be entangled again with a yoke of bondage." (Gal. 5:1)

Freedom from Bondages:

- Standing fast in freedom

In conclusion, don't forget that Jesus Christ's primary mission in the world is to set us free. To do this, He had to be filled, anointed, and live by the Holy Spirit. The price He paid for our freedom was His blood. Hence, He wants His children to be free from all yokes of the devil, humans, self, and traditions. Put on His easy yoke and stay free.

It is up to us, individually, to receive His gift of freedom, abide in Him, live by the Spirit and His Word, and stand free.

Failure to do these things entangles us into bondage again, which may be difficult to be free from.

Therefore, stand fast in the liberty by which Christ has set you free and enjoy your freedom in Him daily.

Have a happy day/night of freedom **loaded** with His **blessings!**

NOVEMBER— FELLOWSHIP

LIVING WORD for TODAY—NOVEMBER 1:

LOADED with DAILY BLESSINGS (Ps. 68:19)-#306

FELLOWSHIP—1

"...that which we have seen and heard we declare to you, that you also may have fellowship with us; and truly our fellowship is with the Father and with His Son Jesus Christ." (1 John 1:3)

Divine Fellowship:

Count down to the last sixty days of the year! May the everlasting arm of the Lord, who has always been there for us, see us through the remaining sixty days of the year and beyond with good health and quality of life **loaded** with His **blessings!**

In every month this year, we have been privileged to meditate on a specific area of God's blessings to us and appropriate some components of that blessing into our lives and situations.

This month, I've been led in my thoughts to consider the gift of **fellowship** in our daily devotional meditations.

Fellowship in the Greek word used in the NT Bible is *koinonia*, which means having same things in common. Another word for fellowship is communion.

No one else could be more qualified enough to write about fellowship with God in the Bible other than these three individuals: Adam, Moses, and John the Beloved.

We start our meditations with the latter. Remember John as one of the twelve disciples of Jesus Christ? He earned the title: "the disciple whom Jesus loved," as he always leaning or reclining on Jesus's bosom (John 13:23–25; 19:26; 21:20).

So later in his life as an old man, when he's writing about Jesus as the Word of life, he had the audacity to say:

"THAT which was from the beginning, which we have heard, which we have seen with our eyes, which we have looked upon, and our hands have handled, concerning the Word of life" (1 John 1:1).

There can be no better way to give an eyewitness account of a person than John's introduction. So, God came down to earth and fellowshipped with humans, and John the Beloved was a key participant in that communion.

The experience he had, he wants us to have as well. What a benefit and special privilege to fellowship with the great God of the whole universe!

Enjoy!

Have a great month of Divine Fellowship **loaded** with God's **blessings!**

LIVING WORD for TODAY—NOVEMBER 2:

LOADED with DAILY BLESSINGS (Ps. 68:19)-#307

FELLOWSHIP—2

"...that which we have seen and heard we declare to you,, that you also may have fellowship with us, and truly our fellowship is with the Father and with His Son Jesus Christ." (1 John 1:3)

Fellowship with God:

Koinonia, having the same things in common, is the foundation of any lasting union. If not, it's just a question of time before everyone goes in different ways. This was in the mind of Amos, a prophet of old, who lived centuries before John, when he asked the Jews of his days the question: "Can two walk together, unless they are agreed?" (Amos 3:3).

This same question forms the basis of the first epistle of John the Beloved. He wrote in his gospel, written years before this epistle, that, "No one has seen God at any time. The only begotten Son, who is in the bosom of the Father, He has declared Him" (John 1:18).

But now, after many years of walking with God, the same John, through the revelation of the Holy Spirit, could now say, yes, we have seen God, we have heard Him, and we have touched Him. God is in Christ! (1 John 1:1). So the same experience that we have we would like to share with you that your joy may be full (1 John 1:4).

Fellowship with God, therefore, is the foundation of true enjoyment of life to the full.

Do you have the same things in common with God for Him to live with you? Keep thinking about this question as we continue in our journey of fellowshipping with God in our daily meditations this month.

Have a great day **loaded** with His **blessings**!

LIVING WORD for TODAY—NOVEMBER 3:

LOADED with DAILY BLESSINGS (Ps. 68:19)-#308

FELLOWSHIP—3

"...that which we have seen and heard we declare to you, that you also may have fellowship with us, and truly our fellowship is with the Father and with His Son Jesus Christ." (1 John 1:3)

Fellowship with the Son:

There are people who say they love God but don't have anything to do with Jesus Christ. But how can you love me and hate my children? This kind of love is a fake love.

Naturally, if you love the father, you also love his children. The same truth applies spiritually.

In fact, Jesus declared to the Jews of His days on earth that, "No one comes to the Father except through Me" (John 14:6). In another encounter with them, they asked Him, and He replied:

"Then they said to Him, 'Where is Your Father?' Jesus answered, 'You know neither Me nor My Father. If you had known Me, you would have known My Father also'" (John 8:19).

So to know God and have relationship with Him is to know His Son Jesus Christ. This is the foundation of having fellowship with God and His Son. We can't choose one and reject the other.

How is your love and commitment to Jesus Christ?

Do you have the same things in common with Him for fellowship? These are foundational questions that must be answered individually in order to enjoy life to the full.

Have a lovely day/evening **loaded** with His **blessings**!

LIVING WORD for TODAY—NOVEMBER 4:

LOADED with DAILY BLESSINGS (Ps. 68:19)-#309

FELLOWSHIP—4

"The grace of the Lord Jesus Christ, and the love of God, and the communion of the Holy Spirit be with you all. Amen." (2 Cor. 13:14)

Fellowship with the Holy Spirit:

We are not only in fellowship with God the Father and God the Son but also with God the Holy Spirit. The early church's benediction consisted of the impartation of blessings from the triune God as recorded in the above text.

Because the Holy Spirit is God's representative in believers in Christ, He enjoys having fellowship with us. So we must always be sensitive in how we live so we don't grieve Him. If we do, He convicts us, and if He does, our duty is to repent and be washed in the blood of Jesus Christ to restore our communion with the Holy Spirit, who is our Great Comforter (1 John 1:7).

My prayer is for us to continue to have the same things in common with the Holy Spirit, day by day, so as to enjoy His fellowship.

Have a lovely day **loaded** with His **blessings!**

LIVING WORD for TODAY—NOVEMBER 5:

LOADED with DAILY BLESSINGS (Ps. 68:19)-#310

FELLOWSHIP—5

"...that which we have seen and heard we declare to you, that you also may have fellowship with us; and truly our fellowship is with the Father and with His Son Jesus Christ." (1 John 1:3)

Fellowship with One Another:

Christianity is not an isolated faith but in connection with other fellow believers.

God came down from heaven in the person of His Son Jesus Christ to seek and save those who are lost, and whenever He finds them, He cleanses them and communes with them as His children and friends.

Of course, there are times when we lock ourselves in isolation to spend time exclusively with the Lord. But the goal of it is to be renewed to serve and fellowship with God and others in new dimensions.

Are you a cave Christian or a community Christian? We are called to live the Christian life in the community.

John the Beloved is calling us to have fellowship with him and other disciples who saw and lived with the Lord Jesus Christ. How wonderful it is to have fellowship with the holy apostles of the Lord! We can do this through their writings in the Scriptures and by sharing the same things in common with them.

May our fellowship with them strengthen our relationship with one another.

Have a great day **loaded** with His **blessings**!

LIVING WORD for TODAY—NOVEMBER 6:

LOADED with DAILY BLESSINGS (Ps. 68:19)-#311

FELLOWSHIP—6

"And these things we write to you that your joy may be full." (1 John 1:4)

Purpose of Fellowship:

The happiest people on earth are not necessarily those who have all the wealth and power.

But the happiest people are those with solid faith in God and surrounded by family and friends in a safe community.

These people tend to live long and healthy, according to social studies.

So our fellowship with God, His Son Jesus Christ, the Holy Spirit, and other believers is a blessing from God, which, if we embrace, would enhance our quality of life on earth and grant us fulfillment with fullness of joy forever.

Our Lord gives us the same prescription for good life in John 15:9–12, and concludes:

"These things I have spoken to you, that My joy may remain in you, and that your joy may be full" (John 15:11).

Do you want to enjoy life to the fullest here on earth and in heaven? The answer is in having the same things in common with the triune God and His community of people.

Don't cut yourself off from this life-stream, but be part of it.

Have a happy day **loaded** with His **blessings!**

LIVING WORD for TODAY—NOVEMBER 7:

LOADED with DAILY BLESSINGS (Ps. 68:19)-#312

FELLOWSHIP—7

"This is the message which we have heard from Him and declare to you, that God is light and in Him is no darkness at all." (1 John 1:5)

Conditions for Fellowship:

While all of God's blessings we enjoy daily are free gifts to us, He, however, established some simple conditions to access them. Just as the laws of nature, so are the laws of the Spirit.

There are some biblical conditions to enjoy fellowship with the triune God and His children.

- Transparency (part one): First on the list in this short epistle by John is living and walking in the light. The world is divided by day and night, light and darkness, and good and evil.

If we're going to share the same things in common with God and all His blessings, we must choose to live with Him and be openly transparent before Him and His children. Despite the fact that God knows all about us, we sometimes hide ourselves from Him, just like our first parents, Adam and Eve, in the Garden when they disobeyed God's instruction.

Is there anything about us that we can hide from our Creator?

None. David says:

"O LORD, You have searched me and known me. You know my sitting down and my rising up. You understand my thought afar off..." (Ps. 139:1, 2). (Read the whole chapter.)

So let us be bare before our Creator and fellowship with Him in the light, with nothing concealing. It is only then that He can reveal Himself to us with His blessings.

Have a victorious day/evening **loaded** with His **blessings!**

LIVING WORD for TODAY—NOVEMBER 8:

LOADED with DAILY BLESSINGS (Ps. 68:19)-#313

FELLOWSHIP—8

"...He who is blessed and only Potentate, the King of kings and the Lord of lords, who alone has immortality, dwelling in unapproachable light, whom no man has seen or can see, to whom be honor and everlasting power. Amen."(1 Tim. 6:14–16)

Conditions for Fellowship:

Transparency (part two)

What does it mean to be transparent before God and His children?

It is one thing to be bare and naked before God, but it is quite a different thing to be totally bare before His children.

Only God is all-knowing, who knows all about us. His children are not and cannot handle each other's secrets. God Himself knows this, and that's why He doesn't expose His children's secrets to each other. So we don't need to know all about each other to fellowship together.

But there are some basic principles of living a transparent life with one another, such as speaking the truth in love (Eph. 4:15, 25–32) and growing up in Christ.

When a Christian demands to know everything about another person, that is not true love but witchcraft and divination. No one has the right to know you as your Heavenly Father because He is the only one dwelling in unapproachable light, who knows the worst about you and still loves you.

So Christians' transparency is living in the truth, speaking the truth in love with one another, and growing up in grace to be like Jesus Christ.

May the Lord help us to continue growing up in grace to be like Him in all areas of our life and relationship with one another.

Have a pleasant day **loaded** with His **blessings!**

LIVING WORD for TODAY—NOVEMBER 9:

LOADED with DAILY BLESSINGS (Ps. 68:19)-#314

FELLOWSHIP—9

"If we say that we have fellowship with Him, and walk in darkness, we lie and do not practice the truth." (1 John 1:6)

Conditions for Fellowship:

- Dealing with the dark spots in our lives

Christians are expected to be holy and spotless, right? But that's not what we see as we fellowship with one another. We see a lot of integrity deficiencies. We have no excuse to make other than the fact that the sinful flesh is still active in our lives.

Because of this, the Bible instructs us to deal with our deficiencies by recognizing them and working on them. If we ignored our shortfalls and excused them in the pretense of grace, we're not walking in the light but in darkness.

Walking in the light means recognizing our fallibility and being open to the infallible God to help us live right.

The Bible says:

"And have no fellowship with the unfruitful works of darkness, but rather expose them" (Eph. 5:11).

Are you hiding your dark spots from the Lord, like Adam and Eve, or like Peter, when convicted by the Spirit of the Lord, or do you break down in remorse and repentance?

Do not hide but expose your shortfalls and weaknesses of the flesh to the Lord in the light of His Word. It is then that you can continue to enjoy your fellowship with Him and His people.

May the Lord open our eyes to see the areas in our lives that need exposure to the light of the Lord for His help.

Have a lovely day/evening **loaded** with His **blessings**!

LIVING WORD for TODAY—NOVEMBER 10:

LOADED with DAILY BLESSINGS (Ps. 68:19)-#315

FELLOWSHIP—10

"But if we walk in the light as He is in the light, we have fellowship with one another, and the blood of Jesus Christ His Son cleanses us from all sin." (1 John 1:7)

Conditions for Fellowship:

- Constant cleaning in the Blood

Walking in the light with the Lord as children of light requires transparency and recognition of our fallibility, but also going to the next level by going to the Lord for His cleansing.

Sometimes Christians take sins for granted without knowing that sins in our lives are like what Solomon calls "little foxes that destroy the vine" (Song 2:15). We must catch the foxes and get rid of them by the blood of Jesus Christ. We must always be on the lookout for new foxes showing up to ravage the vine and apply the same cleansing power of the blood of Christ.

Notice the verb tense in 1 John 1:7 for the blood is continuously present (Gr. aoris tense).

"Cleanses" indicating a perfect past action with a continuous effect in the present. The reality of this to us who are in Christ is the blood of Jesus Christ shed on the Cross over two thousand years ago still has the same effect on any sinner today and forever who believes in it to make him or her holy. That is the basis of our acceptance for fellowship with God and His people.

So let us get out of the darkness of sin and walk in the light with His cleansing blood daily. "For you were once darkness, but now you are light in the Lord. Walk as children of light" (Eph. 5:8).

Have a great day/evening **loaded** with His **blessings**!

LIVING WORD for TODAY—NOVEMBER 11:

LOADED with DAILY BLESSINGS (Ps. 68:19)-#316

FELLOWSHIP—11

"If we say that we have no sin, we deceive ourselves, and the truth is not in us."
(1 John 1:8)

Conditions for Fellowship:

- Acceptance of God's truth

One of the deadly sins God hates is pride. Pride makes people to think and exalt themselves more than who they are. Arrogant people like to publicly show off to hide their inferior and insecure complexes.

The spirit of pride manifests more in religious practices as illustrated by our Lord in Luke 18:9–14. "Also He spoke this parable to some who trusted in themselves that they were righteous and despised others" (Luke 18:9).

So if we're going to fellowship with the triune God and His people, we have to empty ourselves of self righteousness and accept what God's Word says about us. We're sinners saved by grace. The grace of God that saves us is best defined in Titus 2:11–14. Please read and meditate on the verses.

As long as we're in this world, our sinful nature will always be in us, and we have to learn to deal with it from time to time by the grace of God. No exceptions!

May the Lord humble us daily under His grace so we can fellowship with Him.

Have a great day **loaded** with His **blessings!**

LIVING WORD for TODAY—NOVEMBER 12:

LOADED with DAILY BLESSINGS (Ps. 68:19)-#317

FELLOWSHIP—12

"If we confess our sins, He is faithful and just to forgive us our sins and to cleanse us from all unrighteousness." (1 John 1:9)

Conditions for Fellowship:

• Confession of sins

This is the fourth on the list of "if we" in this epistle. In it, John the Beloved encourages us to confess our sins to our Heavenly Father if we're going to fellowship with Him. It is not enough for us to acknowledge our sins, but we must go further by confessing it to God with contrition. God in His mercy forgives us because of the blood of His Son, and He also uses the same blood to cleanse us from all unrighteousness.

Confession of sins must have an important place in our daily devotional prayer because God demands it from us.

"He who covers his sins will not prosper, But whosoever confesses and forsakes them will have mercy" (Prov. 28:13).

So don't take God's forgiveness for granted. But follow His requirements of true repentance and confession to obtain His mercy and cleansing to enjoy fellowship with Him and His children.

Have a pleasant day/evening **loaded** with His **blessings**!

LIVING WORD for TODAY—NOVEMBER 13:

LOADED with DAILY BLESSINGS (Ps. 68:19)-#318

FELLOWSHIP—13

"If we say that we have not sinned, we made Him a liar, and His word is not in us."(1 John 1:10)

Conditions for Fellowship:

- Accepting our past sinful condition

Do you think back to thank God for saving you from your past sins? God doesn't see us with the past sins He had forgiven but as new creatures in Christ; it is, however, necessary to occasionally reflect on the dangerous roads to destruction which we were traveling before Christ intercepted us by His grace and changed our directions. To deny this fact is to rationalize our sinful nature and make God a liar.

His Word says: "for all have sinned and fall short of the glory of God" (Rom. 3:23).

So we can not say that we've never sinned, but be thankful that God found us in our sinful state and saved us by His grace through faith in Christ Jesus. That's worth celebrating as we put on our new garments of salvation and praise the Lord who chose to fellowship with us.

Have a lovely day/evening **loaded** with His **blessings!**

LIVING WORD for TODAY—NOVEMBER 14:

LOADED with DAILY BLESSINGS (Ps. 68:19)-#319

FELLOWSHIP—14

"BEHOLD, how good and how pleasant it is
For brethren to dwell together in unity!" (Ps. 133:1)

Call to Fellowship:

• In the body

Fellowship, *Koinonia,* having the same things in common, is the spirit and attitude of unity in the body of believers. If we're going to fellowship with one another, we must be in one accord with each other.

Since unity and fellowship cannot be separated, it is necessary to foster the spirit of unity in the body to enjoy a free flow of fellowship.

This is good and pleasant for the health of the body.

But unity must flow from the head before it can affect the body. "It is like the precious oil upon the head" (Ps. 133:2).

If a leader of any group or family is divisive, there cannot be unity in the group or family. Hence, group or church leaders must always pray for the anointing of unity to flow through them to the body. This is the primary purpose of the five-fold ministry in the church (Eph. 4:11–14).

Our God is a God of unity; that's why He's the perfect example of unity and fellowship.

In contrast, Satan and his agents specialize in division.

They divide to conquer. Watch out for those who cause division in the fellowship. They need to be counseled and delivered from the snares of Satan.

Where there's unity, there's fellowship and God's blessings flow.

"...For there the LORD commanded the blessing—life for evermore" (Ps. 133:3).

May the anointing oil of unity flow through us to fellowship with God and one another for maximum experience of His blessings in our lives.

Have a happy day **loaded** with His **blessings!**

LIVING WORD for TODAY—NOVEMBER 15:

LOADED with DAILY BLESSINGS (Ps. 68:19)-#320

FELLOWSHIP—15

"These all continued with one accord in prayer and supplication, with the women and Mary the mother of Jesus, and with His brothers." (Acts 1:14)

Components of Fellowship:

- With one accord

There are many alignments to be made in our lives if we're to enjoy the benefits of fellowship. The early church was quick to make these adjustments with one another in their meetings.

The first priority is to be in one accord. In the typical Jewish religious system, women were usually segregated from men—no interaction whatsoever. The ministers (priests) were also distanced from other worshipers. But in the fellowship of the disciples of Jesus Christ, as they gathered in the upper room of one of the women, (Mary, John Mark's mother), there was no class nor gender distinction, but they were all "with one accord and one place" in their meetings.

This one-accord fellowship runs throughout the Book of Acts. There were no more arguments of who would be the greatest among them. Thank God for the Lord's prayer for their unity in John 17.

The number one problem of fellowship among believers today is the lack of unity. The Lord cannot dwell and operate in a house divided against itself. No wonder we're not witnessing God's miraculous acts in our fellowships. When we're together with one accord, He promises, "And whatever you ask in My name, that I will do, that the Father may be glorified in the Son" (John 14:13).

So let us put aside our differences and be in agreement with those we're in fellowship with to experience divine visitations in our lives and situations around us. May the Lord grant you your heart's desires as you fellowship with Him and other brethren.

Have a great day **loaded** with His **blessings!**

LIVING WORD for TODAY—NOVEMBER 16:

LOADED with DAILY BLESSINGS (Ps. 68:19)-#321

FELLOWSHIP—16

"Now in the morning, having risen a long while before daylight, He went out and departed to a solitary place; and there He prayed." (Mark 1:35)

Components of Fellowship:

- Prayer

What is prayer?

Some define prayer as talking to God and others as talking with God. While these short definitions are good, there is another definition, however, which we usually ignore but forms a key component to prayer.

I would define prayer as having fellowship with God. Have you ever spent an hour or more before God in prayer without saying a word and just reflecting on His goodness and mercy? That is fellowshipping with God. Until we grow up to this level in our relationship with God, we cannot be deeply connected with Him in the Holy of Holies, where He reigns.

When our Lord got up early in the morning and went to a solitary place to pray, what was He praying about? And when He spent forty days and forty nights fasting without food in the wilderness, what was He praying for? We don't know. But what we do know is His intimate fellowship with the Father made Him spend more time with Him alone.

May our relationship with the Lord grow to the level where it wouldn't just be our problems that always drive us to Him in prayer but our love to spend time with Him in fellowship.

Have a lovely day **loaded** with His **blessings**!

LIVING WORD for TODAY—NOVEMBER 17:

LOADED with DAILY BLESSINGS (Ps. 68:19)-#322

FELLOWSHIP—17

"When all the people were baptized, it came to pass that Jesus also was baptized; and while He prayed, the heaven was opened.

And the Holy Spirit descended in bodily form like a dove upon Him, and a voice came from heaven which said, 'You are My beloved Son; in You I am well pleased.'" (Luke 3:21–22)

Components of Fellowship:

- Prayer

In prayer, we:

- Cry to God for help and for our needs (examples of Hannah and David);
- Converse with God for others (examples of Abraham for Lot and Moses for Israel); and
- Commune with God and other believers (examples of Jesus and the early church).

Communion is fellowship.

It was Pastor Jentezen Franklin, the founding pastor of Free Chapel, one of the churches that I fellowship with in Irvine, California, who made an insightful observation recently in one of his messages about prayer. He referred to God and Adam's meetings in the Garden of Eden as a form of prayer meetings. He asked, what would Adam be asking from God when there was no sin, sickness, family, nor need for anything? Definitely, Adam's meetings with God in the cool of the day were more of fellowship than asking. Most of our prayers today hinge on needs, but to be more effective, prayer time should be more of fellowshipping with God our Maker.

At Jesus's baptism, He prayed, and heaven was opened to Him. What did He pray for? We don't know. But I think He could be worshiping or fellowshipping with His Father.

Let us learn to turn our prayer time to fellowshipping with God in the beauty of His holiness as we enter into His presence in reverence. This will make our prayers more effective. When we're in His presence, He reveals things to us and teaches us how to pray about them.

Have a beautiful day **loaded** with His **blessings!**

LIVING WORD for TODAY—NOVEMBER 18:

LOADED with DAILY BLESSINGS (Ps. 68:19)-#323

FELLOWSHIP—18

"A new commandment I give to you, that you love one another; as I have loved you, that you also love one another.
'By this all will know that you are My disciples, if you have love for one another.'"
(John 13:34–35)

Components of Fellowship:

- One another in love

Without selfless love, we cannot fellowship with one another. Our fellowship is not only with God but also with one another.

- Love is the foundation upon which Christianity is built by our Lord. Just as He demonstrated it by giving Himself to us, He's commanding all His followers to follow His footsteps of love.
  • Fellowshipping with one another in love confirms who we are to the world around us.
- Love and unity are the most important components of our faith and fellowship, which the enemy is always eager to attack first because he knows how potent they are to crumble his kingdom. So whenever we cannot get along with one another, let us remember we are enabling the satanic kingdom and must quickly repent.
- Love is the major fruit of our life in Christ. Nothing, no charismatic gifts can ever replace it (read 1 Cor. 13).

I pray that we would grow to be like our Master in love for one another.

Have a lovely day **loaded** with God's **blessings**!

LIVING WORD for TODAY—NOVEMBER 19:

LOADED with DAILY BLESSINGS (Ps. 68:19)-#324

FELLOWSHIP—19

"Now all who believed were together, and had all things in common, and sold their possessions and goods, and divided them among all, as anyone had need." (Acts 2:44–45)

Components of Fellowship:

- Sharing of substance

It was a joyful experience to be saved and part of the early Christian community in Jerusalem. It was the risen Lord in action through the Holy Spirit's presence.

Believers in Christ Jesus were:

- • Living together in love;
- Having all things in common;
- Selling their possessions and goods; and
- Dividing the proceeds according to each person's need.

What a true Christian fellowship in action. Please note that this kind of fellowship and community is not man-made but divine through the Holy Spirit.

Many human attempts had been made to replicate the early Christian community at Jerusalem in some parts of the world and had woefully failed after some trials.

While we may not duplicate this community in our complex modern society, we can, however, learn some principles from it and pray that the Holy Spirit pours His fresh love into our hearts to have all things in common to share with each other without taking advantage of one another.

This kind of *koinonia* is possible in the church today with the Lord's presence and the operations of the Holy Spirit in our gatherings. Let us yield our hearts to Him for His fresh outpouring of agape love upon us.

Have a great day/evening **loaded** with His **blessings!**

LIVING WORD for TODAY—NOVEMBER 20:

LOADED with DAILY BLESSINGS (Ps. 68:19)-#325

FELLOWSHIP—20

"So continuing daily with one accord in the temple, and breaking bread from house to house, they ate their food with gladness and simplicity of heart, praising God and having favor with all the people. And the Lord added to the church daily those who are being saved." (Acts 2:46–47)

Components of Fellowship:

- Eating together

There was life in the early church that made it very attractive and comfortable to join. Church time was not boring because everyone had something to share with somebody. That was the breaking of barriers of the religious practice of the day where there was segregation by gender and citizenship in the houses of worship.

There were the apostles' teachings and doctrines to keep balance from extremism.

There were edifying testimonies to share of the Lord's miraculous acts in people's lives. There was the breaking of bread, which is the Lord's Supper or the Holy Communion. But their Holy Communion was different from our practice today. It was the real celebration of the Lord's Passover, which was perfectly fulfilled by Jesus Christ as the Lamb of God. It was celebrated with a real dinner for all to enjoy. So there was plenty of food and wine too. This got out of control later in the church of Corinth (1 Cor. 11:20–22).

But the abuse did not negate the importance of this fellowship.

So they ate together from house to house with simplicity of heart. No wonder the Lord added to the church daily to those who were being saved.

Your local church can have the same result if the leaders and members would be humbled and simplify church fellowship for everyone to feel at home and connected to one another in the bond of love.

Have a great day/night **loaded** with His **daily blessings!**

LIVING WORD for TODAY—NOVEMBER 21:

LOADED with DAILY BLESSINGS (Ps. 68:19)-#326

FELLOWSHIP—21

"Now the multitude of those who believed were of one heart and one soul; neither did anyone say that any of the things he possessed was his own, but they had all things in common." (Acts 4:32)

Consequences of Fellowship:

- Common welfare

Being in fellowship with God and among fellow Christians is beneficial for our wellbeing.

We're not called to be islands to ourselves but interconnected. Loneliness is one of the silent killers in the modern world. God created fellowship to deal with this problem, and there is no better place to be actively involved and connected than within the Christian community. Though imperfect, there's flow of God's grace within the body of believers to keep us healthy and happy.

Isolation is one of the tricks of the evil one to take advantage of the children of God. And in these days of the pandemic, the fellowship of believers is adversely affected. Although we can communicate and minister to one another through the internet, there's no substitute to believers in Christ Jesus coming together in unity to worship the Lord and fellowship with one another. May the Lord grant the world a total solution to the COVID-19 virus and bring a complete end to the spread of the virus so that Christian fellowships can resume fully all over the world.

The devil trembles anywhere the children of God gathers together in unity to praise and worship Jesus Christ. So this practice must continue.

"...not forsaking the assembling of ourselves together, as is the manner of some, but exhorting one another, and so much more as you see the Day approaching" (Heb. 10:25).

Have a great day **loaded** with His **blessings!**

LIVING WORD for TODAY—NOVEMBER 22:

LOADED with DAILY BLESSINGS (Ps. 68:19)-#327

FELLOWSHIP—22

"And with great power the apostles gave witness to the resurrection of the Lord Jesus. And great grace was upon them all." (Acts 4:33)

Consequences of Fellowship:

- Great power (part one)

Ministry becomes very easy and smooth running when there's a release of the Holy Spirit's power among a group of believers in Christ Jesus. But what a drag with difficulty when we try to make things happen with our own power and expertise!

When believers are in one accord, focusing on the Lordship of Christ, the Holy Spirit is present, and where He is, He releases the resurrection power of Jesus Christ for miracles. That was the case of the early church. Their one-accord fellowship attracted the Holy Spirit with His power among them; not just ordinary power, but His great power for miraculous acts.

Do we want to see the great power of the Holy Spirit operating in our fellowships today? Let us close ranks and fellowship with Christ and His people with one heart and one soul and have all things in common with one another. It is then that we can witness the surpassing great power of Christ among us to save souls and turn people from the power of Satan into the glorious light of the gospel.

Let us pray for the outpouring of God's great power to bind us together in love and manifest His power through us to the world around us.

Have a refreshing day/night **loaded** with His **blessings**!

LIVING WORD for TODAY—NOVEMBER 23:

LOADED with DAILY BLESSINGS (Ps. 68:19)-#328

FELLOWSHIP—23

"And with great power the apostles gave witness to the resurrection of the Lord Jesus. And great grace was upon them all." (Acts 4:33)

Consequences of Fellowship:

- Great power (part two)

The power of the Christian church does not flow from a political party nor the statehouse but the Holy Spirit. It is when the church has lost its touch with the Holy Spirit that it seeks to substitute it with political influence and power. The power base of any community where a local church is shouldn't be from the local government but the church. Of course, we're not talking about the civil authority empowered by the people to administer justice and equity to all. But the real power that commands obedience in heaven, earth, and hell must flow through the church. That's how Christ designed His church to be, and that's how the early church operated.

Please also note that their great power was not in the excellency of speeches but in the demonstration of the Holy Spirit's power.

"And my speech and my preaching were not with persuasive words of human wisdom, but in demonstration of the Spirit and of power" (1 Cor. 2:4).

May the Lord help us to set our priorities right and focus on them for the release of His power in our lives and fellowships to affect our communities.

Have a great day **loaded** with His **power** and **blessings**!

LIVING WORD for TODAY—NOVEMBER 24:

LOADED with DAILY BLESSINGS (Ps. 68:19)-#329

FELLOWSHIP—23

"So great fear came upon all church and upon all who heard these things. And through the hands of the apostles many signs and wonders were done among the people. And they were all with one accord in Solomon's Porch." (Acts 5:11–12)

Consequences of Fellowship

- Great power (part three)

The church of Jesus Christ has the mandate and authority of God to be the power-base in any community where it exists. The political powers must bow to the authority of Christ and not vice versa.

A church leader who feels called to seek for a political office should resign from the pulpit and devote his or her time to politics. There's a great difference between the power of Caesar and the power of God. Whenever the two are mixed together, there's always a conflict (my biblical viewpoint).

In the fellowship of the early Christian community, there were:

- Great fear of God upon all the people;
- Great signs and wonders among the people;
- Believers were highly esteemed by the outsiders;
- Believers were increasingly added to the Lord;
- Cities were greatly impacted by the gospel; and
- The power of the government of the day was threatened by the operation of the Holy Spirit (Acts 5:12–17).

It was just a question of time before the power and principles of the kingdom of Christ affected the pagan conducts of the world and brought about some changes.

The most effective way to change the world for the better is through the power of the gospel and not the other way around.

Let us fellowship with one accord and witness for the Lord in the power of the Holy Spirit to change our communities with better results.

Have a better day **loaded** with His **blessings!**

LIVING WORD for TODAY—NOVEMBER 25:

LOADED with DAILY BLESSINGS (Ps. 68:19)-#330

FELLOWSHIP—25

"And with great power the apostles gave witness to the resurrection of the Lord Jesus. And great grace was upon them all." (Acts 4:33)

Consequences of Fellowship:

- Great grace (part one)

One of the signs to watch for in our lives as well as in our ministries of God's presence and approval is favor. God's favor upon our lives and ministries is unsolicited, but poured upon us freely by God to empower us to do His will.

Whenever you find yourself dragging the wheels of your life and ministry, maybe it's time to go back to the drawing board and ask the Lord if He's in what you're doing. Maybe He has a different direction for your life and ministry. God has not called us to live and serve Him in our own efforts. It is, "Not by might nor by power, but by My Spirit, Says the LORD of hosts" (Zach. 4:6).

This was the situation with the early church. With the outpouring of the Holy Spirit on the Day of Pentecost, everything about their lives and gathering together changed. The same Spirit who released great power for the miraculous, poured great grace upon them for favor before the world around them.

Do people around you, where you live, and the ministry you fellowship with look at you with favor? Do they smell the sweet aroma of God's grace in your life, which makes them want to associate and fellowship with you?

Despite what else may be happening, there must be testimonies of God's unmerited favor upon your life and ministry as a sign of His presence and approval upon you. Watch out for this sign!

Have a happy day/night **loaded** with His **great grace!**

LIVING WORD for TODAY—NOVEMBER 26:

LOADED with DAILY BLESSINGS (Ps. 68:19)-#331

FELLOWSHIP—26

"And with great power the apostles gave witness to the resurrection of the Lord Jesus. And great grace was upon them all." (Acts 4:33)

Consequences of Fellowship:

- Great grace (part two)

The foundation of Christian faith, gifts, and character is grace. We're saved by grace, live by grace, and the operation of spiritual gifts through us is by grace.

In fact, the gifts of the Holy Spirit being demonstrated by the apostles in this passage (Acts 4:33, 5:12–16) are called "charismata" (the gifts of grace) in 1 Corinthians 12:1. So the grace of God is what makes the difference in our lives and ministries. Without it, ministry can become a theatrical performance. "For by grace you have been saved through faith, and that not of yourselves; it is the gift of God, not of works, lest anyone should boast" (Eph. 2:8–9).

So God can do it again as He did in the early church. There are many countries today where Christians are experiencing the outpouring of Christ's gifts of grace in their midst. All it takes is a one-accord fellowship, focusing on the Lordship of Jesus Christ.

Therefore be sure to be in a Christian fellowship where grace can be released into your life from time to time. That's the only power that would sustain you through life's challenges.

Have a great day **loaded** with God's **great grace!**

LIVING WORD for TODAY—NOVEMBER 27:

LOADED with DAILY BLESSINGS (Ps. 68:19)-#332

FELLOWSHIP—7

"Nor was there anyone among them who lacked; for all who were possessors of lands or houses sold them, and brought the proceeds of the things that were sold,

and laid them at the apostles feet; and they distributed to each as anyone had need." (Acts 4:34–35)

Consequences of Fellowship:

• No lack

The community of Christians is supposed to be a prosperous community because everyone is expected to be generous in sharing with others in need. This is a great principle laid down by the Lord as part of His new commandment of love.

But in practice, it is challenging due to human imperfections. Even in the early church where the Holy Spirit was active in the apostles' lives as they operated this system of common wealth distribution, it didn't take too long for complaints of discrimination and neglect to set in (Acts 6:1). The expectation of the imminent return of Jesus Christ to take over the kingdoms of the world compelled His early disciples to practice this common wealth distribution community in Jerusalem.

The principle of supporting each other where there's lack was ideal, but the method of practicing it was faulty. Jesus did not ask His disciples to set up a large church community in Jerusalem but to go into all the earth and spread His love (Acts 1:8).

The Lord later allowed persecutions to disperse their koinonia community into all the world. But the principle of believers meeting each other's needs is relevant throughout church history and to us today. Let us always pray for God's direction and be sensitive to how He's leading us to meet people's needs in our fellowships.

Have a prosperous day **loaded** with His **blessings!**

LIVING WORD for TODAY—NOVEMBER 28:

LOADED with DAILY BLESSINGS (Ps. 68:19)-#333

FELLOWSHIP—28

"But concerning brotherly love you have no need that I should write to you, for you yourselves are taught by God to love one another..." (1 Thess. 4:9)

Commands to Fellowship with One Another In:

- Love

The New Testament is full of commands to Christians to fellowship with one another in various circumstances. There are scores of references to doing something for "one another." Because of limited time, I will reference just a few of them.

We're commanded by the Lord and His apostles to:

- Love one another (John 13:34; 1 Thess. 4:9). This is the greatest of all the commands;
- Honor one another (Rom. 12:10);
- Build up one another (Rom. 14:19);
- Accept one another (Rom. 15:7);
- Admonish one another (Rom. 15:14; Col. 3:16);
- Care for one another (1 Cor. 12:25); and
- Be of the same mind toward one another (Rom. 12:16).

There's no way we can carry out these biblical commands if we're not in fellowship with one another (to be continued).

May the Lord unite our hearts together in love so we can fellowship with one another in many areas of need.

Have a happy day **loaded** with His **blessings**!

LIVING WORD for TODAY—NOVEMBER 29:

LOADED with DAILY BLESSINGS (Ps. 68:19)-#334

FELLOWSHIP—29

"For you, brethren, have been called to liberty; only do not use liberty as an opportunity for the flesh, but through love serve one another.
For all the law is fulfilled in one word, even in this: 'You shall love your neighbor as yourself.'" (Gal. 5:13, 14)

Commands to Fellowship with One Another In:

- Service of love

As we continue in "one another" fellowship commands, let us remember that every command from the Lord to us is built on His love.

His love must be spread abroad in our hearts by the Holy Spirit before we can fellowship with one another in love. Here are more commands of love in fellowship for us to:

- Serve one another (Gal. 5:13);
- Bear one another's burdens (Gal. 6:2);
- Forgive one another (Eph. 4:2, 32; Col. 3:13);
- Speak the truth in love to one another (Eph. 4:15, 25);
- Be kind and compassionate to one another (Eph. 4:32);
- Speak to one another in Psalms, hymns, and spiritual songs (Eph. 5:19);
- Submit to one another in the fear of God (Eph. 5:21; 1 Pet. 5:5);
- Comfort one another (1 Thess. 4:18);
- Bear with one another (Col. 3:13); and
- Look to the interests of one another (Phil. 2:4).

These are duties of the Holy Spirit through us to one another as He dispenses His love from us to support and enrich others in our fellowships.

May we yield to Him to be used as His vessels for others, and may we be humbled enough to receive these ministrations from others in our fellowships as the needs may arise from time to time.

Have a lovely day **loaded** with His **blessings**!

LIVING WORD for TODAY—NOVEMBER 30:

LOADED with DAILY BLESSINGS (Ps. 68:19)-#335

FELLOWSHIP—30

"Confess your trespasses to one another, and pray for one another, that you may be healed. The effective, fervent prayer of a righteous man avails much." *(James 5:16)*

Commands to Fellowship with One Another:

- Confession and prayers

As we conclude our meditations on fellowship, I want to touch on an important aspect of praying for healing in the body of believers. But before we go, let us review the grounds we've covered so far on fellowship.

1. Our Fellowship is with the:

   - Triune God-Father, Son, and the Holy Spirit and
   - With other Christians.

2. Our Purpose of Fellowship is to have fullness of joy.
3. Conditions to Fellowship with Others:

   - Transparency, dealing with our sins, past and present, and constant cleansing in the blood of Christ.

4. Call to Fellowship

   - with the pleasantness of unity in the body.

5. Components of Fellowship

   - Prayer as a means of fellowshipping, sharing of substance, eating together, and having all things in common.

6. Consequences of Fellowship

   - There's release of great power, great grace to minister to the world, and no lack among believers.

7. Commands for One Another Fellowship:

- In service of love in various areas of need to one another.

The command in our text today relates to praying for one another to be healed. One missing link in healing prayers today is the biblical command to confess our sins to one another to be healed.

This is crucial and must be handled with the utmost confidentiality by the elders or ministers involved in praying for the sick person. Let us apply this command strictly in our fellowships as we pray for one another, and we shall see God's breakthroughs.

Have a great day/night **loaded** with His **blessings**!

Living Word for **today** with James E. Temidara

DECEMBER—FUTURE

LIVING WORD for TODAY—DECEMBER 1:

LOADED with DAILY BLESSINGS (Ps. 68:19)-#336

FUTURE—1

"For I know the thoughts that I think toward you, says the LORD, thoughts of peace and not of evil, to give you a future and a hope." (Jer. 29:11)

What about the Future?

Thinking about the future is normal for all humans as it helps us plan and live realistically.

But being inundated about the future can be so troubling and eventually lead people to probing into the realms of the supernatural beyond their control.

During our meditations in the last month of this year, it is proper to look at the subject of the future to give us emotional and spiritual strength in biblical perspectives as we step into the new year.

Let me assure you by the Word of the Lord, who made the heavens and the earth, that your future is great and full of hope. Live by hoping for better things to happen in your life and family as you face your future.

Have a happy end of the year with His **loaded blessings!**

LIVING WORD for TODAY—DECEMBER 2:

LOADED with DAILY BLESSINGS (Ps. 68:19)-#337

FUTURE—2

"For I know the thoughts that I think toward you, says the LORD, thoughts of peace and not of evil, to give you a future and a hope." (Jer. 29:11)

Worries about the Future :

Are you worried about the future of the world? Your nation? Your family? What will happen to them after you're gone? And what about yourself? Relax, God is in control.

Carrying the burdens of the future can lead us to unnecessary fears. Fears about the future can lead and are leading many to consult with false prophets, diviners, dreamers, soothsayers, and sorcerers, who are all operating from the same spiritual source of Satan.

Any backslidden society is infiltrated by these groups of spiritual forces prophesying falsehood to the populace.

That was the situation in the time of Prophet Jeremiah. Nebuchadnezzar, king of Babylon, had invaded the land of Judah and sacked the Jewish religious government as a punishment for their disobedience to God's laws after years of repeated warnings from the **Lord**. Many Jews, the king, and the nobles were carried captives to Babylon. But Nebuchadnezzar appointed a regent to oversee the remnant of the Jews he left in Judah.

But instead of the remnants repenting and returning to the **Lord**, many false prophets rose up among them, giving them false hope of a quick fix by God to restore them back to their homeland and rebuild it. Jeremiah came to the stage as a mouthpiece for God to correct and warn the people of God not to listen to the false prophecies peddling around them.

"For I have not sent them, says the LORD, yet they prophesy a lie in My name..." (Jer. 27:15).

Does the situation around you today resemble their case? If so, no worries; the Lord will guide you through His Word and build your faith and hope upon His real plan for your future.

Have a restful day/night **loaded** with His **blessings!**

LIVING WORD for TODAY—DECEMBER 3:

LOADED with DAILY BLESSINGS (Ps. 68:19)-#338

FUTURE—3

"For I know the thoughts that I think toward you, says the LORD, thoughts of peace and not of evil, to give you a future and a hope." (Jer. 29:11)

Worries about the Future:

What's in your future? What are your thoughts or the media saying to you about the future? Regardless of what you may be hearing or thinking, you need to get your information from the right source to direct your thoughts appropriately.

There were many environmental prophets and preachers telling people what they wanted to hear during the time of Prophet Jeremiah.

But God said He did not send them. They promised false hope. Beware of false hope! God has a way of prospering and preserving His people in any generation regardless of the systems of governance around them.

Therefore, God told the remnants of the Jews at home and in exile not to expect a sudden change of the government to restore a godly state, but to settle where they were, build houses and live in them, establish businesses, get married and raise godly offspring, and seek the peace and pray for the government of the day, whether conservative or liberal—because God had ordained seventy years of cleansing before any restoration (Jer. 29:4–10).

The message for us today is that it doesn't matter who is in control of the nation where God has planted us; let's feel secured, support the government by doing our civic duties, pray for the peace and prosperity of our nations, raise godly families, and get involved in any lawful business or investment. Because the hope of our future is not in what the government does but what the Lord has planned for us, and He has a bright and fulfilling **future** for us and our seeds.

Have a happy day/night **loaded** with His **blessings**!

LIVING WORD for TODAY—DECEMBER 4:

LOADED with DAILY BLESSINGS (Ps. 68:19)-#339

FUTURE—4

"Therefore, when they had come together, they asked Him, saying, 'Lord, will You at this time restore the kingdom to Israel?'" (Acts 1:6)

Worries about the Future:

If you're worried about your future, you're not alone. Even the apostles who wined and dined with our Lord Jesus Christ were not immune from this pandemic of worry.

They had left their jobs, houses, land, families, and friends to follow the Lord, whom they thought was the Messiah of their nation. They had hoped that He would use His divine miraculous power to overthrow the evil empire of oppression and establish the godly empire to be ruled by justice, equity, and abundance of Messianic blessings. Their hopes were dashed by His defeat and death on the Cross. But suddenly, their hopes came back to life again when they saw His resurrection from the dead.

After living off and on with them for forty days, He gathered them together for a farewell speech without setting up any revolutionary plans. What a disappointment on their faces as they asked when His kingdom would come.

It's been over two thousand years since they asked that question from our resurrected Lord, and we're still waiting.

So relax, God is not in a quick-fix business, and there's no amount of prayer and screaming out of fear on our part that can change His plans for the future of the world, our nations, families, and ourselves. So let's live with hope and faith in Him to know that, as the lyric of one of our contemporary songs puts it:

"Even when I don't see it, You're still working; yes you're, yes you're working; You never stop, never stop working."

He will make a way for you as you navigate through His process for your **future**.

Have a lovely day/night **loaded** with His **blessings**!

LIVING WORD for TODAY—DECEMBER 5:

LOADED with DAILY BLESSINGS (Ps. 68:19)-#340

FUTURE—5

"And He said to them, 'It is not for you to know times or seasons which the Father has put in His own authority.'" (Acts 1:7)

Who Holds the Future?

Be careful how you ask God a question because the answer you might get from Him may be different from what is in your mind. Check this out in the Bible from all those who asked God questions.

While Christ's disciples asked a question about the future of the Kingdom of Israel from their Master out of confusion and perplexity, He, however, calmed their perplexities with His words of hope. He assured them, and He's saying the same to us today:

• It is not for us to know everything about God's future plans. "It is not for you to know."

While God has revealed some things about the future of the earth in His Word, there are many details He never disclosed to anyone. Jesus Christ, while in the flesh, even said He didn't know the day and hour of the end, not even the angels know except the Father (Mark 13:32).

But we, in our pride, presume to know and probe to know all about the future. Jesus said, "It is not for you to know." What is true about the future of the end time is also true about our individual future. Only God knows all about your future, and He has not revealed it to anyone.

So let us be humbled before Him to know that, "The secret things belong to the LORD our God, but those things which are revealed belong to us and to our children forever, that we may do all the words of this law" (Deut. 29:29).

Have a peaceful day/night **loaded** with His **blessings!**

LIVING WORD for TODAY—DECEMBER 6:

LOADED with DAILY BLESSINGS (Ps. 68:19)-#341

FUTURE—6

"And He said to them, 'it is not for you to know times or seasons which the Father has put in His own authority.'" (Acts 1:7)

Who Holds the Future?

What's in your future, and who's controlling it?

The last days of "this present evil age," which started on the Day of Pentecost when the Lord poured out His Spirit to inaugurate the Christian church, are marked with times and seasons. The world has witnessed various negative and positive events socially, politically, technologically, and spiritually. And we've yet to see many more dramatic times before the end.

But whatever may come, God, our Father, has it under His authority. Things may get ugly in the world, but God has a better and brighter future for His own; "Plans of peace and not of evil, to give you a future and a hope" (Jer. 29:11).

So the best approach to the future is to place our daily lives in the hand of God who holds and controls our **future**. Let Him lead you.

Have a pleasant day **loaded** with His **blessings!**

LIVING WORD for TODAY—DECEMBER 7:

LOADED with DAILY BLESSINGS (Ps. 68:19)-#342

FUTURE—7

"But you shall receive power when the Holy Spirit has come upon you; and you shall be witnesses to Me in Jerusalem, and in all Judea and Samaria, and to the end of the earth." (Acts 1:8)

Personal Responsibility for the Future:

The disciples of Jesus were more concerned about the future of their nation, while the Lord was more concerned about their lives and responsibilities. They were talking about the Kingdom of Israel, but the Lord was talking about their empowerment to build God's kingdom on earth.

After they were filled with the Holy Spirit and empowered on the Day of Pentecost, they never talked about the Kingdom of Israel again. Their language changed to the global expansion of the kingdom of Christ and their roles in the expansion.

Until we shift our focus and understanding from the happenings around us to the greater overall future purpose of God's plan and our personal involvement, we cannot realize our purpose in life. Once the disciples of Jesus were filled with the Holy Spirit, nothing else in life was more important to them than the spreading of the good news of Christ's kingdom on earth.

You and I have a role to play to make the future of our lives and the world meaningful and fulfilling. And we cannot play that role unless we're constantly empowered by the Holy Spirit.

Let us pray daily for the Holy Spirit's fullness in our lives, to live the life of His kingdom, and to show others how to enter and function in the kingdom of Christ. That's why we're alive.

Have a great day **loaded** with His **blessings!**

LIVING WORD for TODAY—DECEMBER 8:

LOADED with DAILY BLESSINGS (Ps. 68:19)-#343

FUTURE—8

"I am the LORD, and there is no other.
There is no God besides Me...
That they may know from the rising of the sun to its setting
That there is none besides Me. I am the LORD, and there is no other;
I form the light and create darkness
I made peace and create calamity;
I, the LORD, do all these things." (Isa. 45:5–7)

Principles about the Future:

What's in the future, and what's ahead of you?

Before you go to a prophet or soothsayer to consult about your future, take time to read your Bible. All we need to know about the future of the world and our future is in the revelation of the Bible.

So let us draw some principles from the Scriptures to calm our nerves and help us walk by faith into our future.

1. The future generally is in God's hand. He is the Creator of all things, and nothing happens in the world or in our lives without His knowledge.

He says: "I am the LORD, and there is no other..." (Isa. 45:5).

"I am the LORD, and there is no other..." (Isa. 45:6).

"I, the LORD, do all these things" (Isa. 45:7).

In this passage, six times, God repeated the personal pronoun, "I" to confirm His sovereignty over the universe.

Because He is the **Lord** who does or allows all things to happen in the world, we can trust Him with our future and feel secure. So live a worry free life.

Have a happy day/evening **loaded** with His **blessings**!

LIVING WORD for TODAY—DECEMBER 9:

LOADED with DAILY BLESSINGS (Ps. 68:19)-#344

FUTURE—9

"I am the Alpha and the Omega, the Beginning and the End,' says the Lord, 'who is and who was and who is to come, the Almighty.'"

Principles about the Future:

1. The future generally is in God's hand; and
2. God is in control of the future.

God did not abandon the world after creating it. He is still in control. There's a philosophical belief known as deism. It is a belief that there is a supreme being who created the world, but after creating it, does not interfere nor involved in running it.

Many American founding fathers were deists.

But when our Lord revealed Himself to John from His glory in heaven, He introduced Himself as the Alpha, which is the first letter of the Greek alphabet, and the Omega, which is the last letter. In the English alphabet, it means, He is, A–Z, the beginning to the end.

Since we cannot write a word, phrase, or a complete sentence without the alphabet, so Jesus Christ is saying that the world, in its past, present, and future, has no meaning nor completion without Him.

So He is in control of sustaining the world He created, and He will do what is right as the Judge of the whole universe. Let us trust Him with the future.

Have a lovely day/night!

LIVING WORD for TODAY—DECEMBER 10:

LOADED with DAILY BLESSINGS (Ps. 68:19)-#345

FUTURE—10

"Jesus Christ is the same yesterday, today, and forever." (Heb. 13:8)

Principles about the Future:

2. God is in control of the future

Jesus Christ, our Lord, who is the Alpha and Omega, the beginning through the end, came to visit the earth and shed His blood to cleanse it from the pollution of sins. He hasn't given up on us regardless of how complex and sinful the world has become. He is alive, the same today in our hi-tech age, and He will be there, the same forever when we're no longer here.

He is in control, and the future of the nations of the earth belongs to Him. He, "the Most High rules in the kingdom of men, and gives it to whomever He chooses" (Dan. 4:25).

So let our mindsets be plugged into His presence and power by faith as we let Him lead us day by day. The future belongs to Him, and He is control.

Have a great day/night **loaded** with His **blessings!**

LIVING WORD for TODAY—DECEMBER 11:

LOADED with DAILY BLESSINGS (Ps. 68:19)-#346

FUTURE—11

"But as for me, I trust in You, O LORD;
I say, 'You are my God.'
My times are in Your hand;
Deliver me from the hand of my enemies,
And from those who persecute me.
Make Your face shine upon Your servant;
Save me for Your mercies' sake." (Ps. 31:14–16)

Principles about the Future:

3. Distinguish between the future of the world and your personal/family future.

People can be so preoccupied with the future of the world that they forget or are less concerned about their own future. Yes, the future belongs to the Lord and He is in control. But what about your own future? What are your plans of action to face the future challenges?

Life is good, but it's also tough and full of ups and downs. When you're down, there are minimal challenges, but when you're up and seem to be making it, going somewhere, that's when enemies of progress rise up against you. If you're in doubt, read about David's experience in Psalm 31 and know that you're not alone in the struggles of life.

But in all our challenges, we can say, like David, our times are in God's hand, and He will deliver us from all our enemies, both now and in the future. So let's place our lives and times in His hand and decide to live daily by faith, and His mercies will sustain us.

Have a healthy day/night **loaded** with His **blessings!**

Living Word for **today** with James E. Temidara

LIVING WORD for TODAY—DECEMBER 12:

LOADED with DAILY BLESSINGS (Ps. 68:19)-#347

FUTURE—12

"And Jesus answered and said to them: 'Take heed that no one deceives you. For many will come in My name, saying, 'I am the Christ,' and deceive many.'" (Matt. 24:4–5)

Principles about the Future:

4. God has not revealed and will not reveal all about the future, general or personal, to anyone, prophet, diviner, seer, soothsayer; not even Satan and his agents.

This is important for Christians to note since we're approaching the last eschatological events of the end of this evil age. One of the major signs of the last days is the outpouring of false prophets and falsehood into the world by Satan. They appear as Christ's apostles outwardly, but inwardly, they are ravenous wolves in sheep clothing (Matt. 7:15).

The Lord warns, "beware," "take heed."

The fact that someone predicts some future events and part of them, or even if all of them come to pass does not make him or her a prophet of God; even when they're performing miracles. Jesus says, "You will know them by their fruits" (Matt. 7:16), and not by their miracles.

Check out their full identity, messages/ doctrines, and methods of operation. Are they getting things done by righteous means or by cohesion, manipulation, and exploitative means, milking the sheep of God?

I pray for the gift of discernment of spirits upon us so we can discern in our spirits the truth of the gospel of our Lord Jesus Christ from the heretical yeast of another gospel of sensation out there.

Have a great day/evening **loaded** with His **blessings!**

LIVING WORD for TODAY—DECEMBER 13:

LOADED with DAILY BLESSINGS (Ps. 68:19)-#348

FUTURE—13

"GOD, who at various times and in various ways spoke in time past to the fathers by the prophets,
has in these last days spoken to us by His Son, whom He has appointed heir of all things, through whom also He made the worlds..." (Heb. 1:1-2)

Principles about the Future:

5. All about the future, general, or personal, has been revealed and can be found in the Bible and in Christ Jesus.

We don't need anyone claiming to have special revelations or dreams about the future and deceiving people.

Although God's anointed preachers may have special insights interpreting God's revelation about the future in the Bible, their authority is limited to what is revealed in the Holy Bible.

There's a lot of information about the future revealed by God to His holy prophets and apostles of old in the Scriptures, but all the revelations are sealed in Christ Jesus, who has been revealed to us in these last days as the fullness of the Godhead.

"For in Him dwells all the fullness of the Godhead bodily; and you are complete in Him, who is the head of all principality and power" (Col. 2:9–10).

So you want to know about the future of the world and yours? Read the Bible and be plugged into Christ Jesus by faith, and live your life in Him by His Spirit daily. You're complete in Him, and He leads His children by His Spirit (Rom. 8:14).

Have a happy day/evening **loaded** with His **blessings**!

LIVING WORD for TODAY—DECEMBER 14:

LOADED with DAILY BLESSINGS (Ps. 68:19)-#349

FUTURE—14

"But he who prophesies speaks edification and exhortation and comfort to men."
(1 Cor. 14:3)

Principles about the Future:

6.   While prophecies in the Old Testament were, more or less, fore-telling the future, prophecies in the New Testament age are forth telling and must meet a threefold test for acceptance (1 Cor. 14:3):

   (a)   The test of edification: Does the prophetic utterance edify or establish people in faith or creating fear in them;

   (b)   The test of exhortation: Are people exhorted in the way of righteousness and in their relationship with Christ; and

   (c)   The test of comfort: Is the prophecy comforting to the souls of the recipients? Notice that whenever God sent an angel to give a message to His people in the Bible, the greeting was always, "fear not" or "peace be unto you."

God's prophecies are never meant to intimidate His children nor to create fears in them but to confirm what He's already telling them about His will.

So there are no secret interpretations about the future (2 Pet. 1:20–21; 2:1–3).

May the Lord establish your faith in Him, exhort and counsel you for clarity, and fill you with His comfort daily.

Have a lovely day/night **loaded** with His **blessings!**

LIVING WORD for TODAY—DECEMBER 15:

LOADED with DAILY BLESSINGS (Ps. 68:19)-#350

FUTURE—15

"And He said to them, 'It is not for you to know times or seasons which the Father has put in His own authority.
But you shall receive power when the Holy Spirit has come upon you; and you shall be witnesses to Me in Jerusalem, and in all Judea and Samaria, and to the end of the earth.'" (Acts 1:7–8)

Principles about the Future:

7. Believers in Christ should not be too focused on the future but live day by day by faith in the Lord who holds the future and be occupied in His kingdom business.

The Lord's Prayer teaches us how to pray for the future.

"Your kingdom come.

Your will be done

On earth as it is in heaven."

(Matt. 6:10)

Our major concern as believers about the future is the full establishment of the kingdom of God on earth, where the will of God is being done.

The Great Commission of Jesus makes us the agents of His kingdom on earth. So we're to be fully occupied in spreading the good news of His kingdom through our lifestyles and words till He comes or takes us home. Once His priority becomes our priority, He will take care of our future. So be a witness for Jesus Christ wherever you're.

Have a great day/night **loaded** with His **blessings!**

LIVING WORD for TODAY—DECEMBER 16:

LOADED with DAILY BLESSINGS (Ps. 68:19)-#351

FUTURE—16

"Now the Spirit expressly says that in the latter times some will depart from the faith, giving heed to deceiving spirits and doctrines of demons, speaking lies in hypocrisy, having their own conscience seared with a hot iron..." (1 Tim. 4:1–2)

Principles about the Future:

The prince of this world, Satan, specializes in distracting people's attention, especially Christians, from what matters most in their lives and communities to things or events of the world that they cannot control.

There are many teachings, prophecies, and information going on in our air waves and social media by eminent Christian leaders that have nothing to do with what God is doing in the world through the Holy Spirit.

What has Christian leaders got to do with predicting who's going to win the US presidential election? When a Christian leader is actively involved in a partisan politics, he or she is dividing the body of Christ. This is a departure from the faith and their holy calling into giving heed to seducing spirits of Satan. Many of them have been proven wrong from time to time, but because they have a large audience with itching ears, they thrive in their divisive and deceptive religious business. If this was done in the Old Testament era, they would have been stoned to death for their wrong predictions.

Let us focus on what matters most to Christ: bringing people from darkness into the kingdom of Christ. God is powerful enough to use any political leader or party to fulfill His will for the future if we stand firm in advancing the kingdom of God as we're called to do by our Savior.

Have a glorious day/night **loaded** with His **daily blessings!**

LIVING WORD for TODAY—DECEMBER 17:

LOADED with DAILY BLESSINGS (Ps. 68:19)-#352

FUTURE—17

"Now the Spirit expressly say that in the latter times some will depart from the faith, giving heed to deceiving spirits and doctrines of demons, speaking lies in hypocrisy, having their own conscience seared with hot iron..." (1 Tim. 4:1–2)

Principles about the Future:

8. The prince of this world, Satan, specializes in distracting people's attention, especially Christians, from what matters most in their lives and communities to things or events of the world they cannot control.

Another distraction of the devil to deceive Christians into buying into his agenda in these last days is spreading conspiracy theories.

Conspiracy theories are lies well prepared to feed the appetites of people who are gullible to unfounded rumors that cannot be substantiated with facts.

Unfortunately, some Christian leaders, including pastors have sold their consciences to the hypocritical lies of Satan to be his agents in spreading conspiracy theories. They are used to destroy facts and people's reputations. And in these days of social media, they spread faster than the wildfire.

Since the day the World Health Organization (WHO) announced that the coronavirus had become a pandemic, some Christian preachers received a new anointing from Satan's kingdom to champion the conspiracy theories of rejecting COVID-19 as a disease. Let us remember that there's no conflict between true science and the Bible. In fact, health science and other sciences have their roots in the Scriptures and the church. If in doubt, study church history, European history, and American history to learn how the church prepared the world for the age of industrial revolution. So let us cooperate with health experts in fighting diseases in our communities instead of being misled by ignorant preachers who downplay scientific facts.

Jesus warns us of the end-time pandemics (Luke 21:11). The Bible is loaded with sound doctrine to nourish us spiritually and establish us in the faith of

our Lord Jesus Christ as we live today and the future. Give yourself time to study and learn biblical truths from qualified preachers and teachers of the word to be equipped.

Have a pleasant day/night **loaded** with His **blessings!**

LIVING WORD for TODAY—DECEMBER 18:

LOADED with DAILY BLESSINGS (Ps. 68:19)-#353

FUTURE—18

"Now the Spirit expressly says that in the latter times some will depart from the faith, giving heed to deceiving spirits and doctrines of demons, speaking lies in hypocrisy, having their own conscience seared with a hot iron..." (1 Tim. 4:1–2)

Principles about the Future:

Focusing on conspiracy theories or the Bible?

9. On conspiracy theories: If preachers were dedicated to teaching the Bible, they wouldn't have time to be talking about lies of conspiracy theories on the pulpit.

Now that the disease control scientists have produced a vaccine to control the spread of the coronavirus, some Christian preachers are busy telling people not to take it and calling it the mark of the beast, 666. Do they really know the Bible? Ask them, has the antichrist appeared? Where is he to be giving people his mark? Have the dead in Christ risen to meet Christ in the sky? Has the church been raptured to join them? These are end time events that must occur before the man of sin, the antichrist, would be revealed to give his mark. Read 2 Thessalonians 2:3–12, 1 Thessalonians 4:13–18, and Revelation 13 to know that the coronavirus vaccine has nothing to do with the mark of the beast, but just like other vaccines that had been developed to control the spread of various diseases, like polio, smallpox, and flu.

If you're offered, please take it for the love of yourself, your family, and others that you're going to be in contact with. In fact, I have been offered and have taken the vaccine. It is safe!

So let us focus on what matters most to us and our Master in these last days, and that is making disciples of all nations for Christ and stop giving heed to the seducing spirits of Satan coming from his agents through lies of conspiracy theories.

Have a lovely day/night **loaded** with His **blessings**!

LIVING WORD for TODAY—DECEMBER 19:

LOADED with DAILY BLESSINGS (Ps. 68:19)-#354

FUTURE—19

"Then many false prophets will rise up and deceive many." (Matt. 24:11)

Principles about the Future:

> 10. One of the major signs to watch out for in the future is the infiltration of false prophets into the Christian church.

False prophets have always been part of the community of God's people since the time of Moses. But as revealed by our Lord and His apostles, there would be more of them as this present evil age draws to a close. False prophets exhibit a lot of charisma and eloquence with some results. Anyone can become a prophet by going into isolation for days or weeks without food and come up with visions, revelations, signs, and wonders. Many of them are empowered by religious demons. There's a lot of the spirit of divination and witchcraft operating in the church today. They will be more pronounced in the future.

Read more about them in 2 Peter chapter 2, the Epistle of Jude, and note their characteristics.

So be watchful in all things and be sure of your salvation.

"But we are bound to give thanks to God always for you, brethren beloved by the Lord, because God from the beginning chose you for salvation through sanctification by the Spirit and belief in the truth..." (2 Thessalonians 2:13).

Have a great day **loaded** with God's **blessings!**

LIVING WORD for TODAY—DECEMBER 20:

LOADED with DAILY BLESSINGS (Ps. 68:19)-#355

FUTURE—20

"Preach the word! Be ready in season and out of season. Convince, rebuke, exhort, with all longsuffering and teaching.
For the time will come when they will not endure sound doctrine, but according to their own desires, because they have itching ears, they will heap up for themselves teachers;
and they will turn their ears away from the truth, and be turned aside to fables.
But you be watchful in all things, endure afflictions, do the work of an evangelist, fulfill your ministry." (2 Tim. 4:2–5)

Principles about the Future:

11. Believers should tune their ears and develop their spiritual appetites for sound doctrines instead of sensations of the evil one through his agents.

In contrast to principle number nine about the infiltration of false prophets and teachers into the church, we must preach the undiluted Word of God, and the people of God must love to listen to the sound teachings of the Bible from Christ's true anointed teachers and preachers. This is the only antidote to being susceptible to false and sensational teachings that lack substance to save and edify.

We must also put into practice the practical applications of the Word of God through love, endurance, and winning of souls to Christ. Fruit bearing is the result of the Word falling into the fertile soil of our hearts to make us grow up and mature. By doing these, we will be able to face the future without fear but by faith.

May the Lord help us to stand firm against all the deceptions of these last days and be active in winning souls to the Lord.

Have a happy day **loaded** with His **blessings**!

LIVING WORD for TODAY—DECEMBER 21:

LOADED with DAILY BLESSINGS (Ps. 68:19)-#356

FUTURE—21

"The voice of one crying in the wilderness:
'Prepare the way of the LORD;
Make straight in the desert
A highway for our God." (Isa. 40:3)

Preparing for the Future:

    1.   With the right heart

As we look forward to celebrating the Advent of the Lord, which we call Christmas, let us use the opportunity to prepare ourselves for what the Lord has for us in the future.

Just as God used Isaiah, a prophet in Israel, to cry out and predict the conditions that must happen before the coming of the King of Glory, which came to pass about 500 years later in the person of Jesus Christ, He is sounding an alarm in our hearts to prepare us for Him.

John the Baptist was born and sent ahead of Christ to preach repentance and get people ready for the Lord's coming (Luke 1:57–79; 3:1–6).

So get ready for what the future holds for you.

The revelation of the Lord is to:

• Comfort His people. If there was any time that we needed God's comfort, it's now. With all we've being through in the years of the pandemic called COVID-19, leading to a bad economy, with the electoral turmoil around the world, it is time for God to comfort His people, and He will. But He needs ready hearts to receive it.

I pray that His presence will fill your heart with His comfort and make you smile as you prepare for His next levels in your future.

"'Comfort, yes, comfort my people!' Says your God" (Isa. 40:1).

Have a lovely day with His **loaded blessings!**

LIVING WORD for TODAY—DECEMBER 22:

LOADED with DAILY BLESSINGS (Ps. 68:19)-#357

FUTURE—22

"The voice of one crying in the wilderness:
'Prepare the way of the LORD;
Make straight in the desert
A highway for our God
Every valley shall be exalted
And every mountain and hill brought low;
The crooked places shall be made straight
And the rough places smooth..." (Isa. 40:3–4)

Preparing for the Future:

2. With a highway for the Lord

As we focus on the last few days of this most challenging year, let us learn to count our blessings and get ready for better years ahead. One of the blessings of our time in the midst of pandemic was the release of COVID vaccine into the world by the medical scientists and civil authorities to fight the spread of the coronavirus disease. Remember, I asked us to pray for this to happen in March during our devotional messages. I was selected as one of the first priority group of people to take the vaccine, and I did. It's pain-free with no reactions. It is a medical miracle we all should take advantage of when it becomes available in your region.

The future is great because we serve a great God who is always comforting His people in their distress. He also wants to end our warfare and give us peace. So His revelation brings comfort and peace.

But for Him to do great and awesome things in us and through us, our hearts must become His highway to flow freely. It is my prayer that His Spirit would lead each of us to get rid of the crooked paths in our lives so we can become the highway for Him to travel in the coming years.

"Speak comfort to Jerusalem, and cry out to her,

That her warfare is ended..." (Isa. 40:2).

I speak the peace of God to whatever warfare you may be fighting now in Jesus Christ's name. It is well!

Have a peaceful day **loaded** with His **blessings!**

LIVING WORD for TODAY—DECEMBER 23:

LOADED with DAILY BLESSINGS (Ps. 68:19)-#358

FUTURE—23

"The glory of the LORD shall be revealed,
And all flesh shall see it together;
For the mouth of the LORD has spoken." (Isa. 40:5)

Preparing for the Future:

3.   With the revelation of God's glory

What's in your future?

Regardless of all the commotions and the traffic jams in your life right now, the glory of the **Lord** is in your future! This is the Word of the Lord to you wherever you are right now. His glory clears all the traffic. All roads are cleared for the president to move freely when traveling.

When His glory is revealed, people around you shall see the difference in you because of the presence of the Lord in your life. You will become unstoppable!

The glory of the **Lord** is the manifestation of His presence in human affairs. God dwells in glory, which no human eyes can see and live. It is unapproachable and the totality of His essence. But to deal with our problems of sin, "the Word became flesh and dwelt among us, and we beheld His glory, the glory of the only begotten of the Father, full of grace and truth" (John 1:14).

May Christ be revealed in you with His glory to erase all your iniquities and deficiencies.

I also pray that people shall see God's glory in all that you do and not your flaws. Your new **future** starts from now.

Have a glorious day **loaded** with His **blessings**!

LIVING WORD for TODAY—DECEMBER 24:

LOADED with DAILY BLESSINGS (Ps. 68:19)-#359:

FUTURE—24

"To them God willed to make known what are the riches of the glory of this mystery among the Gentiles: which is Christ in you, the hope of glory." (Col. 1:27)

Preparing for the Future:

4. With hope

God's promise to give us a future in Jeremiah 29:11 includes a hope. To live without hope is like trying to live without oxygen. It's not going to last. Hope is our oxygen for the future and a spinal cord that joins our present with the future.

But what do we hope for? We hope for a better and glorious future. That's why Jesus Christ was born. He came to reveal God's glory to us, and through His finished work on the Cross, dropped a deposit of that glory in those of us who believe in Him (John 1:18; 17:5, 22).

So if you're in Christ, the deposit of God's glory resides in you, and as you're being transformed by the renewing of your mind daily, His glory is being revealed in you more and more until that glorious day when you enter His unlimited eternal glory.

"Christ in you, the hope of glory" (Col. 1:27).

So let us celebrate Christmas, which is Christ's festival, with the hope of a glorious future. May Christ be revealed in us more and more.

Have a merry Christmas with His **loaded blessings!**

LIVING WORD for TODAY—DECEMBER 25:

LOADED with DAILY BLESSINGS (Ps. 68:19)-#360

FUTURE—25

"'Behold, the virgin shall be with child, and bear a Son, and they shall call His name Immanuel,' which is translated, 'God is with us.'" (Matt. 1:23)

Preparing for the Future:

5. With Immanuel, God with us

Merry Christmas to you and your loved ones! As the first Christmas in Bethlehem brought fulfillment of hope to many, I pray that this Christmas will start the fulfillment of what you have been hoping for over the years.

God is faithful to His promises. For centuries, people in Israel were waiting for the ultimate fulfillment of God's prophecy through Isaiah (Isa. 7:14), but they never saw it happen during their time. However, in God's fullness of time, it came to pass, and a virgin, called Mary, conceived by the Holy Spirit, bore a child named Immanuel, meaning, God with us and the Savior of the world (Matt. 1:23).

As you prepare for your future, ensure that you include Immanuel with it because He is the One who is timeless and eternal, who is able to do all that you're hoping for, and can even do exceedingly and abundantly, above and beyond all you can ever hope for (Eph. 3:20).

He is God with us, who wants to go through your future with you and be with you through the thin and thick of life's journey. God with us, and if God is for us, who can be against us? Nobody and no circumstances, for He makes "all things to work together for good to those who love God, to those who are the called according to His purpose" (Rom. 8:28, 31).

So your future is firmly secured with Immanuel!

Have a joyful Christmas with His LOADED BLESSINGS!

LIVING WORD for TODAY—DECEMBER 26:

LOADED with DAILY BLESSINGS (Ps. 68:19)-#361

FUTURE—26

"Take heed, watch and pray; for you do not know when the time is." (Mark 13:33)

Preparing for the Future:

6.   With prayer and watchfulness

While looking forward to the future, either personal or general, the Lord holds the future in His hand and gives us a matching order, which, if followed, would keep us prepared and ready to rise up to the challenges of the future. His command is: "watch and pray."

"Watch" means to live carefully and not loosely, putting His kingdom principles into practice in our daily living.

Prayer is the fuel that keeps our engines running. When we pray, we're fellowshipping with our Lord and showing our dependency on Him for wisdom to live productively.

Watchfulness and prayer also give us the strength we need to overcome temptations of the flesh and the devil.

Jesus told His disciples in the hour of temptation: "'Watch and pray, lest you enter into temptation. The spirit indeed is willing, but the flesh is weak'" (Matt. 24:41).

So watchfulness and prayer empower the flesh to be in tune and agreement with our spirits when faced with temptations.

May the Lord grant us obedient hearts to heed His commands.

Have a great day **loaded** with His **blessings!**

LIVING WORD for TODAY—DECEMBER 27:

LOADED with DAILY BLESSINGS (Ps. 68:19)-#362

FUTURE—27

"'Watch therefore, and pray always that you may be counted worthy to escape all these things that will come to pass, and to stand before the Son of Man.'"

Preparing for the Future:

7. With a ready mindset

Everything around us in the world is telling us the end is near. The world events, pandemics, and moral failures are all signals of living in the last days of this present evil age. For Christians, none of these things should surprise us because our Lord and His early apostles had forewarned us in the Scriptures.

However, as the Spirit of God is actively moving all over the world, so also is the evil one making his snares so attractive and socially relevant to dull the spiritual sensitivity of Christians. So as we look into what is ahead in the world, we know that the world will go through rapid technological advancements that will deceive many to feel at ease with the system of this world. Our Lord's warning to His own to be in readiness for His coming is to be taken seriously. No matter how attractive this world may become, it is stored up for destruction.

"But take heed to yourselves, lest your hearts be weighed down with carousing, drunkenness, and cares of this life, and that Day come on you unexpectedly. For it will come as a snare on all those who dwell on the face of the whole earth" (Luke 21:34–35).

But we're not of this world; we belong to the Lord, and He will take His own to be with Him before His wrath is poured out. So be ready always for His coming.

Have a great day **loaded** with His **blessings!**

LIVING WORD for TODAY—DECEMBER 28:

LOADED with DAILY BLESSINGS (Ps. 68:19)-#363

FUTURE—28

"Go to the ant, you sluggard!
Consider her ways and be wise, Which, having no captain, Overseer or ruler,
Provides her supplies in the summer,
And gathers her food in the harvest." (Prov. 6:6–8)

Providing for the Future:

    1.   Through provisions

The Bible is full of many paradoxes. While God says He will give us future and hope, He also instructs us to plan and provide for our future. In fact, Paul, the apostle, in the Epistles, commanded Christians who were not working under the guise of the imminent return of the Lord to stop being idle and work with their hands. Though God promises to bless us and not worry about the future (Matt. 6:24–34), He also teaches us to be wise like the ants and provide for the raining days.

"Go to the ant... and be wise."

The ants are feeble insects, but they are very organized in their storage of food and supplies they need in winter during the summer time.

The fact that God is in control of our future does not eliminate our initiatives to plan and know that there are seasons in life we have to go through. So pray for the wisdom of God to guide you in providing some resources for the future when the strength diminishes to work. In your planning, don't forget this:

"Even to your old age, I am He, and even to gray hairs I will Cary you!" (Isa. 46:4).

Have a happy day **loaded** with His **blessings**!

LIVING WORD for TODAY—DECEMBER 29:

LOADED with DAILY BLESSINGS (Ps. 68:19)-#364

FUTURE—29

"'...Do business till I come...Why then did you not put my money in the bank, that at my coming I might have collected it with interest?'" (Luke 19:13, 23)

Providing for the Future:

2.   Through savings and investments

Our Lord keeps us in this world for a purpose: to advance His kingdom.

Doing this involves money and resources for our lifetime. Hence, He instructs us to invest.

Some Christians live from hand to mouth and see savings and investments as worldly affairs. Let us learn from the lessons Christ taught us though the Parable of the Ten Minas distributed by a certain noble man to his servants before he went to a far country to receive a kingdom for himself (Luke 19:12–27).

When he returned, he called his servants to account for the money he gave them for business. Those who invested and profited were further rewarded with more. But the unprofitable servant was punished for his stupidity and indolence.

The Lord is the noble man, and the Christians are the servants

He wants us to use the skills, resources, and opportunities He gives us from time to time to make gains. So let's learn how to invest wisely for our future. It is the will of God for us to have savings and investments according to our individual ability. "...to each according to his own ability..." (Matt. 25:15).

May the Lord grant us wisdom to invest for the future.

Have a lovely day **loaded** with His **blessings!**

LIVING WORD for TODAY—DECEMBER 30:

LOADED with DAILY BLESSINGS (Ps. 68:19)-#365

FUTURE—30

"But if anyone does not provide for his own, and especially for those of his household, he has denied the faith and is worse than an unbeliever." (1 Tim. 5:8)

Providing for the Future:

    3.   By raising children

One of the ways to provide for the future as taught in the Scriptures is raising children.

When children are properly raised and provided for by their parents in their childhood, when they grow up and their parents are old, it is biblical for the grown-up children to reciprocate and pay back by taking good care of their parents. This is part of the honor children owe their parents, which comes with twofold blessings from God.

"Honor your father and mother, which is the first commandment with promise: 'that it may be well with you and you may live long on the earth.'" (Eph. 6:2–3).

When children honor their parents by taking care of them, they are blessed by God with longevity and prosperity.

Children are our future generations, so we must provide for their needs and raise them properly so they, in turn, can take care of their parents later in life.

Of course, there are many modern insurance programs parents can buy into, but the best future security is raising quality children.

Have a happy day **loaded** with His **blessings!**

LIVING WORD for TODAY—DECEMBER 31:

LOADED with DAILY BLESSINGS (Ps. 68:19)-#366

FUTURE—31

"Blessed be the Lord,
Who daily loads us with benefits,
The God of our salvation! Selah
Our God is the God of salvation;
And to GOD the Lord belong escapes from death." (Ps. 68:19–20)

Provisions and Protections for the Future

Today is the last day of the leap year. What a year this has been!

If you would recollect my message and scriptural text from Psalm 68:19 at the beginning of the year, I said, this psalm starts with the battle cry for God to arise and scatter all His enemies. If the daily blessings promised in verse nineteen were to be realized, the Lord would have to go into battle for us. And He did. That's why we're among the living today.

On December 28, 2020, I was in a fatal hydroplane auto accident on a busy California freeway during the rain. The solid Mercedes SUV I was driving lost control and rolled over many times from one end of the freeway to the other. It broke the dividing rails and rolled over to the opposing traffic side before rolling through the hill to the ditch in the bush. The vehicle was totaled. All through the episode, all I could do was call on the Lord Jesus for help, and He did. I can say with David in our text that, "Our God is the God of salvation; And to God the Lord belong escapes from death."

This is real. The CHP officer and toying truck driver who came to the scene of the accident could not understand how I escaped without being crushed dead in the vehicle. To God be the glory! About an hour later, the toying truck that was sent to remove the vehicle from the ditch decided to take me from the rain and drop me off in the toying truck to their office, which was nearby. As we were on the freeway to their office, the same hydroplane accident happened again. The toying truck lost control, and the vehicle was taken to the other side of the road until it hit a big tree. The truck driver was shouting, but I was calling on the name of the Lord. Thank God, He delivered both of us without injuries. The enemy meant to take me out on that day, but the Lord said "no." God is real to those who trust Him.

There are many great things the Lord did for His own despite the sad events of the year. So be thankful for loading you with His daily **blessings**, which we studied throughout the year, such as the blessings of life, love, health, redemption, forgiveness, favor, family, friends, food, freedom, fellowship, and future.

These are all blessings and many more that the Lord, our Warrior, loads us with daily as we journey through life to our eternal home.

Let us celebrate our victories as we move on and commit our battles to the Lord daily, knowing that He makes all things work together for the good of His elect.

Have a great day **loaded** with His **blessings**!

Living Word for **today** with James E. Temidara

CPSIA information can be obtained
at www.ICGtesting.com
Printed in the USA
LVHW020716160222
711266LV00008B/365